Praise for Cathy Salter's *Notes from Boomerang Creek:*

"In this *delicious* book Cathy Salter leads us through the full scope of life's adventures. Columbia, Missouri has known her for years, and now we share her with a wider world of readers. We follow her down country roads, into U.S. and foreign cities, and enter intimate corners of her life. Be grateful to be showered with luminous words as you turn these pages."

Margaret Sayers Peden, Award-winning Translator, 2012 Winner of PEN/Ralph Manheim Medal for Translation

"Armchair traveler or vagabond, those who wish to swim in uncharted waters must read Cathy Salter's lovely chronicle of days filled with the richness, surprises, and downright love of country living and world travel in all their glory. In *Notes from Boomerang Creek,* she has created a kind of Tao of Writing (thank you, Mr. Theroux), which can be used as a springboard for one's own personal note-taking. Have paper and pen at the ready as you take in these informed and intimate glimpses into a very abundant life.

Suzanne Dunaway, Author/Illustrator of *No Need To Knead,* and *Rome, at Home*

"To call a catastrophe serendipitous seems odd. But Cathy Salter found her writer's voice in the roiling waters of the Great Floods of 1993. Her chance encounter with that natural disaster, plus an equally opportune meeting with the wise and discerning editor Jane Flink of the Boone County Journal, has led to more than two decades of delightful columns and, now, a second volume of their compilation. No one else can describe life in Southern Boone County like Cathy does. Her story-telling lens is tinted with a lifetime of world travel and appreciation of arts and literature, and she puts her country life into that context. Charming."

Jim Robertson, Managing editor, *Columbia Daily Tribune* 2015 President, Missouri Press Association

"I'd almost rather see the world through a beautifully clear, unselfconscious page of prose like that of Cathy Salter's than to see the world itself. This is a fine book, and a gift to its readers."

"Cathy Salter has an artist's eye, a poet's ear, and a lover's heart. Her essays invite the reader to partake of a wondrous life filled with the joys of country walks, great books, travel to distant locales, and good food shared with dear friends. Pour yourself a cup of coffee or a glass of wine and settle in by the fire: You won't find a more rewarding place to spend time than Boomerang Creek."

Notes from Boomerang Creek

Cathy Salter

Published by
AKA-Publishing
Columbia, MO 65203

Trade Paperback ISBN 978-1-942168-46-1
Hardback ISBN 978-1-942168-41-6

Material previously published in the *Columbia Daily Tribune* and the *Boone County Journal* used with permission.

Compass Flower Press
an imprint of AKA-Publishing

NOTES FROM BOOMERANG CREEK

CATHY SALTER

Dedication

To Kit (E.B.), with whom I share my life and thoughts described within this book. I'm not sure what being in cahoots means, but I can't imagine being there without him.

"*There is a story, always ahead of you. Barely existing. Only gradually do you attach yourself to it and feed it. You discover the carapace that will contain and test your character. You will find in this way the path of your life.*"

Michael Ondaatje, *The Cat's Table*

Coming Home

*K*IT AND I MOVED TO A SEVEN-ACRE PARCEL in the country in southern Boone County, Missouri in October of 1988. Having just been in Australia the prior month, we named our new homestead 'Breakfast Creek' after an historic tavern we had encountered near Brisbane. As was the case with our arrival in Australia, we had landed in a new world with plenty of territory for us to explore. After a decade of urban living, first in Los Angeles and then in Washington, D.C., we were eager to grow into country living, though at the time we hadn't a clue what that would entail.

Kit dove with energy into his role as Chair of the Department of Geography at the University of Missouri-Columbia, while I began learning all I could about life in the country. After a teaching career and years of consulting with the National Geographic Society in their effort to improve the teaching of K-12 geography in America's schools, I was entering a new chapter in life and eager to record every detail of it with my camera and in journals that gradually came to reside on writing tables in practically every room of the house.

Following the Great Midwest Flood of 1993, I picked up my pen and began chronicling not only the flooding and its aftermath, but also stories of the seasons, friends, family, our countless animals, and the world as seen from my window at Breakfast Creek. These writings first appeared in a weekly newspaper column, "Notes From Breakfast Creek," in *the Boone Country Journal* in Ashland, Missouri early in 1994. In 1997, the column began to also appear weekly in *the Columbia Tribune*.

Cathy Salter

Thus began my writing life, one that continued to capture experiences both at home and out in the world for the next decade. Then, just as suddenly, the writing stopped. The story of why Kit and I left Missouri for New Mexico and then moved back seven months later would take longer than this introduction will allow. The short of it is this. After returning from a weekend visit to Albuquerque in November 2004, we set in motion a move to New Mexico. In early March 2005, the country life we had known for sixteen years came to an end.

We simply decided it was time for a change, sold Breakfast Creek, packed up our possessions, and left the Heartland behind for life in the American Southwest. With our three cats Pooh, Fanny, and Scribbles nested in their cat carriers, the five of us traveled a thousand miles through Missouri, Oklahoma, the Texas Panhandle, and arrived two days later in Albuquerque, New Mexico.

When the dust settled—a curious phrase when applied to a desert landscape where dust is a regular part of life—we found ourselves living in the pulsing heart of a city once again, this time two blocks off historic Route 66, where it makes its way along Central Avenue in the Nob Hill neighborhood of Albuquerque. As a cultural geographer, Kit was eager to walk along Route 66 and be engaged in urban life again. There were coffee shops, an independent bookstore or two, the Buffalo Exchange consignment shop, a vast range of restaurants, specialty shops, and kitschy 1940s-era Route 66 motor hotels. I also had family—my sister Molly and brother-in-law Jim—who had retired there a year earlier. Upon arrival, we began the task of unpacking and settling into a totally new life. Like the final scene of the movie *The Graduate*, we had dashed onto a moving bus without a real clue as to where we were headed.

Kit and I had both moved often while growing up. In the months before our Missouri departure, I had carefully wrapped and packed every cup, saucer, plate, wine glass, platter, and breakable family treasure into boxes for the moving van that would be coming after our final Christmas season at Breakfast Creek. Over those months Kit flew to Albuquerque and bought a house that was within walking distance of Central Avenue and my sister's home. An unusual aspect of the property was its two parallel lots—one that included a curiously assembled house and a detached garage, and another of virtually the same size that held the fossilized remains of a rambling, abandoned garden. It was an odd house, one that had been built and added onto three different times. Loosely configured like a shotgun house, it was narrow and deep, stretching from the original 1940s structure that fronted on the street through two additions to a narrow alley in the back.

The adjacent lot was in fact a garden that had years ago evolved into a world of pathways, walls and fountains created out of grey concrete rip rap. It had been designed by the same woman who had added a modern wing to the back of the house with a loft wrapped around two sides of an open room that I came to think of as a glass fishbowl.

Had the garden not been located in a desert environment and had the drip irrigation system once in place still worked, the lot might have come back to life, and covered up the concrete bones that were the garden's frame and design with a layer of green. But both the garden and house had been unattended for two years. When I first saw it in the dead of winter, it was haunting. Dried grasses were frozen and white. I remember wandering along its gray stone pathways as if I had stepped into the Charles Dickens novel, *Great Expectations*. Like Pip entering Miss Havisham's long-neglected estate, I had entered a world of cobwebs, broken chunks of concrete, and dead wedding flowers. Entering it for the first time, I found myself enmeshed in a dream that had long ago died. With each passing day, I felt myself disappearing deeper and deeper into the heart of the maze.

Before long, I came to feel that I was dying. Something had not made the journey with me from the green Heartland we had left behind. Nonetheless, we busied ourselves with moving in. Kit set up an office and library in the loft and got right down to the business of writing. I on the other hand, rarely entered my office, and found that for the first time in my life of many moves, I had little desire to hang pictures or unpack boxes. Most days, I busied myself instead in Miss Havisham's haunted garden, hidden from the urban world of traffic and the proximity of other houses by a stucco wall that felt too insulating and confining.

Albuquerque has been described as "the city at the end of the world," and it was not long before I felt that distance to my core. The ten-thousand-foot peaks of the Sandia Mountain range separate Albuquerque's high desert landscape from all that lies to the east. When friends from Missouri and family members came to visit, Kit and I took them on the tram ride to the top of Sandia Peak and out of Albuquerque on road trips to Santa Fe, Taos, Roswell, Carlsbad Caverns and the Laguna Pueblo Indian Reservation forty miles west of Albuquerque. When they left, their absence added to the void I was already feeling.

I found I could no longer write. And because I could not write, I felt like I could not breathe. Like a bird that has flown into a glass window and been momentarily stunned, I needed someone to pick me up, hold me until the shock wore off, and then release me to fly back home.

During the spring and summer months following our arrival, I rose early and sat at the highest point in our garden where I faced east as the sun rose over the Sandia Mountains. In those solitary moments, I allowed myself to grieve over what I felt I had lost as a result of our move. Upon leaving the world I'd been nurtured by and thrived in, I had suffered a kind of death. To overcome my sense of loss and sadness, I set out to make the desert garden we'd inherited bloom again. If it could be coaxed back to life, then perhaps there was hope for me as well.

Some mornings while moving about in my desert garden, I felt myself enter the pages of Michael Ondaatje's beautiful novel and film, *The English Patient*. When Count Laszlo de Almásy and Katharine

Cathy Salter

Clifton are stranded after their jeep slides down a sandy embankment in the Egyptian desert, I dug and dug and dug in my sandy garden, trying to find the heart-shaped desert plant filled with water that Almásy told Katharine he would search for.

"There is a plant," he told Katharine, "I've never seen it but I'm told you can cut a piece the size of a heart from this plant and the next day it will be filled with a delicious liquid."

"Find that plant," Katharine replied. "Cut out its heart." There in that desert garden where I sat in the early pre-dawn light, I told myself that if I kept digging, my heart would be full again. Then I would start to write again, breathe once more, and finally be able to get on with my life.

By late spring, I'd planted twenty-five fruit trees, assorted roses, strawberries, herbs, and native perennials. I was breathing, but had not willed myself to put down roots of my own. As a result, Kit's life and mine moved out of sync. In June, Kit sent me back to Missouri to find a property in southern Boone County where we could resettle. Happily, I found that magic place seemingly waiting to welcome us home. June was incredibly green that year and the Missouri River deep and strong. During that brief return visit, I moved light as a feather through familiar landscapes that my eyes and spirit retraced and embraced. After months in the desert, curl returned to my hair and my skin drank in moisture until I was myself again, and once more felt alive.

We both knew it was time to leave New Mexico and go home. Moving back to Missouri meant making the painful decision to leave new Albuquerque friends, and family members dear to us—a choice never intended or welcomed. It had been a year of monumental upheavals and extremes both emotional and geographic. But in our return journey of a thousand miles taken not once but twice over the course of seven months, Kit and I found ourselves instantly at home on five acres of woods, meadow, gardens, glade and meandering creek. We named our new home 'Boomerang Creek.' We live in a rustic house at the edge of a wood with porches and views of our wandering, boomerang-shaped creek. In a detached structure across a shaded glade, we each have a studio filled with art and books.

A decade has now passed and we cannot imagine ever moving again. We have planted a fruit orchard, put in a serious asparagus bed, reconnected with old friends and made new friends and connections in the incredibly exciting film, book, and arts community in Columbia. We helped begin a farmers market in Ashland, We also frequent our community's branch library and YMCA.

But perhaps most importantly, we have each rediscovered the joys of a writing life. From the moment we returned a decade ago, I began writing my weekly newspaper column again—renamed "Notes From Boomerang Creek." With Kit's encouragement as my partner in life and the best editor a writer could hope to find, I published my first book, *Notes From Breakfast Creek* in 2008. It is the story of the world I discovered when we first moved to Missouri in 1988, fresh from decades of life in the city—when simply put, I didn't know the difference between a bale of hay and a bale of straw.

This second book, *Notes From Boomerang Creek* is its bookend. It is the story of how writing has come back into my life and how my writing has evolved. Like the first book, it is a collection of essays written over a decade, capturing perspectives on writing, seasons and gardens, conversations actual and imagined, food and family, travel, and thoughts on local and world events. From where I sit on our screened porch here in the country—down a gravel road located midway between the banks of the Missouri River and Highway 63, and halfway between Columbia and Jefferson City, the capital of Missouri—it is the perfect place to be at this particular chapter in this writer's life.

BOOMERANG CREEK

TABLE OF CONTENTS

Part One
MY WRITING COMPASS

*I*N MY OWN WRITER'S JOURNEY, I have found myself again and again turning to Jill Ker Conway, an extraordinary historian who spent the first eleven years of her childhood on a rural sheep station in the Australian bush. The first chapter of Conway's childhood memoir, *The Road from Coorain*, is devoted to the physical and cultural geography of western Australia. This place—the vast, drought-prone grasslands region of New South Wales where Coorain is located—was equally as important in shaping the author's experiences and world view as a child as were the members of her family.

"In the west," Conway wrote, "most men who acquired title to western land leases in the 1920s spoke broad Australian: picturesque in image, laced with the rhyming slang of Cockney London and the poetic black humor of the Irish. Their manners and their clothes were deliberately working-class. At night when they sat with their wives beside their crackling static-blurred radios, they waited for Big Ben to chime and then heard the impeccable British accents of the BBC announcer reading the news. With that voice they absorbed a map of the world which placed their neighbor, Japan in the Far East, and located distant Turkey in the Near East."

And, "so far as Australia was concerned, its map was also clear and idiosyncratic.... There were really only two places in the westerner's consciousness: the bush and the metropolis at the end of the railway where the wool was sold."

At the age of eleven, Conway's world was transformed by a "fury of the elements"—a catastrophic eight-year drought that led to the death of her father and her family's relocation from the bush country to Sydney. By the time she graduated with honors from the University of Sydney, the stultifying atmosphere created by her mother's increasingly depressed mental state and Jill's passionate desire for a scholarly career in history, beyond what existed for women in the Australia of 1959, led her to a transformative decision. She left Australia for good for America where she earned a PhD in American History in 1969 from Harvard University.

After Harvard, she moved with her husband and soul mate, John Conway to his native Canada where she taught and rose to Vice President at the University of Toronto. That intellectually and personally fulfilling period of her life is the subject of her second memoir, *True North*.

In *True North*, I came upon a passage written when she was thirty-nine. She wrote, "I knew I wanted to quit administration by the time I was fifty, because my life would never be fulfilled if I didn't do the writing I knew was in me. I'd been in love with words since childhood, and I craved the sensation of clarity that comes from working to shape a text.... I missed...the sense of discovery as one made the connections between parts of one's experience which one wasn't even conscious were linked until they appeared on the page."

For twenty-six magical years, I've followed my own writing compass—for sixteen years at Breakfast Creek and for the past decade here at Boomerang Creek. It is what Jill Ker Conway had come to miss until, in her fifties, she penned her brilliant memoir of growing up Australian—"the pleasure of sitting alone at my desk, focusing the mind, and finding out what I knew through what appeared on the page."

(June 2015)

Chapter One
ON WRITING

"Part of the excitement is that I never know beforehand where a story will take me. That makes writing a fascinating journey of discovery every time."

C.S. December 2008

A CIRCLE OF WRITERS

*I*N APRIL 2002, I MADE A SOJOURN to France where I joined the company of a small group of writers in Provence. Our glorious hideaway at Aux Deux Soeurs—an extraordinary country Bed & Breakfast in a renovated stone farmhouse—was proximate to the picturesque perched village of Gordes, the Roman ruins in Arles, rows of ancient olive trees once painted by Van Gogh near Saint-Rémy-de-Provence, and incredible French country restaurants scattered throughout the Luberon region. The setting provided a peaceful base for a week of exploration, a delicious world of material for writing, an immersion into the cuisine of Provence, and evenings of stimulating conversation.

My conundrum was this. I had come to write. However, while I did get up very early each morning to make notes about the prior day's travel events, I could not pull myself away from a single planned outing to remain behind at our idyllic lodgings to write. The dilemma was both delicious and bothersome. While I wanted to write, I also wanted to work with my camera, enter into conversations with my fellow travelers, and absorb absolutely everything I could of Provence in the short time I was there. Writing, I told myself, would happen just as soon as I returned to my patterned writing life back in Missouri.

The reality, of course, is that patterns quickly fall apart when they are broken. After returning to Breakfast Creek—our country home in Missouri—it rained for what seemed like an eternity that May. Day after soggy day, more rain fell—at times torrentially—worrying those who live along the river and flooding basements of those of us who live on higher ground. Gardening was impossible unless the task was pulling invasive weeds.

In the absence of sun and the sense of joy that comes from gardening, I tried to get back into my old familiar rhythm and get down to the business of writing about my travels. To slip back into writing seamlessly, as though I were walking alone in the lavender fields that surround the Abbey Sénanque tucked peacefully into in the Luberon Mountains of the Vaucluse near the village of Gordes. Or to walk again to the mysterious spring-fed source of the Sorgue River that draws tourists from around the world to the lovely Provençal town of Fontaine du Vaucluse.

However, instead of sharing a leisurely *dejeuner* with my writer friends at the Café Lou Fanau at the edge of the crystal clear Sorgue, I found myself dealing with repairs on our veteran Maytag washer *and* dryer—trouble-free until now for thirteen years running. The week of my return was also the week I had scheduled for our annual rug cleaning inside, and deck weatherizing outside. Furniture had to be moved, and books piled around the edges of the library temporarily shifted to surfaces already filled with the stuff of earlier writing projects. More critically, area rugs needed to be beaten, washed, and hung somewhere to dry.

Some obscure part had to be ordered for the dryer. The wait would be a week, and still it rained. This I decided was a test—my payment for having spent an enchanting, sunny week exploring Provence in late April when I would otherwise have been home dealing with repairs on my truck, a computer printer that died an early death, and our ailing Maytags.

At that dark, damp moment when I was afraid to ask what else could possibly go wrong, the clouds of May parted and a mysterious, tubular box arrived in a brown UPS truck. The package was from a distant acquaintance who had re-read a piece that I wrote in 1994 just after "Notes from Breakfast Creek" became a weekly column. Out of the blue, this dear soul had sent the perfect gift for this particularly gloomy moment—a collapsible, umbrella shaped clothesline mounted on a single aluminum pole.

"Where would you like it?" Kit asked. "Let me think on it," I responded, mentally searching for the ideal location. That evening, we had dinner in the garden—surrounded by strawberry and lettuce patches, pea vines, roses, two fruiting pear trees, and pots of culinary herbs. As we shared news of the day, my eyes came to rest on a relic steel satellite dish post anchored just beyond the garden fence. "There," I said, "is the perfect place for the clothesline."

The clothesline was our "yard art installation." It was our ever-changing plein air canvas that artfully captured patterns and designs constructed and deconstructed with each new collection of fabrics hung on the line. On washdays, I carried my wicker laundry basket and clothespin bag to the garden. In the magical exercise of hanging the wash, I was instantly re-connected to the circle of writers with whom I discovered Provence under a sky so blue it made our hearts ache.

(June 2002)

A Good Radio Conversation

*J*UST BEFORE MY RECENT INTERVIEW WITH KFRU's radio talk show host, David Lile, I put on the headphones I'd been handed and adjusted the volume knob. There wasn't time to get nervous. I felt like I was on an airplane that was about to take off. I love flying and spontaneous, in-flight conversations with fellow passengers. When David's voice came through my headset, I leaned forward as if I were in the cockpit with him, and we were on the air, about to travel who knew where?

Our radio conversation began with a question I am often asked when readers learn that I have been writing a weekly newspaper column since 1994. "Do you ever have trouble coming up with something to write about?" he asked. My answer is always the same. "No, not ever. The mind is like a piece of Velcro," I explained.

"How do you know what you are going to write about?" David went on. "Do you take notes all week or keep a journal?"

"I don't take notes or keep lists of thoughts," I answered. "When I am not actively writing, I move about Boomerang Creek, the community, and beyond. In these daily interactions with people and the landscapes that I move through, shards of information on a world of fascinating topics attach themselves to my mind. When I sit down to face a blank monitor on my computer screen the following Monday, threads of this and that always resurface. Weaving the threads into a story is my weekly challenge. Part of the excitement is that I never know beforehand where a story will take me. That makes writing a fascinating journey of discovery every time."

Holding a copy of my 2008 book, *Notes From Breakfast Creek:*

A Look At The World, David began leafing through the pages from back to front. He admitted that this is how he approaches whatever he reads. Because he was moving through the book's contents backwards, David noted with interest that I'd written about a conversation with Denzel Washington at the Sundance Institute and that two of my chapters of essays were about travel. "You've written about Saigon, and so many other fascinating places, but you also write about commonplace events like family auctions."

Picking up that thread, I said that I love traveling, and have had a wonderful life as a result. My experiences as a Peace Corps volunteer in the late 1960s positioned me in the heart of Southeast Asia in the middle of the Vietnam War. I was in my early twenties, full of hope and optimism without a jot of fear. Everything seemed possible.

Fast-forwarding to when I moved with Kit to Missouri in 1988, I turned the conversation back to David's mentioning of commonplace events that find their way into my writing. "I had never been to an auction before moving to Missouri," I told him. "I didn't understand 'auction speak' the way someone does who grows up going to auctions. In fact, I bid against myself three times in my first attempt to buy a quilt twenty years ago."

Then I added, "Something in my genetic makeup told me I wanted to learn everything that I could about life in the country. Clotheslines, auctions, floods, the cycle of the seasons, gardening, canning, quilting circles, small communities, trees and wildlife, planting and harvesting, neighbors and the nature of families with deep roots in the Heartland—all of these themes fascinated me."

"Have you always been a writer?" David asked.

"I've always loved reading and appreciated the craft of writing. But for much of my adult life, I have thought of myself as a teacher. Writing didn't begin for me until the Great Midwest Flood of 1993. When the flood cleanup that had begun in August 1993 in Hartsburg finally ended around Thanksgiving, I picked up my pen and wrote about the affects of the flood on the small, river-bottom farm community that was our postal address. Three months later, I began writing the weekly newspaper column that continues to this day."

Midway through the radio interview, a caller came on the line. "You wrote a piece that I remember about your father on Memorial Day."

"I often write about my father," I said. "Dad grew up on a dairy farm in Pennsylvania and had four daughters. I am the one who loves digging in the dirt and wants to know everything farmers seem to grow up knowing and being able to do instinctively. What I know about farming, canning, floods, and community spirit, I've learned from our friends in Hartsburg and Boone County where Kit and I have put down roots of our own these past twenty years.

"What will you write about next Monday?" David asked as our twenty-minute radio conversation came to an end.

"Honey bees," I answered speculatively. "But then, I just never know."

(December 2008)

Assignment: A Writing Primer

*W*HEN DOES WRITING BEGIN? This is a question that I put to twelve classes of students over the course of a school day at Columbia's New Haven School. I'd been allotted twenty minutes with each class, beginning the day with precious kindergarteners and ending it with fifth graders—a range that proved fascinating given the subject, the nature of writing.

I took along an illustrated copy of E. B. White's 1952 classic, *Charlotte's Web*, and two collections of books written and illustrated by children. One collection published by Landmark Books of Kansas City fell into three age groupings—books written and illustrated by children from six to nine, ten to thirteen, and fourteen to eighteen. The other collection was of books written and illustrated by our daughter Heidi Salter from the time she was in kindergarten until young adulthood.

What could I possibly say to a classroom of children on a warm, late May day when summer vacation was already on their minds? I had twenty minutes with each class—five more than Andy Warhol would have given me—to make an impression on their fertile minds on the subject of writing. To reach the inner writer inside each of their heads, and convince them that they too can write if they sit down without the TV on, put aside headphones, turn off their cell phone, and let their young imaginations soar.

I began with E. B. White who was relatively—from a child's perspective—my same age cohort when he left New York City for life on a farm in Maine—a move not unlike my own when Kit and I moved in 1988 from urban life in Washington, D.C. and Los Angeles to the rural world of Southern Boone County, Missouri. *Charlotte's Web* is a book beloved by children and adults alike. When White wrote his endearing book about a little girl, a pig and a barn spider that wove words into her web, I was five—the age of the kindergarteners that assured me enthusiastically that they knew and loved the story.

I then showed them the Landmark books, impressing on each age group that they had all had been written and illustrated by a school child as part of a national "Written and Illustrated By" competition. Depending on the age of the class, I shared sample books biographic sketches of some of the child-authors. As a segue into the second collection of the books that I'd brought along, I held up one of the three national winners of Landmark's 1988 competition—*Taddy McFinley and the Great Grey Grimley*," by Heidi Salter when she was eighteen years old.

With the twenty-minute clock ticking, I attempted to answer the question that I began this essay with—When does writing begin? For Heidi, I explained while holding up a tiny, handmade book entitled "The Talking Shoe," writing began with her pre-school fascination and facility with language. Written and illustrated in pencil and bound in a brown construction paper cover, "The Talking Shoe" is the charming story of a left-foot shoe named Scrabbles and his girlfriend Jessie—the other half of a pair of lace-up leather shoes that lived in a little boy's closet. It is a simple and utterly adorable tale. Every student and teacher was charmed as I read it aloud to one class after another that day.

I then picked up a handmade book entitled "Tad" that Heidi wrote, illustrated and assembled within a cover for Kit on Father's Day when she was around ten years old. The little girl depicted in the story is Heidi as I remember her at that age—an impish, barefooted, independent-minded little girl with a full head of curly brown hair, dressed in a red tee shirt and yellow shorts. "This little book," I told each class, was the one that Heidi redrew eight years later and entered in Landmark's 1988 book competition. *Taddy McFinley and the Great Grey Grimley*, was the result of her revision of "Tad"—the handmade book about a curly-haired little girl who lived in her ten-year old's imagination.

At this point of each session, an aide passed out a pencil and a single piece of writing paper folded the size of "The Talking Shoe" to each student. On the cover, I had them each write a single letter as their title and put their name as the book's author at the bottom of the cover page. Holding up one of the Landmark books, *A to Z*, I asked them to think of an animal. Then between the book's covers, they were asked to illustrate the animal on one side and compose a brief poem about the animal on the opposing page.

At the end of each class, these books were collected, put in a folder for the teacher, and I encouraged the students to write books of their own over the summer. As one boy left, he asked where he could find a copy of *Taddy McFinley*. His teacher wrote down the title and promised to try and locate it. If New Haven Elementary School's library doesn't have a copy," I assured the boy, "I know where to find one."

(June 2007)

A WRITER'S WORLD

ECENTLY, MY FRIEND BETTY LITTLETON ASKED if I had by chance read "My Father's Suitcase," an article by Orhan Pamuk that had appeared in the December 2006/January 2007 issue of *The New Yorker*. "No," I told her. It is an annual literary issue that I normally read with relish, but this year the double issue had inadvertently been buried in the perpetual pile of magazines that covers the barnwood coffee table in front of our fireplace. Orhan Pamuk, a name that I did not know I knew, was buried somewhere along with our copy of the magazine.

I live surrounded by books and still buy newly published and out-of-print books online. Kit and I subscribe to a range of weekly and monthly magazines that cover subjects from cooking and gardening to news from Kabul and the disappearing world of the Marsh Arabs of Iraq. We read the *Columbia Tribune* daily, the *Boone County Journal* weekly, and the *New York Times* online every morning. But in the flow of life and information, I had forgotten a TV interview that I had seen of a Turkish novelist who was awarded the 2006 Nobel Prize in Literature.

Betty kindly mailed Pamuk's *New Yorker* article to me, noting that from one writer to another, she felt certain I would find it interesting. A year ago, not long after first meeting Betty, I read her 1965 novel, *In Samson's Eye*, written during her career as a Professor of English at Stephens College. I remember being captured by Betty's characters, and beautiful prose that I found reminiscent of Willa Cather. I shared my reaction to the book with the author as well as a group of twelve women with whom I meet once a month. After reluctantly returning

Betty's novel to the library, I ordered a copy from an online bookstore for my own writer's studio library.

When Pamuk's *New Yorker* article arrived I read it immediately, noting that it was in fact, the author's 2006 Nobel lecture, translated from Turkish. The accompanying black and white photograph of Pamuk in New York City, October 12, 2006, triggered a memory of a taped interview of the author in the streets of Istanbul, the city that is the center of Pamuk's world. Still, I could not find a single book title in my mental data bank to connect to this Nobel Laureate.

And so I began a journey into this writer's mind and world. "Two years before my father's death," Pamuk's story begins, "he gave me a small suitcase filled with his manuscripts and notebooks." The father understood that his son, a writer for twenty-five years, would not open the suitcase and read its contents until after his death. The stage was set for a fascinating revelation. For a while, Pamuk admitted that he could not even touch the suitcase—one his businessman father had taken with him on prior trips. "Whenever he came home," the author recalls, "I'd rush to open this little suitcase and rummage through his things, savoring the scent of cologne and foreign countries."

As Pamuk grew older, the weight of the little suitcase represented the weight of literature. His fear was that by opening the suitcase, he might discover that his father was indeed a good writer, "a man entirely different from the one I knew."

Pamuk then turned inward. "A writer," he believes, "is someone who spends years patiently trying to discover the second being inside him, and the world that makes him who he is. To write is to transform that inward gaze into words, to study the worlds into which we pass when we retire into ourselves, and to do so with patience, obstinacy, and joy."

Now, several weeks later, I am in my study surrounded by *My Name is Red*, *Snow*, and *Istanbul*—three of Orhan Pamuk's literary works. Next to the three works as yet unexplored, is a familiar, dog-eared second edition of Charlotte Brontë's *Jane Eyre* and Betty Littleton's novel *In Samson's Eye*. How fortunate readers are who visit worlds crafted by writers such as these—worlds Orhan Pamuk describes as "at once familiar and miraculous." For it is there that we, like the writer, find ourselves one with humanity.

(February 2007)

ILLUMINATING CAVES OF OTHER LANGUAGES

*I*FOUND MYSELF DRAWN to the entrance of a cave filled with a babble of languages. Unable to resist the distant voices from within, I entered. Then guided by three who have explored here before me, I am connected with past cultures, great minds, and languages in which I am not fluent. Yet, not for a moment do I feel lost.

My first guide through this cave of other languages is linguist Geoffrey Khan of the University of Cambridge. Following his lamplight, we emerge in Niles, Illinois—a suburb of Chicago. There, we speak with elderly immigrants who once lived in mountain enclaves in Iraq, Syria, Iran, or Turkey, and grew up speaking a dialect of Aramaic—the three-thousand-year old language of Jesus.

Along the way, light from Khan's torch reveals writing on the cave walls, going back to a time when the Middle East was the crossroads of the world and Aramaic was the *lingua franca* of commerce— connecting people from Egypt and the Holy Lands to India and China.

Khan is racing against time to document the words of the few remaining native speakers of this language of ancient desert nomads before they die off, taking the language with them. Many "pure dialects," Khan tells me, are already extinct. "Others are down to their last one or two speakers."

At this juncture, I feel a hand on my arm, guiding me down another corridor. Kati Marton, author of *The Great Escape: Nine Jews Who Fled Hitler and Changed the World*, leads me into an interior chamber of another cave where I experience Budapest in its golden years in the late nineteenth and early twentieth century. "The language," Marton tells me, is "Hungarian"—Magyar, her mother tongue—"impenetrable—a member of the Finno-Ugric family, not similar to other European languages."

In a dark narrow passageway of the cave of other languages that I am now exploring, we witness a diaspora of Hungarian Jews who fled the Nazi terror in the 1930s. Escaping with them into a larger cave filled with space and brilliant light, Marton points out nine twentieth- century giants— Leo Szilard, physicist and inventor; Edward Teller, Manhattan Project theoretical physicist; Eugene Wigner, theoretical physicist and mathematician; John von Neuman, applied mathematician, physicist, and inventor; Arthur Koestler, author of *Darkness at Noon*; Andre Kertesz, pioneer of modern photojournalism; Robert Capa, the first photographer ashore on D-Day; and iconic filmmakers Alexander Korda and Michael Curtiz (*Casablanca*). Each had fled Budapest for Paris, London, and America, where they reinvented themselves and changed the world.

Staggered by what I didn't know but now have had revealed, I barely realize that a new guide, Margaret Sayers Peden, has taken the torch from Marton and led me back in time to the seventeenth century, to a cave of yet another language and time.

Here I learn the remarkable story of Sor Juana Ines de la Cruz, a Mexican nun born in 1651 to a Spanish father and creole mother. A child genius, she could read and write at the age of three. She had read every volume in her grandfather's extensive library after five years of primary school. After becoming a nun at the age of sixteen, Sor Juana wrote influential works of poetry and prose that led some scholars to compare her to another prodigy, John Stuart Mills—another apostle of individual liberty and enemy of dogma.

Margaret Sayers Peden—awarded the 2012 PEN-Ralph Manheim Medal for Translation—has led millions before me to this cave to read the language of Sor Juana and other great Spanish and Latin

American writers—Pablo Neruda, Octavio Paz, Carlos Fuentes, and Isabel Allende.

At the Saturday morning book gathering in Columbia in February 2013, Peden spoke eloquently to a rapt audience of sixty about her life in translation and of "swimming in a sea of dictionaries" in search of the other language's pure meaning—*the word beneath the word.*

Peden's more than sixty-five translations of Spanish to English works, Marton's personal celebration of nine extraordinary Jewish Hungarian exiles, and linguist Khan's quest to document disappearing ancient Aramaic dialects all brilliantly illuminate caves of other languages we might not otherwise have ever explored.

(February 2013)

THE LANGUAGE OF TRAVEL

A CONVERSATION IS UNDERWAY. Eleven of us have begun gathering once a week to share thoughts on travel and travel writing. Why? Perhaps it is the word itself. *Travel*...six-letters flowing like melted French brie across two syllables. *Travel...* a variant of *travail* meaning a sense of toil and fatigue. *Travel*. A word filled with a passionate language of its own.

The word travel is both a verb and a noun. My dictionary, as if impatient to get going, begins with the verb travel—to go from one place to another; journey: *She is traveling in Europe this summer. He travels fastest who travels alone* (Rudyard Kipling); to move, proceed, pass: *Light and sound travel in waves*; to walk or run: *A deer travels far and fast when chased*; to pass through or over: *to travel a road*.

Then, like a seasoned traveler, my worldly multi-lingual lexicon introduces the noun travel—the act or fact of going in trains, ships, cars, and the like, from one place to another; journeying: *to spend a summer in travel. She loves travel.* (Indeed! I agree.) Travels—journeys: *Soon after, we find him on his travels in Italy* (Samuel Taylor Coleridge.) Travels—a book about one's experiences, visits, or observations while traveling: *We possess the travels of a native of... India in the fourth century* (Mountstuart Elphinstone).

The various meanings of the word travel anticipate our conversation. Parsing its meanings in my dictionary, words jump off the page. *Journey, Europe, summer, Kipling, Coleridge, India, Italy, alone, light, waves, far and fast, pass through, love, experiences, visits, observations, the fourth century.* Like countless travelers over the centuries who have kept journals, woven travel tales and left their footprints in the sands of distant deserts or carved into sandstone, I too could write my own travel stories with these words.

Months ago, I talked with Lucille Salerno—the indefatigable and creative Director of the University of Missouri Extension's Osher Lifelong Learning Institute—about teaching another class on travel writing, expanding on one I had offered for the first time a year earlier. As my enthusiasm for such a class grew, I began to compile an annotated list of travel writing from the library that surrounds me in my studio at Boomerang Creek. An innocent task at first, my list has become a monumental journey of its own. Mark Twain's *Innocents Abroad* is one among a host of other well known writers, along with a few forgotten ones, who felt the need to capture *light, waves, experiences, observations,* and *love* as they *passed through or over* worlds either *alone* or with other fellow travelers.

On the first day of class, our group took turns reading aloud a short travel article by master storyteller Pat Conroy. "In the last days I would ever feel like a young man," Conroy wrote, "I went to Paris to finish the novel I was writing at the time." After going into an "uncontrollable rapture" reading Ernest Hemingway's *A Moveable Feast,* Conroy reveals, "I could think of no finer way to spend a part of my life than by writing a book in the storied, uncapturable city of literature and light."

Just hearing the word *Paris* through Conroy's writer's voice was an intoxicating invitation to travel. Riveted, we listened to Conroy's delicious language of travel as it continued to work its magic on us all. As each person in our circle read a passage aloud, images of Paris entered our heads. Gamely, we tackled the pronunciation of French words, hoping not to sound like a donkey (Conroy's own assessment of his French that summer).

Our senses were stirred at the mention of *croissants, brioche,* and *escargots, the Seine, the Louve, the Rue Mouffetard, Les Deux Magots, Sartre* and *Beauvoir.* But it was Conroy's description of a picnic lunch with friends—*two cheeses, Chaource and Camembert, hard sausage, duck paté, a baguette, and a bottle of Rosé d'Anjou*—that drew a collective sigh. Without a single reservation, our travels had already begun.

(September 2011)

The Tao of Travel

*I*N THE EARLY MORNING, when a light September mist transforms our meadow filled with native purple grasses into a field of French lavender, I find myself lost in thoughts of travel. Transported, my train of thought moves rapidly to the subject of travel writers, and in particular, Paul Theroux.

For Theroux, travel has been a way of life, providing him with rich insights and first-hand material for the author's long list of fiction and travel books. His latest, *The Tao of Travel*, is both enlightening and clever in its design and intent. It is, Theroux writes, "a book of insights, a distillation of travelers' visions and pleasures, observations from my work and others' that is based on my reading travel books and traveling the earth."

Bound in the fashion of a nineteenth century journal, it is soft in the hand like an oft-read Bible. To the eye and touch, it speaks of Moroccan leather embossed with gold leaf lettering, and is lined with an antique world map on the inside of the front and back cover. Theroux intended it as a guidebook designed to be carried around and referred to often, a how-to, a miscellany, a reading list, and for the writer himself, a reminiscence.

On the book's cover, a hand extends from the gilded sleeve of a traveler holding a carpetbag ringed with rays of light. Its contents, "Enlightenments from Lives on the Road," are notions on the subject of travel, "often a metaphor for living a life"—penned by fellow travelers across the ages and interspersed with others by Theroux himself.

In the final chapter of the book, Theroux lists his "Essential Tao of Travel":

   1. Leave home.

   2. Go alone.

   3. Travel light.

   4. Bring a map.

   5. Go by land.

   6. Walk across a national frontier.

   7. Keep a journal.

   8. Read a novel that has no relation to the place you're in.

   9. If you must bring a cell phone, avoid using it.

   10. Make a friend.

As the titles of Theroux's twelve travel books hint, no mode of transportation offers more opportunities for observation than the railway train. "While every airplane trip is the same," he notes, "every railway journey is different." The traveler can walk around, trips are not stressful, and anyone who cares to can write down their impressions of the passing landscapes and record conversations with often-companionable fellow passengers.

In a quote from Theroux's book, *The Old Patagonia Express*, he recalls, "There is nothing more perfect in travel than boarding a train just at nightfall and shutting the bedroom door on a riotous city and knowing that morning would show me a new latitude. I would leave anything behind, I thought, for a sleeper on a southbound express."

Reminiscences of one of my own distant railway travel experiences resurfaces in a pocket-sized journal that I treasure these decades hence. I am in Thailand on the Bangkok-to-Nongkhai evening express sleeper train. It is February 26, 1975. Time disappears as snapshots, once penned in a small, pocket-sized journal while traveling by railway, resurface as if captured only yesterday—

The lights began to dim around 8:30 p.m. as the bed maker made his rounds and arranged the sleeper compartment for us. The upper berths are lowered and mattresses within are arranged with crisp white sheets and a cover. Then the bottom berth is extended, the bed made up, and drapes are hung. Very neat and tidy.

I had a lower berth—much cooler as it was a particularly stuffy night and the fan didn't work. Also, it gave me a chance to sit up as we pulled into various stations and observe the night activities of hawkers and food sellers.

The moon was full and the night magical. The smoke of fires inside small dwellings scattered among the darkened hills made a beautiful picture that I will carry with me throughout the journey and for all of my life.

As Paul Theroux has done over his life as a traveler and writer, I had left home, though not alone. I had traveled light with journals and maps. Traveling by railway, I had crossed the Mekong River—the national border between Thailand and Laos. Cell phones did not yet exist. I made friends along the way. *Tao. The way.* Indeed, my travel life was well underway.

(September 2011)

THE SOLITARY NATURE OF EXPLORATION

TANDING AT THE EDGE OF OUR SHADE GARDEN, I see the world in miniature. A riverine flagstone path winds through its center, dividing it into equally lush hemispheres that beg to be explored. On a solitary mosey along the pathway; I pause near an ornamental bench where Fanny, our calico Manx cat, sits still as stone, stoically waiting for a gecko to move out from under a giant hosta leaf where it has taken cover.

Fed by abundant spring rains, this verdant garden has exploded with treasured perennials forced into hiding beneath towering undesirable invader species. To have the garden appear natural while at the same time allowing its beauty to be fully appreciated, there must be an investment of time each May in weeding every inch of this delicate, shaded plant world by hand.

Armed with gloves and a large two-handled plastic tub, I venture from the flagstone path into a region of the garden's geographic interior and begin my morning exercise. Alone with birdsong, I'm watched by bluebirds nesting in a Thai spirit house. Set quietly back a foot from the flagstone path's center, it is an auspicious vantage point from which the bluebirds can watch all activities taking place around them.

For an hour, I bend and extract weeds by the handful, filling the generously expansive tub two or three times in the process. One by one, assorted irises, peonies, feathery astilbe, cinnamon ferns, Asiatic lilies, ornamental strawberries, columbine, bleeding hearts, ox-eye daisies, lambs ear, coral bells, and celandine poppies emerge from the heavy foliage that has by now overshadowed their footprint. When at last the warmth of filtered under-story light is again felt, each plant breathes a sigh of airy thanks and rewards my labors with endless blooms.

The solitary nature of this exercise sets my thoughts traveling to women who have undertaken remarkable journeys. Amelia Earhart, answering a phone call one afternoon in April 1928 from book publisher and publicist George P. Putnam, was asked, "How would you like to be the first woman to fly the Atlantic?" Without hesitation, Earhart accepted the challenge, accomplishing the landmark twenty-one-hour flight across the Atlantic Ocean two months later with another pilot and a copilot/mechanic. Upon their return to the United States, the team was greeted with a ticker tape parade in New York City and a reception at the Calvin Coolidge White House.

My thoughts then travel back to a time forty years earlier, when Nellie Bly—a fearless investigative reporter for the *New York World*—and Elizabeth Bisland—a journalist writing for the monthly *Cosmopolitan* magazine—both received similar calls in November 1889 from their publishers proposing that they leave immediately on a record-setting race to circumnavigate the globe in under eighty days. The feat had never before been accomplished, save by the fictional Phileas Fogg in Jules Verne's popular 1873 novel, *Around the World in Eighty Days*.

Conceived in an atmosphere of competitive, male-dominated journalism, the race of these two unaccompanied, Victorian-era women was followed by the entire world through daily news releases. But unlike Amelia Earhart a generation later, their remarkable accomplishments are hardly a footnote in today's history books. This, however, may change. Author Matthew Goodman's grand book, *Eighty Days: Nellie Bly and Elizabeth Bisland's History Making Race Around the World*, published in 2012, has once again shed light on this remarkable, long-forgotten story.

After reading *Eighty Days*, I sang its praises in two newspaper columns and then invited author Matthew Goodman to come to

Columbia in October 2013. Working with a group of local women and organizations, plans immediately got underway that include an author's reception hosted by the Boone County Museum, campus talks for students and the public at the University of Missouri Reynolds Journalism Institute, and a panel at the Daniel Boone Regional Library of four Columbia women who have made extraordinary journeys of their own.

Standing alone in my quiet country shade garden, I am in awe of the solitary nature of these journeys and the remarkable accomplishments of Amelia Earhart, Nellie Bly and Elizabeth Bisland. Like the plants I am surrounded by, I am eager for the stories of these three women to continue to receive the air and light they so richly deserve.

(June 2013)

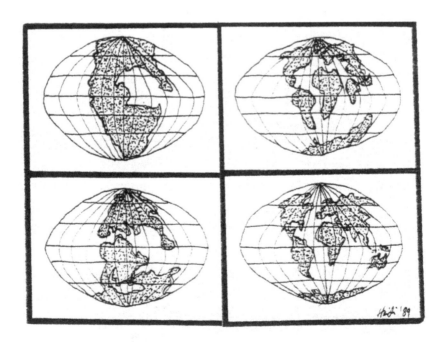

Cathy Salter

Chapter Two
A Writer's Imagination

When I was a child, maps were alive with pink and green and yellow shapes labeled with exotic country names. As I grew older, maps grew more detailed, adding lines representing rivers and relief, and dots of varying sizes representing cities and historic sites. History books were filled with detailed maps and fascinating stories layered across time and vast expanses of the world's continents. Without maps, history's stories were incomplete. With maps, I could navigate my way back through time.

C.S. October 2009

A Scene From Above

WERE I A BLUEBIRD THIS SPRING MORNING viewing Boomerang Creek from above, I'd have noted a solitary woman walking with trekking poles along the quarter-mile mown pathway that rings an open grassy meadow surrounded on three sides by woods and glade. She has spotted me, "carrying the sky on my back" as Henry David Thoreau was wont to say—"a traditional symbol of hope and happiness."

I flit ahead of this woman whose hair is a softer shade of the reddish brown plumage that covers my throat and breast. Rounding the south end of the meadow, past a row of six tall sweet gum trees, *liquidamber styraciflua*, this woman stops to note the return of their leaves, lobed like a maple but forming a more regular, five-pointed star. She remembers their colors as they mark the changing seasons— green in summer, streaked with crimson and yellow by autumn.

Like a sunset, an admirer once noted, "The tree is not a flame, it is a conflagration!"

Rounding the corner at the path's southeastern edge, the walker leaves woods and sweet gums behind and follows a series of fence posts linked by stretches of barbed wire. The fence line is the eastern boundary of this property's meadow—a mix of tall native grasses partially encircling tilled berry and herb beds, a rose garden and a small orchard.

Atop two of the round fence posts, the woman's husband has affixed bluebird houses, one of which the walker is rapidly approaching. As a diversion, I fly several posts ahead of her, landing and then flying on ahead of her until she passes the wooden house where two bluebirds nest each spring. The woman makes a point of not looking into the hole of the wooden house as she passes, sensitive to my rouse that was intended to focus her attention on me.

When she has completed six laps and headed back to the open deck of her house, two other bluebirds catch her attention. This pair has made the extraordinary decision to think outside of the traditional, open meadow bird box and instead, take up residence in a Thai spirit house. It sits atop a high, thin persimmon tree stump in the back of a shaded hosta garden with a central flagstone pathway and wooden bench nearby for moments of quiet reflection in this peaceful garden beneath a canopy of persimmons, oaks, maples, cypresses, and ash trees.

Cousins or offspring, perhaps of the very bluebirds now inhabiting the meadow bird box, this pair wing hither and yon, working their way indirectly to the spirit house's front porch and entrance. Once inside, they hop past an eight-inch high alabaster statue of an Egyptian cat, a small Buddha, and a large petaled silk lily. Their nest lies hidden from view at the back of this honey-colored teakwood house—hand crafted by a Peace Corps friend from the woman's life some forty-seven years earlier.

Two small blue-green, plastic geckos once stood guard at the entrance of the spirit house but mysteriously disappeared when a pair of house wrens nested in this same spirit house a year ago. Noting that wrens are the very symbol of small, vulnerable life forms, eighteenth century poet William Blake wrote, "He who shall hurt the little wren / Shall never be beloved by men." Perhaps the spirit of the poet himself dispatched the menacing-looking geckos that spring in an effort to welcome in the diminutive wrens with their upcocked tails and bubbling, musical birdsong.

A bluebird then emerges from the spirit house and wings toward feeders hanging in a glade between the house and studio at Boomerang Creek. The woman settles into an Adirondack chair on the deck.

"Ready for a coffee?" the man asks the redheaded meadow walker.

"Absolutely," she replies, eager to share news on her bird sightings. "Can you believe the exaltation of bluebirds out on a lark this morning? I circled the meadow six times and they hardly seemed to notice I was there."

(May 2013)

A Flight of Fancy

THERE IS SOMETHING MAGICAL about a great blue heron. It is a solitary fisher bird—prehistoric in form, graceful in flight, haltingly slow when wading on its stilt-like legs, tapered and stealthy in aerial motion, still as a frozen pond when focused on spearing its piscatorial prey. Was this ancient marsh bird, I wonder, named for Heron—a Greek geometer and mechanician—because he believed its assemblage of oddly angled and curiously measured body parts must surely have fallen from one of heaven's starry constellation?

I once surprised a great blue heron that had dropped down like a silent night on the pond when we lived at Breakfast Creek. Legs extended, the heron inched around the frozen edges of the pond, finally stopping near a corner where our paddling of ducks and geese were floating in open water. There, it shape-shifted down to half its prior size, assumed a perfectly balanced one-legged stance, pulled its feathery coat up over its hunched shoulders, and settled in for the night.

The following morning, I came face to face with the heron, taking it for a twiggy branch frozen solid to the pond's icy surface. For an instant that I've never forgotten and often revisited, we both stopped breathing. Fueled by instinct, some internal gear shifted within the heron, releasing an expansive pair of wings. Then, in one wide-eyed blink, the now fully alert creature initiated an impossibly slow, virtually vertical liftoff from the ice.

More than a decade later, as I am temporarily grounded by foot surgery, I relate this story to my grandson Nicolas who lives in Madrid, Spain—far away as the heron flies. In this period of arrested motion

Cathy Salter

that began three weeks ago, my mind travels about unfettered but my forward motion requires that I balance like a heron at rest on one leg.

"Recently," I tell Nico, "your grandfather, *Abuelo* Kit, transported me across the mulch pathway from our house to my writing studio in a grandly appointed wheelbarrow—my bandaged and trussed toes pointing the way."

Nico wonders what I do all day. "Rest a lot," I tell him.

I have spent hours reading my way through the pile of books assembled weeks ago for this initial month of post-op healing. Funny how we dream of house arrest, away from the noise of the world, but when it happens, it is not easy to sit still and watch impassively as the minutes and hours move in circles and complete their calendar days. Humans are not nearly as patient as herons.

Nico also wonders how I can endure sitting for a month with one of my feet elevated. "Simple," I say. "Whenever I'm tempted to rush things, I just close my eyes and beckon the magic blue heron. Please take me aloft, I whisper, before drifting into a quiet meditation that to no one's surprise resembles a napping cat."

"Now," I tell Nico, "I will to take you along on a magical flight of fancy." And so it begins—

> Perched weightlessly atop the bird's long feathery back, I look down as the blue heron slowly arches up and over the woods and hollers until somewhere five miles to the west, the bird and I become a solitary shadow cast from high above the Missouri River as it courses along its mighty way. Like light dancing on water, we sparkle.
>
> With wings, I feel graceful again. Together, we move like the wind, traveling wherever my mind wishes to go. Emerging from an unexpected dance with a capricious thermal, I feel delight.

"Describe something that you see down below," Nico asks. So I describe the chalky white dome of a Burmese Buddhist stupa seen from high above a hill in Mandalay. But then the stupa moves.

"What was it that moved?" Nico asks. "It is actually Pooh," I tell my darling grandson, "our snow white feline with one blue eye and one golden, emerging from a catnap of her own." Just then a shadow flits quickly past a window across the room. "My magic heron is on its way to fish in a nearby pond," I tell Nico, "so we must say goodnight.

"Buenos noches," Nico.

"Buenos noches, Abuela Cathy."

(December 2010)

Snow

THE SILENCE OF FALLING SNOW IS OTHERWORLDLY, erasing colors from the canvas outside my window. Blurring all in a swirling wash of white. Birds and squirrels, and I as well, retreat. But, to where? Squirrels to their high-flying aerial nests revealed when the last of the autumn leaves finally fall. Birds to sheltered berry thickets and brush piles at the edges of the woods. Me to feed the Buck stove another log from our rapidly diminishing woodpile on the porch.

Kit flew to Boston just hours ahead of a snowstorm that brought much of the Midwest and the South to a halt for two days. Snow fell throughout the night and due to predicted sub-zero temperatures, area-wide announcements of school closings came early. And so, I awoke to silence. No school bus rumbled by at seven-twenty as is its normal schedule. No cars or trucks hazarded the gravel road that connects Boomerang Creek to the nearest paved artery into Ashland. The snow erased all lingering traces of green that had remained in the yard.

Inside, I filled the hours near the fire reading Marianne Wiggins's novel, *John Dollar*, mesmerized by the images this powerful author creates with language. The cats slept as if there were no day at all. No welcoming sun emerged to draw them out onto the porch to bask and warm their belly fur. They simply curled inward and traveled to another imagined season and time.

That day, I traveled to colonial Burma circa 1917 with Charlotte Lewes, a young English woman widowed by the Great War, who hopes to begin a new life there. In Rangoon, Charlotte swims with dolphins and loves a sailor named John Dollar. On an ill-fated outing to one of the Andaman Islands, she witnesses the phosphorescent arrival of sea turtles laying eggs on the beach before an earthquake and tsunami erases the world and creates a new one in which things are not where or as they'd been before.

Like a tsunami, snow can be disorienting. Brilliant. Blinding. Blue. Cut diamond sparkling white. Light and powdery. Slow motion and silent falling. Avalanche compact and deadly loud like a train wreck. Throughout the day, I'm aware of powdery snow falling from the distance of time and geography into which I retreat as I read. Tropical heat and colors described in the story's telling rekindle memories of my own travels in Burma more than three decades ago. Time, like the snowy canvas outside, temporarily disappears into night.

Dangerous, sub-zero, bone-chilling winds finally die down to stillness. All is calm. All is white. Birds come out. Squirrels still do not. I dress in layers until I am nondescript. A turtle wearing Ugg boots with only a nose and two eyes exposed. If Kit is to find his way to the garage when he returns from Boston late Saturday night, the driveway must be shoveled.

For the next two hours, I become a snow mover. Energized by cold sunlight that is nonetheless dazzlingly bright and renewing, I push and toss snow until strands of hair that have escaped from my Nepalese wool hat are frozen stiff. Surprisingly, I am not at all cold. Instead, I am warmed by thoughts of all things green. The seed catalogues I've just ordered. The green energy drink I blended that morning before my outdoor labors—romaine, spinach, pears, green apples, celery, ginger and an entire fresh pineapple.

Later, back indoors, I felt wonderful, but needed to create something colorful after working in blinding white light for hours. Kit called with news that his evening St. Louis arrival would be an hour late. To pass the time, I made a batch of my mother Alice's spaghetti sauce. Cooking kept my mind off the possibility that Kit might return and be faced with an unplowed airport parking lot or a dead car battery, but neither was the case.

At eleven that night, Kit pulled into a driveway that looked as if Martha Stewart had shoveled it with a butter knife. Outside, Boomerang Creek remained cold and white. Inside, where I had just added another log to the fire, all was cozy and bright.

(January 2010)

Maps and Flights of The Imagination

*A*s the daughter of a career Air Force pilot, I grew up around air-planes, although I never learned to fly. What I love even more is maps. Early on, I was a navigator at heart. Each time my father was transferred from one base to another, my parents packed our household belongings into an Atlas van and loaded my sisters and me into the family car—a Studebaker shaped like an airplane in the years after World War II, and later a more kids-appropriate Chevy station wagon in the late 1950s. Before I understood what road maps were for and how to read one, I was certain that my parents knew every road and highway in the country by heart. Never once did I worry that they might get lost. They were simply the two smartest navigators on the planet.

At school, classroom wall maps were worlds I was eager to explore. Africa hung the length of a wall, yet somehow the Nile River was able to run vertically north from the continent's heart up through Egypt where it emptied into the Mediterranean without a drop of the Nile spilling onto the classroom floor.

In textbooks and atlases, maps were alive with pink and green and yellow shapes labeled with exotic country names. As I grew older, maps grew more detailed, adding lines representing rivers and relief, and dots of varying sizes representing cities and notable sites. History books were filled with detailed maps that enhanced fascinating stories layered across time and vast expanses of the world's continents. Without maps, history's stories were incomplete. With maps, I could navigate my way back through time. That is how I learned geography.

Recently Kit and I visited the Art Institute of Chicago which was exhibiting original artwork from 2006 to 2009 Caldecott Award books. My friend, Uri Shulevitz, who has been writing and illustrating children's books since 1963, was among the artists. His 2008 Caldecott Honor Book, *How I Learned Geography*, is a beautifully illustrated and poignant story of Uri's own childhood memories of World War II.

I first met Uri in the mid-1970s when I was teaching in Los Angeles, soon after he had published his first illustrated children's book, *Dawn*. Over the years, he and I have reconnected in New York City where Uri has lived since immigrating to the United States in 1959. He fled with his parents from Warsaw in 1939 at the age of four, and spent the next six years living in the Soviet Union, most of that time in Central Asia, in the city of Turkestan in what is now Kazakhstan. In *How I Learned Geography*, Uri tells and illustrates his own childhood story—

> *Fleeing with nothing, we traveled far, far east to another country, where summers were hot and winters were cold, to a city of houses made of clay, straw, and camel dung, surrounded by dusty steppes, burned by the sun.*

Food was scarce. Uri had no books or toys. One night, his father returned from the bazaar carrying a rolled up map instead of supper. Uri went to bed hungry and angry with his father. The following day, a colorful world map filled an entire wall of their small dirt-floored room. "I spent long hours looking at it," Uri recounts, "studying its every detail and many days drawing it on any scrap of paper that chanced my way."

He made rhymes out of strange-sounding names on the map, repeating them "like a magic incantation," and was transported far away without ever leaving the room.

"*Okazaki Miyazaki Pinsk,*
Pennsylvania Transylvania Minsk!"

"And so," Uri writes, "I spent enchanted hours far from our hunger and misery."

The book, dedicated to the memory of Uri's father, is a magical journey of the imagination and spirit. Whether you are four or sixty-four, it will touch your heart and give you hope.

(October 2009)

Literary Ramblings on a Rainy May Morning

*M*AY RAIN IS FALLING AND PEONY TUBERS DORMANT during winter have sent delicate stems up through layers of mulch in search of light. A final hard freeze in early April reminded impatient gardeners that one should never rush spring's clock in a Missouri garden.

In this state of eager anticipation of greener, warmer days, Kit and I momentarily let our thoughts ramble. "Fancy a trip to London sometime in the fall?" it begins. "Or what about flying to Brooklyn to visit our author friend, Matthew Goodman?" Oh, delicious dilemma! Such thoughts fills my head this rainy May morning.

I close my eyes and imagine a world of possibilities. Everything I read takes me somewhere and involves me in the explorations of and with others. Even the most mundane of outings becomes an adventure when the telling is given proper life. The following is Virginia Woolf telling her diary what happened to her on February 15, 1915—

> *Leonard (my husband) and I both went up to London this afternoon—*
>
> *L to the Library, & I to ramble about the West End, picking up clothes. I am really in rags. With age one's less afraid of superb shops. I swept in Debenham's & Marshalls. Then I had tea & rambled down to Charing Cross in the dark, making up phrases & incidents to write about. Which is, I expect, the way one gets killed. I bought a ten & eleven penny blue dress, in which I sit at this moment.*

My eyes remain on the brief diary excerpt, and I find myself transported across the Atlantic to the London of Virginia Woolf. Then, as quickly as spring, I am in the tearoom at the Basil Street

Hotel in Knightsbridge, London. Ms. Woolf is sitting alone in an overstuffed chair drinking tea and nursing a small glass of sherry. A basket of scones, pots of strawberry jam and rich *crème fraîche* have been wheeled on an elegantly appointed cart to her table—part of the daily late afternoon ceremony of high tea so utterly irresistible to Londoners on rainy spring afternoons.

I note the blue dress the English author is wearing and after reading the passage in her diary, feel that I'm the one sitting in the dress and sipping tea. There I am, rambling on about the falling rain, and noting phrases and incidents to write about. But Virginia Woolf is far too removed for the conversation about writing and gardens that I imagine us having. Back from my London literary ramble, I stir my own cup of tea momentarily. Just as quickly, I'm in a café in Lower Manhattan.

The idea of a week in New York City in the fall had begun to surface in my consciousness during the final lingering weeks of winter. Browsing online through the *New York Times*, I check out bargain flights and begin to mentally map out routes on foot across the Brooklyn Bridge to Matthew Goodman's Park Slope neighborhood.

I am convinced that the anticipation of travel is as exciting for me as the actual adventure itself. Perhaps it is the same with spring. Just as suddenly, I look out as a flock Canada geese fly overhead in the rain. I cannot imagine missing spring at Boomerang Creek. In the meadow garden, packets of squash and zinnias need to be planted and asparagus spears require daily harvesting. In the orchard, three fruit trees—an orange quince, a Montmorency cherry and a brown turkey Fig—await planting. At the house, the screened porch, unused over winter, needs dusting and freshening up for the coming open-air seasons.

But on this delicious, rainy May morning, Kit and I—two writers-in-residence at Boomerang Creek—are on a literary ramble. Nearby, our cats, Fanny and Pooh, stare out at the rain from under the covered porch where we are lost in dreams of travel and sun-filled gardens.

(April 2014)

An Imagined Conversation with Eudora Welty

*M*iss Welty died on July 23, 2001 at the age of ninety-two. In *Smithsonian* (April 2009), the magazine includes a feature article, "The Writer's Eye," by T.A. Frail, illustrated with sepia-tone photographs taken by Eudora Welty during the early years of the Depression. Frail reminds us that Miss Welty, born one hundred years ago, "was one of the grandest grande dames of American letters—winner of a Pulitzer Prize, the National Book Critics Circle Award, an armful of O. Henry Awards, and the Medal of Freedom." The photographs remind us that Welty was also a gifted photographer years before she published her first short story.

I remember now that my friend Sandy Crow and I had imagined a conversation with Miss Welty just months before her death. I actually called Sandy and suggested we meet in Jackson and simply appear on the writer's doorstep on April 13, 2001 to celebrate her ninety-second birthday. We would arrive at four, in time for afternoon high tea with some lovely Southern pastry from a local bakery, having been assured that it was Miss Welty's favorite. For good measure, we would be certain to bring a bottle of fine, aged Kentucky bourbon as a birthday gift. Then, it would be entirely up to Miss Welty where this imagined meeting and conversation would go.

There were so many questions I wanted to ask Miss Welty. I knew that she'd graduated from the University of Wisconsin, studied a year at Columbia University in New York City, and had ambitions to become a published writer. But instead, she had returned to Jackson in 1931 when her father was diagnosed with leukemia and remained there with her mother following his death. Though she took occasional trips back to NYC relating to her writing and photography, Jackson remained Miss Welty's home throughout the remainder of her long and productive lifetime.

Why, I wanted to ask Ms. Welty, had she chosen not to move back to Manhattan where she had been part of a circle of bright, young, aspiring writers? What kept her in the South following the Depression after she'd experienced life in the big city? Why did her brief career as a photographer end once her first two short stories were published? How did her photographer's eye instruct her writer's imagination?

In this imagined conversation, Ms. Eudora would at this moment sip the cup of tea that I had poured for her, praise the cake my friend and I served, and then settle comfortably into a reflection on her beginnings as a writer. She would do so as easily as she had once moved though the scenes in her photographs—each one capturing a time and place that no longer exists. "My father gave me a camera when I was fifteen," she began. "During the Depression, one of my part-time jobs was taking pictures for the Jackson Junior Auxiliary and writing for the *Jackson State Tribune*. In the early 1930s, I began documenting scenes I'd been born into and until then had taken for granted. "

Although Welty had grown up in a fairly privileged white family in Jackson, Eudora Welty's photographs captured the lives of everyday laborers and African-Americas with the same humanity that she later penned into her stories. "What did photography teach you," I heard myself ask, "when you traveled around the Deep South with your camera two decades before the civil rights era?"

"I learned," she responded, "that life doesn't hold still. A good snapshot stopped a moment from running away. Making pictures of people in all sorts of situations, I learned that every feeling waits upon its gesture; and I had to be prepared to recognize this moment when I saw it."

A nod of understanding on my part prompted Miss Welty to proclaim that, as it was her birthday and now past the five o'clock cocktail hour. It was therefore high time we gave that fine bottle of bourbon a try. Then, taking a deep breath and slowly exhaling, she made reference to the connection from her photographer's eye to writing in words penned by the author in her 1984 memoir, *One Writer's Beginning*:

> *These (gestures and moments) were things a story writer needed to know. And I felt the need to hold transient life in words—there's so much more of life that only words can convey—strongly enough to last me as long as I lived.*

Last week, I had lunch with a circle of friends who shared thoughts on books and writers they enjoy reading and rereading. Ms. Eudora Welty was there in spirit as we toasted her one hundredth birthday. This grand lady's sense of place, photographic eye, and writer's imagination continue to inspire conversation, real and imagined— the mark of a truly gifted storyteller.

(April 2009)

Chapter Three
CONVERSATIONS: REAL AND IMAGINED

I am certain Mr. Jefferson was in the garden with us that night, planting seeds of change in our conversation for this meadow garden's future.

C.S. May 2010

A CONVERSATION WITH THE MAYTAG MAN

LAST WEEK, A MAYTAG REPAIRMAN ARRIVED to replace a part in our dishwasher. Maytag appliances have a reputation for rarely needing repairs, but in this case the faulty part was part of a national recall. It was a Thursday, my pie-baking day, so the kitchen was filled with pecan pies, chess pies and vegetable quiche pies wrapped and ready for that afternoon's farmers market in Ashland.

The repairman, replete with ponytail and one arm covered from wrist to shoulder with colorful tattoos, went straight to his task, but not before spotting the pecan pies. "Pecan pies are my favorite," the colorful character let me know. "Grew up in Arkansas." There is always a connection somewhere when you begin a conversation with a stranger, and with us, Arkansas was it. "I was born in Hot Springs," I responded, "but never actually lived there."

Our Arkansas connection, thin as it was, led us to his family's rural, predominantly white Arkansas hometown and a discussion of race. I cut to the chase and asked him what he thought about the presidential candidates and issues. "Frankly," he said, "I probably won't even vote. I don't believe anything politicians say anymore. And believe me, there are people in parts of Arkansas who'll never vote for a black man. I moved up here to be in a larger city where there's some diversity."

Cultural diversity is a rich geographic theme. Being a geographer as well as a teacher and writer, this conversation reminded me of a handy booklet entitled "Why Geography is Important," published by the Gilbert M. Grosvenor Center for Geographic Education in San Marcos, Texas. The booklet is part of the National Geographic's effort to enhance the teaching and understanding of geography in America. "Geography," it contends, "requires awareness of the importance of cultural diversity—that is, area differences in language, race, religion, and politics."

It explains: "When American citizens appreciate cultural diversity, many issues and problems may be addressed in a positive manner. This awareness is valuable when we try to make sense of worldwide situations, as well as those in our own country. Our political, military, and economic leaders need to be well versed in cultural diversity, and geography offers a sensitive pathway to such understanding."

My conversation with the Maytag man happened in an atmosphere of political attack ads filled with carefully crafted innuendo and outright lies. Critical issues affecting the average American citizen have been sidelined in editorials, TV and newspaper punditry and national magazines by the hot-button issues of sexism, elitism and personality.

It took a disastrous week of falling dominos on Wall Street to refocus the political dialogue on the economy. Treasury Secretary Henry Paulson asked Congress to move immediately and approve a staggering $700 billion bailout to end the nation's banking crisis. It will help Americans (like the Maytag repairman), Paulson insisted, because the economic crisis on Wall Street affects Main Street America as well as markets and commodity flow around the globe.

We live in a world where "economic globalization and job mobility require that Americans understand the nature of foreign cultures who represent, on the one hand, a labor force, and on the other, a market area for our products." Issues and problems can be addressed in a more positive way when American citizens better appreciate cultural diversity. With advances in communication technology and the Internet, the lives and economies of Americans and populations around the world have become interwoven.

That fall, while the media seemed focused on the economy, I was even more concerned about an issue rarely talked about: race. I would be sixty-three years old when I cast my vote for America's first black president on November 4, 2008. I was born at the very end of World War II when segregation still existed in America's schools. In the spring of 1967, I heard Martin Luther King speak at a church in Lincoln, Nebraska. As a Peace Corps volunteer during the Vietnam era, I experienced life while immersed in a foreign culture and gained a fresh perspective on how much of the world's population lives. Up close, my eyes were opened to worlds that changed my life and priorities forever.

From afar, I witnessed heartbreaking events taking place in America. Robert Kennedy and Martin Luther King were both assassinated in 1968 while I was teaching in Thailand. Four years after returning home to a teaching job in Bellevue, Nebraska, I migrated from the Midwest to southern California. A year later, I began teaching ninth grade geography in south central Los Angeles. For more than a decade, my life was greatly enriched by thousands of students of color. So when someone tells me forty years after the assassinations of Robert Kennedy and Martin Luther King that segments of the American population still won't vote for a candidate solely for reasons of race, I am angered and moved to say so.

Geography teaches us the importance of cultural diversity and having an informed world view. History compels us to judge a person by the content of his or her character. The degree to which race is a factor in future presidential elections, relations between the

White House and Congress, and relations with local police within America's racially divided and underserved neighborhoods will tell us just how much we have heeded or chosen to ignore these critical lessons.

(September 2008)

CONVERSATIONS AT THE TABLE

*M*ARCH HAS BEEN FILLED with memorable conversations exchanged at a variety of local tables. Surrounded by gardens and an orchard exploding before our eyes into full spring bloom, Kit and I have hosted several March meals at Boomerang Creek where conversations over the course of leisurely meals touched on writing, art, politics, wine and how to prepare Brussels sprouts.

These evenings of lively discourse around our harvest table were matched by noteworthy conversations and shared meals in Columbia during the recent MU Life Sciences and Society Symposium, "Food Sense." Free and open to the public, the three-day symposium offered a rich menu of food for thought by local, national and international experts. Topics included eating behavior, the nature of food writing, cooking wisely, mindlessly eating and marketing nutrition, the communal aspect of breaking bread, the dining experience as a visceral narrative, how sensory scientists analyze the flavors of wine, and the clash between food cultures in America today.

Months earlier, when spring's arrival was still but a winter dream, a series of actions set in motion a serendipitous series of conversations that took place during the symposium weekend. As is so often the case, the story behind the conversations began with a book that I had read several months earlier—Todd Kliman's *The Wild Vine: A Forgotten Grape and the Untold Story of American Wine.*

Having lived in Missouri now for over two decades, I knew a bit about the historic role that early nineteenth-century German immigrants living in Hermann, Missouri and the Norton grape played in the story of American wine. Kit and I also have a personal history

Cathy Salter

with the Beckmeyer Vineyard in Hartsburg where gorgeous Norton and Chambourcin grapes grow on sunny, south facing hillsides lined with acres of vines lovingly planted, tended and picked by hand.

Several winters ago we invited Orion and Barbara Beckmeyer to join Terry and Mary Neuner, owners of the Westphalia Vineyard, for dinner and a conversation about wine at our table. After sampling bottles of Norton wine from each of their vineyards, a friendship linking the two families took root and continues to this day.

Reading Kliman's *The Wild Vine*, I was reminded that the Norton, a native American grape virtually forgotten after Prohibition, was the same grape used to make an earlier Missouri wine that won a gold medal at an international wine exhibition in 1873 and that later, when French vineyards were hit by phylloxera, it was the Norton that came to the rescue of the French wine industry.

From there, Kliman took me on a journey back in time, filled with twists and turns, tales of earlier efforts and failures, historic characters and a contemporary champion who has reintroduced the Norton to Virginia. In the telling, I learned the amazing story of Dr. Daniel Norton—the largely forgotten man who created the hybrid grape that ultimately produced a good, drinkable American wine where others from Jamestown to Thomas Jefferson had failed.

As chance had it, Kliman—food and wine editor and restaurant critic of *the Washingtonian*—was among the invited speakers at a "Food Sense" Symposium held recently at the University of Missouri. I attended his session on food writing at the journalism school, and that evening shared a late dinner with Todd, Kit, Nina Furstenau and other symposium planners at Sycamore Restaurant in Columbia. The following day, before Todd headed for the airport, we shared an impromptu picnic of World Harvest Market cheeses and olives, and toasted the symposium organizers with a bottle of Beckmeyer Vineyard 2009 Chambourcin/Norton wine.

I love Todd's brilliantly researched and beautifully written book and hope the Norton grape story will have a further chapter—one that brings Kliman back to Missouri to harvest grapes in Hartsburg and listen to those wildly earthy, sweetened-on-the-vine, Norton grapes hum happily while fermenting in open bins at Terry Neuner's winery. Most of all, I hope we continue to gather at tables near and far to share meals and exchange ideas. This food and wine conversation has only just begun.

(March 2012)

Conversing with Mr. Jefferson About Gardening

*T*HERE COMES A TIME EVERY SUMMER when I wonder why it is that I so love planting an annual vegetable garden, but then don't properly tend it. It happened recently on one of those deliciously breezy July mornings when it is cool enough for me to contemplate reclaiming my carefully planned and laid out garden, now full of invasive meadow grasses that insinuate themselves between rows and plants no matter how much straw I lay down on the pathways.

Then there is the matter of the volunteers. Late last fall, I arrayed the tilled garden with spent squash and pumpkins after the first hard freeze. Over winter, they slowly imploded, spilled forth their seeds, and fed the winter birds. In early May, their bleached and brittle shells were tilled under, rich mulch was applied to enhance the garden's tilth, and a vegetable garden was artistically planted.

Looking at the garden now, it is clear that it wants to be a rambling squash and pumpkin patch, not a fussy collection of geometrically shaped herb and vegetable beds. After reading Anne Raver's recent *New York Times* article "At Monticello, Jefferson's Methods Endure," I sat on a garden bench, imagining a conversation with Thomas Jefferson about his lifelong love of gardening.

Mr. Jefferson explains that success and failure are both part of the deal when one chooses the life of a gardener. From the time he left the White House in 1809 and returned to his beloved Monticello until his death in 1826, Jefferson grew, according to Raver's article, one hundred seventy varieties of fruits and three hundred thirty varieties of vegetables and herbs.

Raver describes walking along Jefferson's "geometric beds—many

---

of them planted in an ancient Roman quincunx pattern." Everyone knows he loved peas and kept careful records of his annual pea harvest. But, when Jefferson traveled, he saved seeds that he later planted in his two-acre kitchen garden. Many were exotic even by today's organic gardening standards—sea kale, Egyptian onions, and an almost black, pre-Columbian tomato called Purple Calabash.

"I feel like your daughter, Martha Jefferson Randolph," I told the President, "who wrote to you in despair in the years you were traveling as Secretary of State and again while you were at the White House. You wrote back that it was the fault of drought, or that a plague of insects had made the crops feeble, brought on by the lean state of the soil."

A weight shifted ever so slightly on the bench we shared, as when a person uncrosses one leg and then crosses the other. "Perhaps it wants to be an orchard," Jefferson offered after a period of thoughtful silence.

"Yes," I said. "You are absolutely right."

Kit and I had inspected the garden the night before, admiring our five pear and apple trees and bemoaning the sorry state of the vegetable garden. Kit favored plowing it under. I suggested letting the blossoming squash and pumpkins flourish wherever their trailing tendrils wander and relocating the herbs to the porch where the rest of our kitchen herbs appear to be thriving.

I am certain Mr. Jefferson was in the garden with us that very night, planting seeds of change in our conversation for this meadow garden's future. This fall, when all the squash and pumpkins have been harvested, we plan to plow it under. In its place, four new fruit trees—a plum, one sweet and one sour cherry, and perhaps a Granny Smith apple tree—will be planted.

We all agree that this is a fine plan. While I continue to do some weeding and water the vegetable garden regularly, I'm quite ready to admit defeat and move on. Peter Hatch, the director of the gardens and grounds at Monticello, said of Jefferson in Raver's article, "He was experimental and had a lot of failures. But Jefferson always believed that 'the failure of one thing is repaired by the success of another.'"

"Amen," I say. "Amen."

(May 2010)

A French Accent in My Library

*S*ITTING IN THE QUIET OF MY LIBRARY, I join in on a conversation now underway, one that spans centuries. The voices are peppered with observations born of personal trials, tribulations and revelations experienced over the course of the conversants' lives. The voices are a babble of French spoken by a sixteenth century French essayist, America's founding foodie, a nineteenth century French novelist, a Hungarian-American journalist and author, and a cowgirl chef from Texas currently cooking with a French accent in Paris.

Recently, I accompanied Kit on a trip to the Columbia Mall, a destination I normally avoid. "Drop me at the bookstore," I asked. "I'll be among friends until you come and find me perusing the aisles or enjoying a café au lait."

When he returned, I was deeply engrossed in Kati Marton's new memoir, *Paris: A Love Story*. Marton writes that Paris has been at the heart of her life for decades—first as a student in the late 1960s studying at the Sorbonne, then as a journalist when she met and married ABC foreign correspondent Peter Jennings, fifteen years later as an award-winning author and wife of U.S. diplomat Richard Holbrooke following a divorce, and now solo following the sudden death of Holbrooke in 2010.

Marton and I are close in age. I follow her in my thoughts, imagining her as she moves through the city's familiar neighborhoods (*arrondissements*), crossing from Left Bank to Right en route to the Place de Voges. She stops at the very café where Kit and I ordered cappuccino and croissant the first morning we experienced Paris together.

"I didn't get to Paris in the 1960s," I tell Kati. *"Life took me instead to Southeast Asia where my high school French resurfaced during my travels to Cambodia and Laos just before communism and civil war closed their borders to the world and changed everything."*

"Richard was there, then." Kati realizes.

Those were the years before computers, email, iPhones and iPads. Kati and I recall writing letters to our parents on flimsy, blue aerograms that were both stationery and envelope wrapped into one. Our mothers saved every letter chronicling our eloquent thoughts and grand adventures. While attending a class at the Sorbonne's Grand Amphithéâtre, a coliseum-sized hall, Kati noted a professor she could barely see who was speaking about Michel de Montaigne— the sixteenth century humanist credited with inventing the literary form of the essay. "I dove into Montaigne's *Essays*," Kati recalls, "and began a lifelong relationship with the man and his words."

Montaigne, alive and well versed in my library, is clearly pleased. "In 1580, I left teaching to travel for a year. Seeking truth, I decided to spend the second half of my life settling the ancient question, *'Who am I?'*"

Upon hearing the very question that plagued the heroic character Jean Valjean in his novel, *Les Misérables,* Victor Hugo joins in:

> *Every French child learns the date February 20, 1571—Montaigne's thirty-eighth birthday, the day when he retreated to the tower of his family castle near Bordeaux and began to write. His one hundred seven 'essays' or 'trials' were utterly original and radical. He was 'the first modern man.'*

America's third President, familiar with the essay form and enamored with everything French, now enters the conversation from the pages of *Thomas Jefferson's Crème Brûlée,* a book by Thomas J. Craughwell. Jefferson recounts his travels to Paris in 1784 with one of his slaves, nineteen-year old James Hemings:

While I studied the cultivation of French crops and grapes for winemaking, James learned the marvels of pasta, French fries, Champagne, macaroni and cheese, and crème brûlée.

At this mention of Paris and food, Texan Ellise Pierce, author of *Cowgirl Chef: Texas Cooking with a French Accent*, kicks the conversation with her signature Texas boots back to the present.

"Let's eat, honey," I can just hear her say. *"I've cooked a batch of cauliflower gallettes with chipotle crème fraîche."*

"And for dessert?" Jefferson queries with anticipation.

"Crème brûlée Mr. President," Ellise assures America's first foodie.

"But, of course," I nod approvingly.

(January 2013)

On Local Wonders with Poet Ted Kooser

BY FIVE-THIRTY, SLEEP IS GONE. Enough sleep, I reckon, although by late autumn it is dark and chill at this early hour. Still, I wouldn't think of missing a moment of the wonders awaiting me as I rise and dress for a dawn walk around the meadow.

The cats are one paw ahead of me as I slide open the door to the porch, our daily match-step-from-memory routine. Their first concern is to awaken with a bracing drink from their water bowl, cold as a snow-fed mountain lake. Mine is to clear the deck of acorns that have fallen onto the porch in the night. Off the little brown nuts go, broomed into a pile that is a tiny offering I have made, free for the taking, for the squirrels.

This done, Kit and I set off in tandem with our trekking poles on a morning constitutional. Then, like skaters moving in an oblong circle, Kit steps to the right and falls in behind me. By now the horizon has begun its magic, early morning light display—the palest of apricot color softly on the rise. In a clear pale sky, a crescent sliver of moon and two stars greet me as I gaze upward. Across the neighboring pasture, as regular as a clock, the lights of a school bus wink yellow and red. No need to wear a watch when you live in the country.

As I round the woods marking the southern border of our mown meadow pathway, a lone female cardinal wings from cedar to cedar, staying just ahead of me and out of harm's way. By the time I begin my second lap, the sky is blue with pink contrails that just minutes ago were invisible in the dawn light. Four laps later, Kit and I head back to the house for a hot coffee on the porch. By now, it is a different morning. A low fog has suddenly rolled in, revealing another wonder of early morning invisible to our eyes in the earlier light.

All across the mown interior of the meadow where our small orchard thrives, gossamers woven by spiders in the night appear. Tiny white sails in an ocean of meadow grass, spiders casting their nets like fishermen long before dawn, hours before the rest of the world is fully awake.

Drawn to a fleet of sparkling threads sailing across the grass in the shadow of a tall pear tree, I spot a long-legged spider feasting on a partially nibbled piece of pear fruit. A strand of memory attaches it to a recent conversation with Ted Kooser—Pulitzer Prize winning poet, former United States poet laureate, painter, and author of *Local Wonders: Seasons in the Bohemian Alps*—the world Kooser observes from his home base in Garland, Nebraska.

Last month, I told Ted that a friend had written, enclosing Kooser's lovely poem, "Porch Swing in September," describing the activity of a spider—

> *...a small brown spider has hung out her web on a line between / porch post and chain, so that no one may swing without breaking it. / She is saying it's time that the swinging were done with....*

I tell him that, coincidentally, we have just spent the past month in close proximity to a golden orb weaver spider that took up residence at the edge of our porch at Boomerang Creek. "We named her 'Ziggy' and became quite attached to her," I noted, "but thankfully never literally."

Upon hearing from me, Ted shared a favorite E. B. White poem, "Natural History"—White's love letter to his wife, Katharine Angell— sent to her from the King Edward Hotel, Toronto after they first met—

> *The spider, dropping down from twig,*
> *Unwinds a thread of her devising:*
> *A thin, premeditated rig*
> *To use in rising.*

And all the journey down through space,
In cool descent, and loyal-hearted,
She builds a ladder to the place
From which she started.

Thus I, gone forth, as spiders do,
In spider's web a truth discerning,
Attach one silken strand to you
For my returning.

"Isn't it fine that fall is coming on?" Ted concluded. "It's my favorite time of the year."

(November 2013)

WHEN CONVERSATION TURNS MAGIC

*D*RIVING FROM ASHLAND TO COLUMBIA, I pass telephone wires stretched taut between straight-arrow poles at the edge of farmland that borders the KOMU-TV Station. Sections of humming communication cables are bundled with criss-cross patterned clips to help stabilize the wires in strong winds. At one point, lines take a detour from the west side of the highway and cross over four lanes of highway traffic, creating a congested jumble of converging cables. This communication hub reminds me of the suspended phone and power lines along San Francisco's trolley car route where it begins a narrow descent to the line's terminus at Fisherman's Wharf. At this busy juncture along Highway 63, birds flock to the wires, line up facing the sun and, I would guess, shoot the breeze.

What do birds talk about at such suspended times? The weather, I imagine, just like the rest of us. Farmers cuss and discuss the persistent April showers that keep confusing their planting calendar. Backyard gardeners debate whether or not to cover delicate plants when a hard frost is forecast. Perhaps birds from various cardinal points of the compass report on flying conditions they have experienced on the wing. *Rainy and cold in Baltimore,* chatters the oriole. *Yesterday's baseball game rained out,* complains the cardinal. *Sunny and bright in the Carolinas,* chirps the wren.

On days when chilly April winds nip with a wintry bite, lighthearted birdsong passed along telephone lines is reduced to wistful musings. The congregation of birds on the wires and the steady stream of commuters passing up and down the highway nearby become one and the same—birds of a feather lost in thoughts of warm water ports. Dreaming of sun-warmed earth, soil ripe for planting, and temperatures that will begin the miraculous transformation of blossoms into fruit.

We are not so different from our fine-feathered friends when it comes to the need to flock together and share conversation. When the opportunity is paired with sweet serendipity, the moment can be delicious. Recently, after a particularly busy week punctuated by raw winds that just wouldn't quit, Kit and I drove to Columbia for a Saturday matinee at the Ragtag Theater's new Cinemacafé on Hitt Street.

As we passed the KOMU-TV station with our seat warmers on and wool scarves around our necks, a light fluttering of snowflakes tried to confuse spring into thinking she had missed her cue and arrived on the scene a month early. At that moment, I noted the telephone lines that are usually packed with birds were virtually empty, confirming in my mind that there was nothing attractive about being buffeted by wind on such an unseasonably cold day. If I had checked the recesses of nearby cedars, perhaps I'd have found an ornamentation of brilliant red cardinals dotting the interior branches. Winter, I said to Kit, is like a dry brown oak leaf that hangs on tenaciously until an emergent spring leaf literally forces it to finally release its hold.

We arrived at the theater an hour before the film—early enough for a glass of wine and a shared plate of hummus with slices of fresh Uprise Bakery bread. One of the many wonderful aspects of Ragtag's new space, designed by local architect Brian Pape, is its comfortable, artsy ambiance that invites conversation whatever the time of day or evening.

When Kit headed over to put in our order, I spotted a friend, author Mary Kay Blakely, whom we had not seen for much too long. She was deeply engrossed in a conversation with another woman who we soon learned was her sister. After being invited to join them at their table, the four of us slipped into easy conversation as if no time has passed at all since our last meeting. When it was finally time movie time, hugs were exchanged and Kit and I left to get in line.

After the film, we were delighted to find our friends still conversing energetically at the same table. A round of wine was ordered and before long the discussion turned to summer plans and travels. I mentioned that the Iowa Summer Writing Festival was celebrating its twentieth season that June and July in Iowa City, and I mentioned various weekend writing workshops that I have attended there in past summers. Mary Kay then hinted that some of her colleagues at MU's School of Journalism might be interested in developing their own summer writing program on campus—one guaranteed to attract interested writers from around the world to Columbia throughout the summer.

This serendipitous conversation that cold Saturday afternoon was pure magic. The idea of a local summer writing festival will hopefully fill future conversations as plans develop over the months ahead. Like Columbia's True/False Film Festival that grew from a local event to an international documentary attraction in just five years, the prospect of an annual summer writing program offered by MU's School of Journalism within walking distance of the downtown district's exciting cultural offerings is one that I think both the city and a world of writers would relish and eagerly support. And mark my words. Within the next decade, Columbia will host a national book festival of its own. Yes, yes, absolutely.

(April 2008)

Postscript: Great News! The Unbound Book Festival, a national book event, will debut April 23, 2016 in Columbia, Missouri.

(September 2015)

Yet Another Exchange with Denzel

*S*CENE ONE: THERE HE WAS. Standing next to me on the porch of the Sundance Institute's Tree Room Restaurant, waiting for a break in the rain. He'd just finished dining with a group of aspiring actors and directors attending a Sundance Institute workshop. Denzel Washington, whom the institute's founder Robert Redford had invited to mentor the attendees, had just stepped out into the night air. Pausing when he saw the rain, the actor/director moved next to a tall woman with red hair.

The rain continued. The woman resisted the temptation to mention that Suzanne Goin, the chef/owner of Lucques—the actor's favorite Los Angeles restaurant—had once prepared *pan chocolat*—a flakey French pastry filled with melted chocolate—in her kitchen when she and her husband Kit lived at Breakfast Creek—their first country home in Missouri. Silence hung heavy in the night air.

Fast forward to Columbia's 2009 True/False Documentary Film Festival. Kit and I have just finished our T/F volunteer shift at the Tiger Hotel's Forrest Theatre after a full day of documentary film screenings. As is now our habit during this unique local gathering of cineastes from around the world, we headed for Sycamore Restaurant for a late evening plate of fried oysters and a glass of Vouvray white wine. Two hours earlier, Michael Odette—the restaurant's chef—had hosted a party at the restaurant for two hundred filmmakers and True/False guests. The energy from their earlier presence could still be felt as our own conversation began to flow.

Over oysters and wine, we discussed the films and conversations shared with moviegoers throughout the day before slipping into our own thoughts. Momentarily, my mind drifts back to the Sundance

Institute where Denzel Washington has broken the silence by asking the tall woman if she too is an actor.

"No," she answers, *"I'm a writer."*

"So tell me a story," the actor responds with a nod of directorial encouragement.

And so she weaves a story that over the space of time and miles ties the actor's life in Los Angeles to her own in Missouri. He listens, following the threads of her tale until both her story and the rain come to an end.

"True or false," he asks.

"You tell me," she answers, for that is exactly her intent.

Intrigued, Denzel Washington turns, looks into the tall woman's face as if tracing it like a map, and flashes a smile to die for and large enough to fill a movie screen. He then kisses the writer's hand and walks off into the night.

End Scene One.

Scene Two: Columbia's 2009 T/F Film Festival has come and gone. Still captured by the power of documentary storytelling, the tall woman now stands on the porch at Boomerang Creek on a cold March morning, warming her hands with a cup of hot coffee. She recalls the actor's fascination with her Sundance tale documenting their culinary connection and then begins weaving a second tale as if he were still listening.

"Last night," she tells the actor, "I was in the audience at the Missouri Theater for the final showing of Director Anders Ostergaard's 2008 political documentary, *Burma VJ*. The film, sure to become a classic, is eighty-five tense minutes of inspiring, heart wrenching, real-life video footage captured inside a closed society repressed for the past four decades by a military dictatorship. It is the nightmare George Orwell, who died in 1950—two years after Burma gained its independence from Britain—captured in his classic novel, *Nineteen Eighty-Four*."

The woman reminds Denzel of Orwell's prescient words: "Who

controls the past controls the future: who controls the present controls the past."

"*Burma VJ* begins in 1988, the year Kit and I moved to Missouri. Halfway around the world in Burma, the country's brutal military junta shot and killed three thousand demonstrators, imprisoned opposition leader Aung San Suu Kyi, and outlawed independent journalism. In the years since, the Democratic Voice of Burma (DVB)—a 'television station in exile' based in Norway—has been broadcasting images of repression in Burma across the globe."

"How do they get the video footage?" Denzel asks, as captured by the story as I am.

"Courageous Burmese journalists," I continue, "move about Rangoon with hidden handicams and cell phones, then transmit footage via short-wave radio and satellite feeds that DVB transmits worldwide. When Burma's Buddhist monks took to the streets in September 2007, followed by tens of thousands of students, DVB allowed the world to watch the courageous event and its brutal aftermath."

Denzel pauses. "*What story should I tell*," the actor asks the woman.

"*Return to the past.*" I say. "Fill in the back story. Read Emma Larkin's 2004 memoir, *Finding George Orwell in Burma*. Larkin spent a year in the 1990s traveling through Burma, using as her compass the life and works of Orwell—the man this repressed country's underground teahouse intellectuals refer to as 'the prophet.' Then find Emma Larkin and document her remarkable journey."

"Will you be in the audience when it comes to the 2010 True/False Film Festival?" Denzel asks, flashing one of his famous killer smiles.

"*Yes, yes,*" I respond in language from *The English Patient*, another film classic, "*absolutely.*"

(March 2009)

Chapter Four
The Magic of a Library

On a winter day when chill winds are about, I visit the shelves of my studio's library and reconnect with Charlotte Brontë and her extraordinary family ....

They had no public library, no Internet, no typewriter and no computer. They had no electricity. Their only heat was from the parsonage fireplace. ...

What a joy it is to be captured again and again by great literature. What a treasure a public library is for a community—whether large or small, and whether urban or rural in its setting.

C.S. April 2007

Finally, Snow

SILENTLY, SOFTLY, UNEXPECTEDLY IT CAME in the night, falling on solitary cedars and the dense stand of woods around Boomerang Creek. Light as an owl's feather necklace, it blanketed winter's dry-as-straw grasses, transforming the meadow into a field of sparkling diamonds in dawn's first light. Finally, weightless as breath to the touch, snow had arrived as a February surprise.

Icy roads and freezing temperatures closed area schools, though there was only an inch of snow accumulation and not a whisper of wind as I made my way across the frozen mulch pathway that morning to my writing studio. Locally the storm was but a parting note at the tail end of a powerful winter system that pounded New

England and mid-Atlantic coastal towns with wind, snow and ice, rattling windows and nerves alike. As January came to an end, the eastern half of the continent once again braced for another foot of heavy snowfall while still digging out from the last late-January blast.

Cozy in the snug confines of my studio's library and reading corner, I open the bag of books I've carried with me from the house. The arrival of snow made this a perfect morning for reading and contemplation. Like a slow food dining experience, I began savoring the evocative collection of volumes now stacked around me. First, I open a massive volume to a red ribbon that marks today's February date. It is an anthology of the world's greatest diarists—*The Assassin's Cloak*, edited by Irene and Alan Taylor—and for the next minutes, I am transported back in time.

Diarists from the eighteenth century to the twentieth century penned thoughts that provide snapshots of their lives and times. On this date in history, John Wesley, Lord Byron, Sir Walter Scott, and three other diarists commented on issues ranging from insomnia, aging, and the unanticipated discovery of nature in a winter garden.

The exercise leads me next to *Midnight at the Pera Palace: The Birth of Modern Istanbul*, by Charles King. For anyone who has experienced or anticipates visiting this fascinating ancient city's architecture, bazaars, streets and waterways, King's masterfully researched and told social and geo-political history is a multi-faceted gem.

For the next hour, I'm back in the mid-1920s when this geographic crossroads on the Bosporus was experiencing a wave of Turkish nationalism as well as a jazz-age cultural revolution. A fascinating cast of historical characters including Russian revolutionary exile Leon Trotsky and the young American newspaper journalist Ernest Hemingway appear as footnotes in Istanbul's transformation into a modern nation. I close King's book as the aging, increasingly paranoid Trotsky flees the intrigues of Istanbul, heading with his books and family for southern France.

From Istanbul, I jump a decade ahead to La Foce—the traditional

Tuscan farm where writer Iris Origo wrote and worked with her Italian husband Antonio for fifty years, improving both the land and lives of local peasants. I return often to Origo's beautifully penned memoir, *Images & Shadows: Part of a Life*, and each time find myself informed by this gifted writer's introspective chapter on the role of writing in her life.

Another small literary gem is novelist Penelope Lively's recent memoir, *Ammonites & Leaping Fish: A Life in Time*. Having arrived at the sage age of eighty, she assembled "views from old age"— meditations on what it is like to be old, as well as how memory shapes us. Finally, just acquired and much anticipated is Christopher Benfrey's memoir, *Red Brick, Black Mountain, White Clay: Reflections on Art, Family and Survival.*

All are books that can be picked up in any order and read for hours or for only a single chapter. On this particular day when snow has fallen unexpectedly and given its gentle permission for me to steal away to my studio, I have traveled across time and the world with fellow writers through their books.

Finally, snow!

What an utter joy.

(February 2015)

Lessons Found in the Rooms of Childhood

ℱOR EACH OF US, THERE COMES A TIME when as a child, we make the momentous journey from the insular familiarity of family to the community of an elementary school. Because my father was a career Air Force officer, the elementary schools that I attended were located within the bounds of the particular military base at which my father was currently stationed. Whenever he was reassigned in a new base, my sisters and I changed not only houses, but schools as well. Thus, when each September rolled around, my classmates were a totally new sea of faces.

In 1958, my father was transferred to the Pentagon, across the Potomac River from Washington, D.C. For the next four years, I experienced life in a classic American suburb. Our rented, split-level house with a yard, back patio and abundance of trees was in the northern Virginia community of McLean, not far from Washington, D.C. My eighth-grade year, I attended a new, progressive high school with a mixture of kids—transient students new to the area like me, and others who had lived in that same neighborhood and attended school together since kindergarten.

For me, the perennial new kid on the block, the idea of attending the first eight grades with the same roster of kids in the same neighborhood school building was a concept I could hardly fathom. That fall, my first season of living in suburban America, I envied my new friends their deep roots in the community and entered McLean High School's spirited academic world eager to study hard and fit in.

Throughout September, community-wide discussions and events are planned for this year's Daniel Boone Regional Library's 2008 One

Read selection, Ivan Doig's *The Whistling Season*. The author—a former ranch hand, newspaperman and magazine editor who was born in White Sulphur Springs, Montana—had the following to say after *The Whistling Season* was selected:

"My narrator in *The Whistling Season*, Paul Milliron, educator and bookman and graduate of a one-room school that he was, would have fully known the value of a community read. In Paul's well-thumbed Latin-to-English dictionary, these several meanings of *communitas* are given: 'sharing, partnership, social ties, fellowship, togetherness.' What better rewards could readers and writers alike ask for, than the common ground of literary fellowship through reading?"

Reviewing Doig's novel for a recent discussion group at the Southern Boone branch library in Ashland, I recalled my own early school settings where many of my life's earliest lessons were learned. In Doig's novel, Paul Milliron points out that the Marais Coulee schoolyard of his seventh grade school year (1909-1910) was divided like a continent of "brawling nationalities"—the Slavs (the Stoyanovs and Drobney brothers) don't get along with the Swedes (the Johannsons and Myrdals), and the proverbial bully (Eddie Turley) doesn't get along with anyone. In this one-room community comprised of the children of Montana dry land farmers, immigrants, and migrant project people, "grudge fights" took on the status of "nationality brawls."

While early twentieth century one-room schools were largely rural worlds themselves, they also offered children a window on a larger world through the subject of geography. In the opening pages of *The Whistling Season*, Paul, age thirteen, is sitting with his father and two younger brothers at the kitchen table. Doig points out that Paul is doing his geography assignment.

In 1987, my father sent me a 1915 Pennsylvania edition of *Dodge's Advanced Geography*, first published by Rand McNally & Co. in 1904. Paul may very well have been studying from an earlier Montana edition of the same geography text. In an attached note, Dad explained that his older brother Bob wanted Kit and me to have it.

> *[This] was issued to your Uncle Bob around 1917 at Cooney Town, a one-room school in West Finley Township, Pennsylvania—not too far from Wheeling, West Virginia. Bob (eighty-two), along with his brother Harry (eighty-seven) and sisters Hazel (ninety) and Pansey (eighty-four) were four of the fourteen students in the one-room school—eight grades.*
>
> *I remember spending hours poring over this book, more than fifty years ago, The pictures leaped off the pages when I looked at it last week. Geography was a major part of our curriculum in those days, along with arithmetic, history and grammar.*

Dad's 1987 recollections of the worlds within that well-thumbed 1915 geography book are mirrored by Paul in *The Whistling Season* when as Montana's State Superintendent of Schools, he returns home in 1957 to Marais Coulee, faced with the dilemma of having to determine the fate of the state's one-room schools.

"Childhood," Paul reflects as he ponders his decision, "is the one story that stands by itself in every soul.... As surely as a compass needle knows north, that is what draws me to these remindful rooms, as if the answer I need at the end of the day is written in the dust that carpets them."

(September 2008)

The Era of Peace Corps Book Lockers

$\mathcal{I}$N 1961, President John F. Kennedy established the Peace Corps, perhaps his most enduring legacy. Fifty years later, President Barack Obama recognized the Peace Corps as "forever changing the way America sees the world and the world sees us." To date, over two hundred thousand current and returned Peace Corps Volunteers (PCVs) have collectively given over a half-century of service to the cause of peace in nearly one hundred forty countries.

Recently, I received a fascinating article, "The Famous Peace Corps Book Lockers," from a former Peace Corps Volunteer who served in Thailand when I did in the late 1960s. The article explained that in the early days of the agency, PCVs were supplied with book lockers when they went off to their country assignments. The books were the idea of Eunice Shriver—a sister of President Kennedy and the wife of Sargent Shriver, the first Director of the Peace Corps.

In an early memo to Volunteers, Sargent Shriver wrote: "We know you need books. This book locker of paperbacks and other inexpensive publications is designed to meet that need." The book collections, wide ranging in scope, served as portable libraries for Volunteers at their isolated sites and were meant to be read and then passed on.

Included in the email from my old friend was a four-page, single-spaced list of titles included in the book lockers as of 1964. There were American classics by authors ranging from Henry Adams to Thornton Wilder and international classics from Miguel de Cervantes to H. G. Wells. Also listed were works of contemporary fiction and non-fiction, reference books, maps, illustrated classics, regional studies, and Ladder Editions—specially prepared editions of well-known American books that would appeal to readers for whom English is a second language.

News of the book lockers soon triggered a buzz of email exchanges among my circle of Volunteer friends, each filled with personal reflections from more than four decades ago. My good friend David who spent two years on the remote island of Koh Samui—a six-hour ferry ride from the southeast coast of Thailand— wrote, *"Man, I loved my book locker!"* Steve Landau's diary from 1967 noted that he had read Kobo Abe's *Woman in the Dunes* and Gunter Grass's *The Tin Drum*. Another friend admitted that he'd received three book lockers!

Thom Huebner remembered, "I too, was introduced to Vonnegut, Abe, Mishima, Mann and James Purdy. The book locker was a terrific networking device, since those of us stationed in northeast Thailand would exchange them and more importantly, talk about them."

One of the three must have been mine, because for the life of me, I can't recall ever having received such a gift. In lieu of a portable library, I spent evenings conversing with my students. Each night before dark I made entries in a journal and composed letters to my parents on blue onion-skin aerograms at my bedroom table.

Having no screens or glass on my plywood windows, a slow-burning mosquito coil balanced on the neck of a Coke bottle burned at my feet. The sun set each evening over a canal winding past a Buddhist monastery and cemetery. When it finally grew too dark to see, I'd duck under the mosquito netting that hung over my bed, accompanied by a flashlight and issues of *TIME* mailed from home.

My Peace Corps pal Tom Hudak, a university linguistics professor, wrote, "The book lockers were there as a stable foundation and support for us when everything else seemed totally alien…and you were about to have a complete meltdown. They were there in the corner watching you and cheering you on."

When asked once by his students how he stood the isolation,

Tom tells them that the book lockers helped to combat that. "In my pre-retirement days, and as I watch students today latch on to their cell phones, I wonder how they would handle the isolation," he commented. "They have a hard enough time in my class since cell phones, computers and Facebook are forbidden in my class."

Shriver's book locker idea—part of the agency's legacy in its infancy fifty years ago—was great but short-lived. In that magical era without cell phones and instant communication, the written word—whether read by flashlight or recorded in fading light in a journal or letter—was an enduring gift that has stood the test of time.

(June 2014)

JUST THIS SIDE OF WINTER

*W*ELL BEFORE THE FIRST HINT OF DAWN, I listen to the sounds that our house makes in the night. *Whirring* overhead fan. *Purring* air purifier. Just barely audible *radio voices*—KBIA at five-thirty in the morning, connecting us automatically to NPR and the world. *Click.* The thermostat register checking its own temperature, set at sixty-five degrees for the night. *Clink.* Ice dropping onto a pile of cubes in the refrigerator's freezer bin.

Then one more sound catches my attention. Unfamiliar, it is curious enough to have me leave the warmth of down feathers, wool blankets and Kit to find its source. But first, I slip my bare feet into chocolate-colored high topped, fleece-lined Ugg boots— replacements for my old pair purchased in New Zealand long before the world decided that these wooly boots from Down Under were in fact not so ugg-ly after all.

Ignoring traditional house robes, I opt for a warm, oatmeal-colored, oversized sweater that almost reaches my knees and add a sleeveless fleece-lined vest the color of Burmese garnets. Catching my image in the glass porch door, my white pajama pants float beneath the sweater and vest like Pakistani *shalwar kameez*. For an instant, I see my beautiful sisters Molly and Kim in the late 1970s. Dressed in traditional pajama-like pants and long tops, they are wrapped in cashmere pashmina shawls as a cold dawn rises over the ancient city of Gabedero in Sindh Province, Pakistan.

That sound again, leading me to the warming room where I discover that the fan switch on the front of the Buck stove has been *blowing* all night over hot embers stowed under a pile of gray ash.

Sifting under the pile, I uncover two live shards of last night's fire, add twigs and a small piece of split wood. Soon, I have the fire *humming* back to life in the stove.

One final sound. A cat scratches at the basement door. Fanny, our sharp-eared calico Manx, has heard me padding around. Still dark outside; nonetheless, morning is underway as far as this cat is concerned. *Feed me*, she insists while weaving in, around and just ahead of my feet—a feline skater executing perfect figure eights on icy linoleum. The *tinny-tight snap* of a tuna can opening, instantly brings our three cats to their bowls. Only then do I push in the coffee button. Clear water runs through dark coffee grounds and cinnamon—*drip, drip dripping* dark brown liquid into the carafe below.

Milk *steamed* and coffee *poured*, I head for the couch across from the now glowing Buck stove, adding a large piece of split firewood before I cozy in. Pre-dawn. My favorite hour of the day. In touch with the house and its living, breathing sounds, I am fully awake and at peace. The fire, a plaid, wool blanket and two sprawling lap cats conspire to keep me warm. Settled in at last, I join the rich cast of characters in two books by Sri Lankan born, now Canadian author Michael Ondaatje, two colorful companions for what remains of the dark.

In Ondaatje's luminous novel, *The Cat's Table*, an eleven-year old boy makes a life altering journey by ship from Ceylon to England in 1954. In an earlier lyrical travel memoir, *Running in the Family*, Ondaatje (then in his early forties) reconnected with his eccentric Ceylonese/Dutch family and the landscape he left as a child, moving first to England, then relocating to Canada in 1962.

Upon arriving back in Sri Lanka (formerly Ceylon), Ondaatje identifies sounds in the night, linking him to his distant childhood. Reading his description of a peacock's disturbed cry when awakened from its perch high in the trees, I'm instantly linked through memory to a mysterious peacock on a walkabout many years ago that spent a night in a walnut tree at our former Breakfast Creek home.

Just then, as light spills from Ondaatje's pen over the flaming tropical *flamboyant* trees of his native Ceylon, dawn surfaces half a world away at Boomerang Creek, just this side of winter.

(December 2011)

Rediscovering the Magic of the Brontës

*I*T IS SPRING, AND I AM OUTDOORS walking again. On winter days when chill winds were about, I chose instead to walk my way through our film library on the treadmill in our basement. It was while there that I reconnected with Charlotte Brontë and her extraordinary family.

Searching a shelf stocked with movie classics, I pulled out an early film version of *Jane Eyre*, starring Joan Fontaine and Orson Welles. For the next hour, I found myself walking in the very world that inspired Charlotte Brontë's writing and that of her sisters, Emily and Anne. In this 1944 black-and-white film, the wind-swept moors of West Yorkshire are as alive with foreboding and mystery as the dark hallways and stone tower of Thornfield Hall.

I then re-read the novel and its introduction. I was fascinated to learn that *Jane Eyre* was originally published in London in 1847 by an *"unknown and unrecommended"* writer by the name of Currer Bell. When the novel took London by storm and went into its second printing, readers who had assumed the author was a man, learned that *Jane Eyre* had in fact been written by Charlotte Brontë—the sister of Emily Bronte, who had just published *Wuthering Heights* under the name Ellis Bell. Readers in England and America were captured by the Brontë sisters' stories then, just as I have been one hundred sixty years later.

There is a timelessness about the Brontë sisters' passionate and beautifully written novels. Recently, I was reading an article on the subject of change in the April 2007 issue of *More* magazine. There were quotes on the subject by three women—Maya Angelou, Dorothy Canfield Fisher, and Emily Brontë. Miss Brontë wrote:

I've dreamt in my life dreams that have changed my ideas. They've
gone through me…like wine through water, and altered the color
of my mind.

When I enter the world of Jane Eyre and Thornfield Hall—
the estate of Edward Rochester who has employed Miss Eyre as
a governess—there is no leaving it until the story is done. The
cover opens, the tale begins, and once again I walk with Miss Eyre
and Mr. Rochester on the grounds of his estate or stand alongside
Jane later as she looks out from a massive rock outcropping worn
smooth and round from the relentless wind that blows across the
treeless moors.

It is to this wild place not far from the Brontë parsonage in Haworth
that readers are physically touched by the lives of the characters in
Charlotte's novel, *Jane Eyre*, and Emily Brontë's *Wuthering Heights*.
In the moors, it is said that visitors to the Brontë Museum hear the
voices of these extraordinary sisters and the characters they created
long ago with their pens—Edward Rochester's anguished call across
the miles heard by Jane Eyre and, in *Wuthering Heights*, Heathcliff's
tortured walks in the moors in search of the ghost of his soul mate,
Cathy.

Recently, Kit and I watched a 2007 PBS *Masterpiece Theater*
production of *Jane Eyre* and we've each re-read the novel. Kit has
checked out *Jane Eyre* (the unabridged audio book on twelve tapes)
from the Daniel Boone Regional Library. In addition, I am re-reading
Elizabeth Gaskell's acclaimed biography, *The Life of Charlotte Brontë*—
published in 1857, two years after Charlotte's death.

The preface to Gaskell's biography begins—

> The dour parsonage of Haworth, on the edge of the moors in
> the North of England, sheltered early in the nineteenth century
> a family of [six] doomed children touched by genius. There were
> Charlotte, who wrote *Jane Eyre*; Emily, who wrote *Wuthering
> Heights*; their sister, Anne, also a published writer; and in the

background of all their lives, the brooding and wastrel brother, Branwell, who might have become a great painter.

The tragic story of the Brontë family as told in Gaskell's memoir to Charlotte is richly illustrated with sketches of the Brontës and their world. Like the fictional character Jane Eyre, the Brontë sisters were rarely idle. After walks together in the moors where tales took shape in their heads, the sisters would scribble prose on scraps of paper and then read their developing dramas aloud to each other late into the night.

These amazing women—Charlotte, Emily, and Anne Brontë — had no public library, no Internet, no typewriter and no computer. They had no electricity. Their only heat was from the parsonage fireplace. What they knew of the world, they learned from books in their father's personal library and experiences in their own lives. Until their novels were published, they had never traveled to London. Their novels are among the most passionate and romantic in the English language. Yet of the six Brontës, only Charlotte would marry— tragically just nine months before her untimely death at the age of thirty- nine.

What a joy it is to be captured again and again by great literature. What a treasure a public library is for a community—whether large or small, and whether urban or rural in its setting.

(April 2007)

A Passage in the Egyptian Desert

I HAVE BEEN ON A LITERARY JOURNEY recently to a place I've never traveled, but now feel that I have. That is the power of words and the magic of *The Names of Things*—a book that recalls author Susan Brind Morrow's years spent tracking the ancient roots of language in Egypt in the 1980s. Part memoir, part travel journal, part commonplace book, part etymological treasure-hunt, the book is a passage to the Egyptian Desert—a world as old as time.

My journey with the author to Egypt's Desert, the Sinai, and the Red Sea was a tutorial in ancient hieroglyphics and finding the origin of words in nature. Sacred words like flags mark tombs, rocks, and trees in the Egyptian desert even now. Ancient words that began as a description of a living thing when the land first became desert, carrying the thing concealed across the millennia. Morrow writes:

> *But the original, the thing itself, would never come back. It had passed away from the world. You could conjure it, though, the emotion that kept it alive inside you, with a trigger: an image, a smell, a combination of sounds that formed it into a picture that stayed in your mind. That was the life of the thing after it died. The only thing that could bring it back. That is what a word is worth.*

As I read Morrow's descriptions of her childhood in upstate New York, Cairo's chaotic streets and alleys, and favorite words remembered and new ones discovered during her passages in the desert, I began my own journal, feeling keenly the need to physically form her words myself with ink on paper. Reading her words, "Nile, Egypt's sweet sea", I record her description in my own notes: "once clotted with papyrus, thriving, gigantic, mobile, filled with bird and animal life as today it only is in the Sudd—a great marsh in South Sudan."

Papyrus. A plant that no longer exists, except in a dead language—the hieroglyph *green.* Environmental extremes in Egypt are defined with colors. The desert is red. The sea is green. Morrow becomes my teacher, just as Steele Commager was her teacher at Columbia University. "He loved words," she recalls, "had us track things, word origins, poetic lines."

Traveling with her into the harsh openness of the desert, I imagine walking barefoot in the sand and dive into a dune, feeling the warmth around me. She warns, "it takes time to learn that refuge in the desert is at best temporary: a shrinking line of shade, the coolness of water or the dark. Intransient things like song or conversation."

Together, the author and I explore starry skies that she observed as a child living in rural, upstate New York. I revisit Egypt's deserts where Morrow travels with nomads and her guide, Joe Hobbs. Referred to as Joe, he is part Indiana Jones and in real life a geography professor from the University of Missouri-Columbia. Morrow acknowledges Joe as "the great desert naturalist…known for his integrity. His name alone can purchase food and shelter almost anywhere in the Eastern Desert and Sinai."

Joe is my friend as well. We share a love of cats, lizards, birds, tortoises, stars, storytelling, maps and curious creatures. Who else, I wonder, has explored the Egyptian desert *wadis* and roads known to Joe and Susan? Are there maps of the landscape and sites that they visited?

Oliver Payne, an editor friend of mine at *National Geographic* magazine, replies to my query that little has been published in the magazine about the Eastern Desert of Egypt. Another friend sends David Rumsey's historic map website where I discover a wealth of historic maps of this region drawn by cartographers from as early as 1742.

I am reluctant to leave Susan Brind Morrow's book and put away historic maps that orient me in this desert world of shifting sand, rock worn by harsh winds, and borders that resist the idea of nations. *The names of things.*

"Maps. Lines traced by the feet of past explorers." (Beryl Markham, *West With the Night*).

These things have been invaluable companions on my literary passage with Susan Brind Morrow and Joe Hobbs in the Egyptian Desert.

(March 2011)

The Sound of a Wild Snail Eating

*D*URING THE FINAL WEEK OF APRIL, I began reading a tiny book that, simply described, is *beautiful*. An old friend sent an email saying, "You must read Elisabeth Tova Bailey's book, *The Sound of a Wild Snail Eating*." Intrigued by the title and a reviewer's description of the book as "the earthly adventures of a woman and a gastropod," I ordered it immediately.

The author, I learned, had suffered from a flu-like virus that within weeks caused a dysfunction of her autonomic nervous system. After successive severe relapses, she was forced to move from her rustic 1830s Maine farmhouse with hand-hewn beams and square headed nails overhead to a small studio apartment with stark white walls. Barely able to move on her own, Bailey missed the golden brown hues of the overhead beams with their "knots that told a history of branches and long-ago wildness" that she had studied for countless hours in the earlier years of her illness when she still lived in her rural farmhouse.

Viruses are embedded into the very fabric of all life.

—Luis P. Villarreal

One day, a friend placed a pot of wild violets on Bailey's nightstand. In the pot was a small snail that the friend had found on a walk in the woods. Initially feeling burdened by the tiny mollusk that she was incapable of caring for, Bailey grew to consider the snail her companion and friend. In her later book, she notes how the snail, when removed from its own natural environment, gradually came out of its shell and began to eat, sleep and reproduce.

Cathy Salter

Each evening the snail awoke and, with an astonishing amount of poise, moved gracefully to the rim of the pot and peered over, surveying, once again, the strange country that lay ahead. Pondering its circumstance with a regal air, as if from the turret of a castle, it waved its tentacles first this way and that, as though responding to a distant melody.

One morning after Bailey awakens to find a small square hole eaten out of an envelope on her nightstand, it occurred to her that the snail might like something more familiar to eat. She began feeding it the dry petals from flower arrangements friends brought as gifts. Bailey wrote—

I put some of the withered blossoms in a dish beneath the pot of violets. The snail was awake. It made its way down the side of the pot and investigated the offering with great interest and then began to eat one of the blossoms. A petal started to disappear at a barely discernible rate. I listened carefully. I could hear it eating.

As I slowly digested each page and chapter of Bailey's book, I felt myself shrinking down in size as if entering the small confined space from which the author observed her tiny snail's anatomy, decision-making, and locomotion. I recalled essayist Anne Fadiman's reaction to the author's observations of her small pet:

As I read Bailey's descriptions of how her snail moved...I felt myself shrinking and shrinking and shrinking, like Alice in Wonderland, until I was snail-sized myself.

Eventually, the snail begins to explore, pressing us to engage in our own exploration of the heart and spirit. Inspired by the tiny snail, I decided to set out myself in soft rain toward our creek where my feet brushed masses of naturalized daylilies, wild Sweet William, stands of May Apple, and lacey native ferns dancing in filtered light across the woodland floor. Observing my every footstep, I searched for morel mushrooms—the favorite food of *Neohelix albolabris,* the common woodland snail.

Elisabeth Tova Bailey's observations of a humble snail are written from a single year of the nearly two decades of her illness. As sparsely and beautifully constructed as a Japanese haiku, the book reveals a courageous journey of survival and resilience as quietly as a prayer.

The natural world is the refuge of the spirit...richer even than human imagination.

—Edward O. Wilson, *Biophilia,* 1984

(April 2011)

Harmony in the Aftermath of a Storm

*W*HEN A DEADLY STORM HITS seemingly out of nowhere, lives are shattered and landscapes altered. Mother Nature's random acts of madness—tornados, earthquakes, hurricanes, fires, and floods—wreak havoc and test our spirit. In the aftermath of chaos, when calm at last settles in, it's up to us to pick up the pieces and carry on.

As a nation, we are tuned 24/7 to all manner of instant news media. We watch scenes of natural disasters with eyes glued and hearts pounding, all the while sending up prayers of thanks to our country's richly multi-cultural host of gods, grateful that we weren't in the latest storm's devastating path.

Recently America's collective attention has been focused on a deadly storm of another kind—one born of racial tensions too long seething under our nation's skin of many colors. Michael Brown, an eighteen-year old unarmed black man, was shot multiple times and killed by a white policeman in Ferguson, Missouri—a predominantly black suburb of St. Louis.

All too often, the deadly spark that has historically ignited racial rioting in American cities and towns has been the same—an unarmed black youth is killed by a white policeman in a minority neighborhood where racial tension and distrust of local police have been festering for decades.

In dark times like this, deep-seated anger divides us. When calm is finally restored in Ferguson, America's monumental task will be to address how we as a nation can collectively heal our racial divide, and begin to revitalize inner city deserts where poverty and unemployment rates are high and potential human energy languishes. Race is not a problem only in Missouri; it is a national problem. If we are ever to achieve racial harmony in America, the rebuilding of trust as well as infrastructure and opportunity must begin now.

But how? What is our collective response when deadly storms strike?

After the Great Flood of 1993, people came to Hartsburg, Missouri from near and far to rebuild the community. Volunteers stayed a day or week or however long they could. Local Amish women cleaned houses. Pennsylvania Amish carpenters, transported by a retired postal clerk, arrived with tools and skills sorely needed. Two African-American plumbers wearing cowboy boots were among a team of New Jersey plumbers who'd seen Missouri towns inundated and homes swept away on their TVs. Grateful that they themselves had been spared, they lent a helping hand to complete strangers. Friendships that continue to this day were fostered.

This month, Boone County's September 2014 One Read selection is Daniel James Brown's *The Boys in the Boat*. It is the true story of an unlikely American eight-man rowing team from the University of Washington and their against-all-odds quest for gold at the 1936 Berlin Olympics. Before arriving as freshmen, they'd spent their hardscrabble youths working in logging camps, fishing towns, and dairy farms. In the depths of the Great Depression, their families struggled through financial hardships and deprivation.

Rowing, a physically and mentally demanding sport, became their solace during hard times. From their dedicated rowing coaches and one extraordinary boat maker, the nine young men learned lessons they never forgot. Rowing is about hard work, pitching in and pulling together—no matter where you come from, or how hard your life has been. Ironically, whenever it seemed weather conditions or life was at its worst, they rowed their best races.

Imagine. If we can come together and rebuild Hartsburg after a flood and Joplin after a tornado, can't we, and shouldn't we do the same in Ferguson? If we as Americans put our collective minds to the task, persevere through pain, and learn to row as one, something extraordinary just might happen.

It is a state of grace called harmony. While fundamental and achievable in nature and rowing, it is sadly all too rare in America today.

(September 2014)

Chapter Five

EMBRACING THE ARTS

...Moving to my own easel, I recalled the feeling I'd had while working on the painting now before me. In the process of capturing a landscape, I step out of myself. I enter the blank canvas, and follow wherever the colors on my palette lead me....

C.S. January 2012

THE THEATER OF LIFE

THERE ARE MOMENTS WHEN THE THEATER of life is as immediate as an early morning storm witnessed from a front row seat on a screened porch. Such was the dramatic beginning to my Monday—my writing day, my weekly stage for reflection in prose. Lightning flashed. Thunderous rumbles followed by sharp cracks drove Fanny, the boldest of our three cats, flying indoors for safety. A nano-second interruption of power sent every digital device in the house into a bothersome blinking mode. It was as if each clock or dial had been captivated by the electrifying plein air performance and together, had joined in a standing ovation.

The evening before, Kit and I were part of an audience of twenty at another brilliant performance—a "Sunday Soiree at Six." The unique program was staged at Carpe Diem, a mini art center co-owned by Dianna Long and Alex Innecco—a gifted Italian-Brazilian conductor who was at the time the artistic director of the Columbia Chorale and the 9th Street Philharmonic Orchestra, as well as the music director at Missouri United Methodist Church (MUMC).

Two years earlier, Kit had returned from one of the splendid performances by the 9th Street Philharmonic that Alex conducted during the winter months. The performance and Alex's infectious banter convinced Kit to purchase two season tickets as a way to support this hugely popular local music program.

The opening of Carpe Diem brought together Alex's many talents—choral conducting, voice, directing an art school in Brazil, and working with community groups in Brazil, the USA, and Europe. The tiny building with cobalt blue trim and festive flowerbeds had a business past as eclectic as the music performed at each Sunday Soiree at Six—having been a diner in the 1930s and more recently, a tattoo parlor.

We arrived just as Dianne was setting out coffee and cookies—a small part of your reward for investing twenty dollars in an hour-long program that makes you feel as if you were being serenaded in your own living room—or perhaps an eighteenth-century salon. Standing on a one-step-high dais, Alex welcomed the audience and introduced his multi-talented piano accompanist, Craig Datz (an organist at MUMC and small animal veterinarian at the University of Missouri's Animal Hospital).

When Craig took his seat at the piano, the magic began. Facing his audience and the occasional passersby strolling Locust Street, Alex opened with "Comfort Ye" from the *Messiah* and carried us back in time to the eighteen-century when Handel's masterpiece might have been performed. Subsequent songs ranged from Schubert's Erlkoing to Gilbert & Sullivan, and from Cuban composer Ernesto Lecuona to tongue-twisting Brazilian songs.

In the theater of my imagination, the buzz of university students in this same intimate space that had been a popular diner decades ago became a background chorus, and the pianist was accompanied by the whir of a tattoo artist's pen. Alex's beautiful tenor voice transported us all to an eighteenth-century, Renaissance salon where culture was music, theater, poetry, political discussions, and conversation performed for intimate groups.

Indeed, that is exactly what Carpe Diem was designed to be. *"Certain music is meant for small spaces,"* Alex wrote on his website, *"and that we can surely offer."* In addition to the Sunday Soiree series, he offered a music appreciation history course called "Bach, Beethoven and the Boys" and later focused on opera in a class he called "Screaming Divas."

When our grandson Nico visited during the summer of 2009, we took him to this tiny treasure in town where we had experienced the theater of wonderfully diverse music across space and time in the course of a single hour. I asked Craig Datz to play "Cordoba," a beautiful piano selection by a Cuban composer that speaks of a city in Spain where Kit and I have walked with Nico's father, Hayden.

In Nico's honor, Alex sang a nonsensical Brazilian tongue teaser and the song "Granada" by a Spanish composer. Nico was as delighted as the Sunday Soiree audience was by the diversity of the musical selections, the technical vocal dexterity of the tenor, the deft touch of the pianist's fingers on the ivories, and the lighthearted *joie de vivre* that Carpe Diem's spirit embodies.

The rain has now stopped. The tenor and pianist are taking their bows on an intimate stage the size of the screened porch I am sitting on at Boomerang Creek. *"Seize the day,"* I hear Alex Innecco sing out to the birds and squirrels that have gathered high in the trees. And with that, I smile at where my writer's imagination has just taken me.

"I live with 'carpe diem' engraved on my heart." —M.F.K. Fisher

(October 2009)

APPROACHING THE DANCE

$\mathcal{M}$ARK TWAIN IS SITTING ON HIS PORCH one summer afternoon in the autumn of his years. A warm breeze moves like a dancer through a nearby grove of trees. The author, dressed in his rumpled, signature summer white linens imagines another scene about to unfold behind his curtain of tired eyes he has closed to capture the drama.

A woman in a clingy, carmine-red dress with a flourish of ruffles at the knees brushes past a dark-haired man in a black suit molded to his pencil thin frame. Their eyes lock, but like the sultry breeze; their bodies pass like cautious strangers, their slight touch only a tease. The author recognizes the move. The couple's slow-building lead-in is the classic approach to the tango—a passionate Latin dance the author witnessed in his years of traveling abroad. He has never forgotten that electric moment, or felt one quite like it since.

When the writer opens his eyes again, the woman and man are nowhere to be seen. In their stead, two butterflies are weightlessly buffeted by the breeze into a spiraling motion like ballet dancers spinning on point. Twain picks up a pad of paper from his lap and dips his fountain pen into the inkwell on a nearby writing table.

Moved by the body language of the strangers and a phantom ache that hides just beneath the heart, words begin to emerge from Twain's sage pen. Only the author knows the identity of the dancers and the outcome of the dance. Wrote Twain—

> Twenty years from now you will be more disappointed by the things
> you didn't do than by the ones you did do. So throw off the bowlines.
> Sail away from the safe harbor. Catch the trade winds in your sails.
> Explore. Dream. Discover.

In 2006, Kit and I join nine other couples in Ashland for an hour of ballroom dancing lessons. Over the next year, we sign up for three ten-week sessions with our boundlessly energized, endlessly patient, Arthur Murray-trained dance instructor, Dale White. We are drawn together by the magic of dance—that moment when passion takes over and the mind stops leading the feet. That fluid sense that as in a dream, you are dancing on air. And the dance you are approaching is the *T-A-N-G-O.*

On the final evening of each ten-week session, couples arrive with an assemblage of potluck dishes that magically will result in a balanced assortment of delicious hors d'oeuvres, salads, entrees, side dishes and desserts. I can't explain how it happens, but it always does in a small town where potlucks and pies with perfect crusts are a regular part of life.

Tables are rearranged and place settings for dining laid out. Toasts are offered and good food is enjoyed by all. Finally, the tables are cleared of food and pushed back against the wall, and for the remainder of the evening, we dance uninstructed, showing off as best we can what we have learned over the past months.

Though still novices, we now move about the floor with a semblance of confidence we did not have when this hour-a-week adventure with ballroom dance began a year ago. Like children pleased with our own progress, we are eager to have our dear instructor see us dancing in a fashion recognizable as the foxtrot, waltz, cha-cha, merengue, or west coast swing.

Kit and I had never before felt the need for formal dance instruction. Every Salter in his family is an uninhibited, razzle-dazzle, natural on the dance floor. But we were moved by the idea of a head-to-toe, low-impact aerobic workout that got us moving about on the dance floor. Swing, we'd read, is "fast, furious and filled with flips, kicks, and twirls that can burns a good three hundred seventy calories an hour."

When I was very small, my father would lift me onto his size-twelve shoes, and dance me around the room to one of his favorite LP albums. He was my favorite partner for years and dancing with him was always magic.

Encouraging my early passion for dance, my parents gave me tap and tumbling classes. Both forced me to learn routines and neither required a partner. I could launch into a solo tap routine, stand on my head, and do backbends whenever and wherever the spirit moved me.

Dancing with a partner happened when I was a fifth grader. One afternoon, my teacher had the class line up by height and pair up (boy, girl, boy, girl) for ballroom dancing sessions. I was tall for my age and there were more girls than boys in the class. Without missing a beat, I partnered up with another girl, and inevitably, took the lead.

Rock 'n' Roll captured my heart and soul as a seventh grader. Back then, boys my age stood around awkwardly while the girls danced together to the latest hits on the jukebox. When the music slowed and the mood changed, there wasn't a girl in the room who didn't ache to be asked onto the dance floor by any one of those silly, adolescent boys.

When Kit and I met, I was a veteran junior high school teacher in South Central Los Angeles, thirty-two years old, and newly enrolled in a beginning ballet class for adults. Dressed in black tights and leotard, I pliéd two nights a week through classic barre exercises at a full-length, wall mirror. Transported by the music and ballet's measured movements, I stood taller and felt more graceful than I ever had before.

Legendary choreographer Martha Graham wrote, "Dance is the hidden language of the soul." I understood this when I saw Rudolph Nureyev and Margot Fontaine dance together in Los Angeles, and later watched in awe when Cynthia Gregory as a beautiful white swan rose on a single toe shoe from the floor to a perfectly balanced arabesque extension. What moved these ballet legends on the stage came from the same place in their souls as my own passion for dance.

In the film, *Shall We Dance*, a ballroom dance instructor feels empathy for one of her students, a businessman hoping to find that magic spark missing from his otherwise highly patterned workday life. As in life, he has learned the dance routines, but still something is missing. The instructor, who had once dreamed of winning the Blackpool International Dance Competition, understood failure and barely masked her own sadness at no longer competing.

When only the two of them remained in the studio one evening, she dimmed the lights, walked directly toward him, and placed his right hand at the center of her back. "Don't talk," she said. " Just dance what you feel." Then, with her left hand on his shoulder, and her right hand high in his, the music and the tango began. It was electric, and neither the dancers nor the movie audience dared breathe until it was over.

In her 2006 travel book, *A Year in the World*, Frances Mayes writes about feeling like a voyeur when she and her husband saw flamenco dancers in Spain. Mayes writes,

> Flamenco lights a brushfire in the blood. All those brightly dressed women twirling and clicking heel-toe, heel-toe, the men in black, thin as whips, the play between them, and the stepping forth for solo dancing. Through the staccato clapping, which times and builds and emphasizes, hands become a musical instrument, powerful punctuation, and raw drive.

For Mayes, flamenco's passion is best expressed by the Spanish word *duende*—a "*summoning of a life-force spirit and the expression of the spirit.*"

Across America, from Ashland to Los Angeles, people are discovering the magic of ballroom dancing. Mark Twain is watching it all from on high, applauding our efforts to throw off the bowlines, to navigate uncharted territory, and to let our inner passions fill our sails as we tango our way like stars around the dance floor.

(December 2006)

Entering the Blank Canvas

$\mathscr{S}$INCE RETURNING FROM A MAY *plein air* painting experience in Tuscany, one end of our screened porch has been reimagined to accommodate two easels, assorted brushes, oils, watercolors and painted canvases. Like a sewing room where everything is conveniently at hand, our open-air art studio stands ready whenever the spirit moves one or both of us to capture images of Boomerang Creek with brush and paints.

On a recent morning, I awoke at four-thirty to distant thunder and flashes of predawn light that announced the arrival of a front moving in from the west. My first thought was to move the canvases we'd worked on in a late afternoon painting session the prior evening if rain was blowing into that corner of the studio. Flipping on the porch light, I stepped out and found that all was dry except the paint on our canvases.

While there, I studied the strong use of primary colors—red, blue and yellow—and bold geometric shapes in Kit's most recent paintings. In describing a landscape, he has always had an amazing ability to capture images brilliantly in his teaching and writing. Painting is a new journey for him, and following his nature, Kit is boldly going where he has never gone before.

Moving to my own easel, I recalled the feeling I'd had while working on the painting now before me. In the process of capturing a landscape, I step out of myself. I enter the blank canvas, and follow wherever the colors on my palette lead me. That early rainy morning, I re-entered a painting begun a month earlier in Tuscany of the wisteria covered façade of a limestone carriage house. Beyond a dark-green hedge where I'd applied sunlight with a horizontal stroke of my brush, I imagined myself walking down stone steps into a terraced vegetable garden that was the source of many traditional Tuscan dishes enjoyed during our weeklong stay at the Spannocchia villa.

When we returned to Boomerang Creek after a two-week absence, I perused our own garden to see what needed tending. First on the list was the strawberry bed that Kit had covered with netting to keep out berry-loving birds, deer and possums. Each morning, I moved along and around the raised bed, reaching under the netting as far as my arm would extend, gathering in fat June-bearing strawberries and their smaller, sweeter French fraise de bois cousins. One morning when my collecting bowl was almost full, I came face-to-face with a four-foot, slate gray garden snake with its head and upper torso fixed in strike position. "The rest are yours, buddy," I said to the hissing snake, quickly pulling my arm back out from under the netting.

The following morning, I found that the snake hadn't moved or changed its posture one jot. It was, in fact, completely entangled in the netting. I groaned and immediately thought of Harrison Ford's line after the character he was playing, Indiana Jones, falls into a pit of deadly vipers—"Why does it always have to be snakes?" I also heard my Mother Alice's imploration when I called to tell her about my conundrum over the snake. "Why don't you just whack him with a shovel!"

Ultimately unable to ignore the sad plight of the entangled snake that I knew would never thank me, I undertook a delicate, thirty-minute rescue operation requiring scissors for the surgical removal of twisted netting from along the snake's long, scaly body. Finally, I freed him.

I have come to see the drama of the snake held at bay from exploring the strawberry bed as a metaphor for my own relationship with art. For decades I've appreciated and collected art, but never once actually attempted oil painting before our recent trip to Tuscany. Finally, having freed myself to explore as an artist, I painted the light of Italy with new eyes and understanding.

American landscape artist Edward Hopper once said, "All I ever wanted to do was capture light on the side of a barn." For the first time, I can say that I know exactly what he meant.

(January 2012)

Vicki WHITE
10/2013

The Brilliance of Crystal Bridges

*N*ORMALLY, JANUARY IS NOT THE MONTH when a road trip to the Ozarks comes to mind. But in fact, that's exactly what happened when the first Wednesday of January arrived feeling like spring. Having recently reread Rebecca Mead's "Alice's Wonderland," a *New Yorker* article (6/27/2011) about Walmart heiress Alice Walton's new Crystal Bridges Museum of American Art, Kit and I made a spontaneous decision to drive to Bentonville, Arkansas that very morning and see it for ourselves.

A trip to Arkansas was long overdue, given that I was born in Hot Springs at the end of World War II. My grandfather was at the time in command of a temporary Army post in Hot Springs, redeploying returning overseas soldiers. My mother Alice and sister Molly had been staying there until I was born while Dad, an Army Air Corps B-29 pilot, was en route home from the Pacific Theater, eager to meet me for the first time.

In 1949, another Alice, the youngest of Sam and Helen Walton's children, was born in northwestern Arkansas where her father had moved his family after returning to civilian life following the war. In 1950 Sam opened Walton's Five & Dime on Bentonville's town square. The rest is global marketing history. By 2010, his company employed 2.1 million associates worldwide and had annual sales totaling more than $405 billion.

Alice Walton's incredibly good fortune has been matched by her longtime love and appreciation of art. Together, these elements have enabled the creation of Crystal Bridges, a world class museum of American art in the middle of the Ozark world of white oaks, pines and dogwoods that has been her home for over six decades.

When Alice Walton first conceived of developing a museum to house her extraordinary art collection, she invited world-renowned architect Moshe Safdie to Arkansas to walk the ravines and hills of a one-hundred-and-twenty-acre site at the edge of downtown Bentonville. She hoped that by understanding the Ozark culture and local sense of place, the architect could better create an architectural design that would complement the surrounding natural landscape.

Crystal Bridges has had its critics, but not for a minute did it disappoint us. After a five-hour drive that January morning, we turned into the graceful, tree-lined entrance of Crystal Bridges Museum of American Art and were greeted by sculptor Roxy Paine's four-story stainless steel sycamore tree. Entitled "Yield," the soaring tree sculpture has become a metaphor for the museum. "To yield," it reminds the viewer, "is to give way, allow another the opportunity to speak; to yield is also to produce something new."

A booklet commemorating Crystal Bridges 11-11-11 Grand Opening describes the heiress and architect's collaboration as a "weaving of the tapestry of Arkansas culture, one that enables conversations of nature, architecture and art under a kind of cultural canopy." The curving walls of the galleries, according to Dr. Kevin Murphy, the Curator of American art for Crystal Bridges, are designed to "entice people to follow the paths of historical conversations in art."

The art museum, free to the public and open everyday except Tuesdays, has sparked spirited conversations among all sorts of people. These include art enthusiasts from the East and West coasts who can't fathom that anything resembling culture exists in the Ozarks; local Midwesterners who love art as much as any New Yorker and think nothing of driving five hours to spend a day surrounded by art, nature, and great architecture; diehard Walmart critics who can't find anything good to say about the company's impact on the landscape; and local working class families and school teachers thrilled that their children now have access to great art in their own neck of the lower Midwest, upper South woods.

The incredible collection of art, ranging from colonial to contemporary and arrayed in an historical flow under the museum's canopy of galleries, left us breathless and hungry to return soon and often. Clearly, our conversations at Crystal Bridges have just begun. Your own await you, thanks to Alice Walton's brilliant celebration of American art—located just down the road in the Ozarks.

(January 2012)

SOLDIER ARTISTS, BLOOD MOONS, AND THAT TWO-THOUSAND-YARD STARE

*I*N THE WEE HOURS OF APRIL 15, 2014, EARTH'S SHADOW crept across the moon's face, covering it completely. It was the first of four blood moons to occur this celestial calendar year. The reddish marbled color comes from refracted sunlight (the reddish portion of the light spectrum) that passes through Earth's atmosphere, bends again, and is sent onto the moon during a total lunar eclipse. Standing on the frosty porch at two o'clock in the morning, barefooted and shivering, I was mesmerized by the moon's transformation from a cold, bluish white to the color of translucent flesh and bone.

The following evening, I attended the 2014 Carlos Perez-Mesa Lectureship in Medical Humanities, an annual free event, thanks to Dr. Perez-Mesa's generous family, at the University of Missouri Center for Health Ethics. The speaker, Dr. Barbara Mathes, presented an illustrated lecture, "Medicine in the Art of War: Stories in the Art of Soldier-Artists."

The works of war artists have illustrated and recorded aspects of wars around the globe for centuries. Over the past two centuries, American and European governments have commissioned war art as both propaganda and to commemorate battles. As a body of work, the art captures daily life of soldiers during wartime and serves as a pictorial record of how war shapes our lives. The visual and sensual impact of war captured in paintings and sketches of war artists are often the very scenes absent in written histories.

The U.S. Army's art program has produced more than fifteen thousand pieces of art since its inception a century ago during World War I. "Unfortunately," Dr. Mathes reported, "this is one of the largest collections of paintings by American artists almost never seen." Currently this collection of paintings, some never framed, is stored in vaults at Fort Belvoir near Washington, D.C. in the care of the Army's Historical Properties Section.

Because soldier artists capture the realities of wartime activities firsthand, the collection has a unique educational value that should be shared. Their art illustrates a scene and a moment in a way that written and spoken words cannot. After a decade of war in Iraq and Afghanistan, art would be an invaluable healing tool for soldiers wounded in battle or suffering post-traumatic stress disorder.

During the lecture, Dr. Mathes showed details from an oil painting completed in March 1919 by American artist John Singer Sargent. Entitled *Gassed*, it depicts the aftermath of a mustard gas attack on the Western Front during the First World War. In this haunting, composition (seven-and-a-half by twenty feet), nine wounded soldiers in groups of three are being led in a line by medical orderlies toward a dressing station. As if in an allegorical frieze, the nearly life-sized, tall, blond wounded soldiers—eyes blinded and bandaged—appear to be guided by guy ropes.

In the unearthly background, the reddish-yellow haze of a setting sun burnishes a rising moon. Overhead, an aerial dogfight is underway in the evening sky. And in the background, a group of soldiers plays football, seemingly detached from the suffering all around. For a brief moment, normality eclipses the dark shadow cast by war.

Dr. Mathes concluded her lecture with a list of war artists from World War I up to Afghanistan and Iraq. Tom Lea was among the World War II artists cited. When Congress cancelled funding for WW II war artists, Mathes related, *Life* magazine stepped forward. From 1941-46, Lea served as an eyewitness reporter for *Life*, traveling over one hundred thousand miles to the theaters of war where American forces were involved. His writings and paintings appeared in *Life* between April 1942 and July 1945.

While visiting my mother in San Antonio shortly after the lecture, she found me poring over her signed copy of *The Art of Tom Lea: A Memorial Edition*. I'd selected it purposefully from amongst the other Tom Lea books in my parents' library. Lea was a native of El Paso and longtime friend of my Great Aunt Helen, and her daughter, my Aunt Jane, Mother's cousin.

For years I've known of Lea as an author and illustrator of novels set in the American Southwest. Not until a month ago did I discover the significant role he had also played as a correspondent and war artist in World War II. Lea's painting, *That Two-Thousand-Yard Stare* is as moving and relevant today as when it first appeared in *Life* magazine the year I was born.

The geographic range and scope of Lea's war art is extraordinary—The Tunisian desert, 1943. Argentia Bay, Newfoundland, 1941. Battleships on the North Atlantic, 1941-42. Air, sea, and land battles in the Pacific. Sketches entitled Across the World with U.S.A.A.F. Flying the [Burma] Hump, 1943. Watercolors of Madam Chiang and Generalissimo Chiang Kai-shek, 1943.

The most personally moving of Lea's war art are scenes captured when the artist accompanied the first assault wave of the First Marines on Peleliu Island in 1944—later collected as a book, *Peleliu Landing*, in 1945. Lea's oil, *The Price*, graphically illustrates what Marine combatants encountered on Peleliu.

In his haunting 1944 oil, *That Two-Thousand-Yard Stare*, a soldier's vacant eyes illustrate the traumatic stress of war. About the real-life Marine who was his subject, Tom Lea wrote—

> *He left the States thirty-one months ago. He was wounded in his first campaign. He has had tropical diseases. He half-sleeps at night and gouges the enemy (Japanese) out of holes all day. Two-thirds of his company has been killed or wounded. He will return to attack this morning. How much can a human being endure?*

Lea's ability to capture both the weaponry and emotions of war is as powerful today as it was in 1945 when my father, then a twenty-five-year-old B-29 pilot in the Pacific theater, was flying dangerous night raids over Japan in the final year of World War II.

Each year on Memorial Day, we remember the sacrifices of veterans from wars past and present. We should also remember the origin of the medical term for PTSD, "the thousand–yard stare," illustrated seventy years ago by World War II artist Tom Lea. Lest we should ever forget, Tom Lea's haunting painting of the same name continues to remind us that war is an unforgiving, living hell.

(June 2014)

INDEPENDENT FILMS BRING THE WORLD HOME

*F*OR AS LONG AS I CAN REMEMBER, I've loved going to the movies. In the 1950s, Saturday matinees entertained audiences of kids with cartoons, serialized shorts, previews of coming attractions, adventure movies and, of course, popcorn and a box of Milk Duds.

By my college years in the 1960s, I had gravitated to foreign films like Ingmar Bergman's *The Seventh Seal* that exercised my intellect and passionate dramas like *Black Orpheus* that transported me from Lincoln, Nebraska in the dead of winter to the steamy Brazilian underworld of Rio.

When Kit and I lived in West Los Angeles during the 1970s and 80s, our favorite Friday night date after an intense week of teaching was a movie followed by a leisurely dinner for two and a lively critique of the film we had just seen.

In the two decades since our move from L.A. to D.C. to "L.A." (Lower Ashland), we have witnessed exciting innovations in Columbia's art and theater community, as well as the growth of an international independent documentary film culture. Together, they have made Columbia's downtown known as "The District," a destination for anyone who loves the arts.

Among the brightest and most welcome innovations was the Ragtag Cinemacafé that opened in May 2000 on 10th Street. Housed in a narrow, brick storefront, it offered a bar with a limited but organically healthy small-plate menu up front, and an intimate theater with seventy mismatched chairs and lumpy couches behind an old red velvet curtain.

Ragtag's primary mission from the start has been to "provide a venue for the best in United States independent and international filmmaking." David Wilson and Paul Sturtz, two of a young, creative, all-volunteer group of film enthusiasts, first envisioned the Ragtag Film Society in 1997 and began screening films at The Blue Note.

In February 2004, Ragtag staged their first True/False Film Fest, attracting four thousand moviegoers to three venues. In February 2008, Ragtag moved to its new home on Hitt Street with two theaters, a bar/café and a bakery. That year, more than nine thousand guests attended the seventh annual True/False Film Fest the final week of February. Over twenty-five thousand tickets were purchased for the films, workshops, and festival-related events staged at eight downtown venues.

Every year, Kit and I join hundreds of local volunteers who work at various T/F venues and events. We also join non-ticket holders in the "Q" (the queue line,) and when space allows, we eagerly attend provocative, often jarring independent films followed by Q&A discussions with the film directors.

For T/F 2010, "co-conspirators" Paul Sturtz and David Wilson selected thirty-six films from over seven hundred submissions that "ask us to be alert to the wonder of open-ended possibilities as we observe non-fiction films that focus on the world, both near and far." Filmmaker/director, Laura Poitras was the recipient of that year's T/F Film Fest's True Vision Award. Her 2010 documentary *The Oath* focused on a cab driver in Yemen named Al-Bahri—the former bodyguard of Osama bin Laden and brother-in-law of Salim Hamdan, a prisoner at Guantanamo and the first person to face U.S. military commissions.

The filmmaker's masterful piece of intimate camera work in *The Oath* moves the audience through the streets of Yemen's crowded capital in Al-Bahri's cab one minute, then segues to the solitary world of Hamdan in his seventh year of confinement without a trial at Guantanamo. And as a small circle of Yemeni youths sit with Al-

Bahri, he counsels them on the consequences of radical jihadism.

During the film's Q&A session, I asked Poitras where she first got the idea for her film. "I'd gone to Yemen to learn about al-Qaeda," she said, "and someone told me to talk to this cab driver who'd once been bin Laden's bodyguard." From that thread, one critic wrote, she wove a story "as filled with reversals as a Shakespearean tragedy."

For more than a decade, True/False has gotten us out of our February funk, and into local theater venues. Championing the best new non-fiction filmmaking, its visionary founders strive to promote art, inspire dialogue, and deepen our community's understanding of each other and the world at large.

Challenging, thought provoking, poignant, informative, comic, romantic, visually electric, often disorienting—this is what documentaries at their creative best can be. "There are no small stories," according to Sturtz and Wilson. With my virtual taxi ride through Yemen's capital still powerfully resonant in my mind a week later, I would also agree.

(March 2010)

Afternoon Tea

*T*HE CEREMONY OF AFTERNOON TEA IS A RITUAL that has brought friends and family together for ages. Cakes and pastries, scones and clotted cream accompany assorted perfectly steeped pots of tea. Two recent events reminded me of the importance of such rituals that over time become treasured rites celebrating friendship and life.

As February ended with a snowy blast, a warm email from a dear friend arrived inviting me to afternoon tea at her home. Though we've known each other for over twenty years, busy schedules have kept us from getting together often enough.

"What kind of tea do you prefer?" Marjo asked, wanting the tea to be perfect for the occasion we both were looking forward to.

"Black tea with milk, no sugar," I responded. "Perfect," she replied. "That is exactly the way I like my tea."

At the appointed time, I arrived with chocolate mints and sesame cookies that promptly joined a sterling silver tea pot and two tea cups and saucers—one her mother's china pattern and the other her mother-in-law's—on a serving tray. For the next two hours, we shared conversation over tea in Marjo's sun-filled library. Time fell away, teacups were refreshed, and not once did our conversation flag.

When the 2015 True/False Film Festival began later that same week, I knew immediately that I wanted to see "Tea Time"—a documentary about five women who met for afternoon tea once a month for sixty years. Chilean filmmaker and director Maite Alberdi talked about her film in a *New York Times* interview (October 20, 2014):

In my home country of Chile, having afternoon tea together with friends and family is a cherished ritual. The custom is far more than just tea: It's a time to catch up with loved ones and share experiences both seismic and mundane. As time goes on, teatime and the conversations it fuels can become the glue that holds.

The five women included the filmmaker's grandmother and four friends who attended high school together. After graduation, they met for tea once a month for more than half a century. Describing this ritual that Alberdi has witnessed since her childhood, the filmmaker added,

It is impossible to overstate the importance of this occasion for my grandmother. She won't skip it for anything.

This year's T/F Film Festival included documentaries on timeworn wars that continue to haunt Afghanistan and Indonesia, and the chaotic messiness of life. On the other extreme, *Tea Time* focuses up close and personal on a time-tested rite grounded in civility and calm. After viewing *Bitter Lake*, this year's kaleidoscopic and haunting True Vision Award documentary about Afghanistan by Adam Curtis, we needed a breather. A documentary entitled *Tea Time* seemed like just the ticket.

Anticipating that it would be a crowd pleaser, Kit and I arrived two hours early to assure a spot at the head of the "Q" line—a full hour before "Q" numbers were given out. Within minutes, the pre-"Q" line had grown into a snaking Disney line of like-minded moviegoers. Ironically, the showing of *Tea Time* that we had chosen to attend was at four o'clock in the afternoon.

When finally through the "Q" line and in the theater, we learned that Alicia, one of the five women in Alberdi's tender and poignant film, was in the audience and would be at the Q&A. Her presence made this sweet and touching gem of a film all the more memorable.

When we talked briefly with Alicia later, I mentioned my recent afternoon tea with Marjo and that for the past decade; I have met for lunch once a month with a circle of twelve fascinating women. Our monthly gathering allows us to converse about films, books, travel, health care issues, opera, world affairs and a wide range of current hot-topic issues that concern us.

In a spontaneous celebration of friendship, Alicia and I linked arms and posed for a picture that I will share with Marjo and my Salon circle—women who understand the value of teatime and conversations that become the glue that holds.

(March 2015)

Chapter Six
Dateline USA

Nowhere is Route 66 more at home than in Oklahoma, where the pavement follows the contours of the land as though it had always been there. In Oklahoma, the West and East collide on Route 66, and the state becomes the crossroads for America's Main Street.

—Michael Wallis, Route 66: The Mother Road

Seizing the Day: Chicago Weekend with Tosca

When Paul McCartney was sixteen, he wrote "When I'm Sixty-Four"—a young man's song to his lover about growing old together. When I first heard it on the Beatles' 1967 album, *Sgt. Pepper's Lonely Hearts Club Band*, I was twenty-two years young and off exploring the Asian continent. What lay in store for me at the cusp of sixty-four? A weekend in Chicago that coincided with President Barack Obama's Nobel Peace Prize, Tosca's opening night at the Chicago Lyric Opera and the 2009 Chicago Marathon.

Magically, Kit and a cast of eleven opera lovers made it happen. On a soggy Friday morning, our spirited band of thirteen organized by Carpe Diem's Alex Innecco and Dianna Long headed in a small caravan for Chicago. When we pulled into our hotel adjacent to the Merchandise Mart on the Chicago River, the skies parted and the setting sun turned the downtown's architectural gem of a skyline into shimmering silver and gold.

The magic had begun. Our location was within walking distance of Chicago's historic theater district, Michigan Avenue's Magnificent

Mile, Millennium Park and the Art Institute of Chicago. Our unique Holiday Inn perched fifteen floors atop the *Chicago Sun Times* Building and Apparel Mart offered a lofty lobby-level Cityscape Bar with a bird's-eye view and the newly opened Italiasia Restaurant.

After nine hours of passengering in the rain in a two-vehicle caravan on Missouri and Illinois interstate highways, Kit and I happily joined our eclectic opera flock for an evening indoors, looking out a wall of glass in the Cityscape Bar spectacularly surrounded by downtown Chicago in sparkling relief. Warmed by wine, delicious Italian/Pan Asian fusion food and the company of friends, it was the perfect first act to our Chicago Tosca weekend.

Saturday was left open for unstructured explorations in the city. Dressed in layers for the crisp, clear October morning air, Kit and I headed on foot up State Street and eventually shifted eastward onto Michigan Avenue. Breezes off Lake Michigan left me thankful for every piece of clothing I was wearing from my neck to my toes. Sidewalks were packed with shoppers and families in town for Sunday morning's annual Chicago Marathon. Streets were jammed with cars, taxis, tourist trolleys, buses, elevated train tracks and a few horse-drawn buggies.

By lunchtime, we had walked from the Merchandise Mart up State Street and over to Water Tower Place, then south on Michigan Avenue to the Tribune Tower near the Chicago River. There, our mental map from prior visits led us down from the crowded streets to the dark underside of the bridge to the legendary Billy Goat Tavern for a cheeseburger and beer with neighborhood locals.

Next was the Art Institute's exhibit of illustrations from Caldecott Award Books from 2006-2009. *How I Learned Geography*, written and illustrated by my friend Uri Shulevitz, is a treasure for all ages. After a brisk walk back to the hotel through the Theater District, we joined our Tosca group and walked to Chicago's Civic Opera Building, a dazzling 1929 Egyptian motif and Art Deco wonder.

The season-opening production of Puccini's *Tosca* was one

created by Franco Zeffirelli for two operatic legends, Maria Callas and Tito Gobbi, at London's Covent Gardens. From our seats near the orchestra pit, we were transported into the Attavanti private chapel of the Church of St. Andrea della Valle Rome in the early nineteenth century where painter Mario Cavarodossi, Floria Tosca's lover, is working on his portrait of Mary Magdalene.

In 1887, actress Sarah Bernhardt, starring in the French play *La Tosca*, inspired Puccini's 1900 opera *Tosca*. A British critic described her then in Act Two: The Supper Scene—"She looked superb, pale as death, Sarah Bernhardt, knife in hand over the dying Scarpia, is the nearest thing to great tragedy that has ever been seen in modern times."

Bernhardt played her last *Tosca* in 1913. Attending my first *Tosca* in Chicago has given new meaning to the Latin phrase, *carpe diem*. And as for "When I'm Sixty-Four," so far it has been absolutely great.

(October 2009)

Exploring a Stretch of Oklahoma's Route 66

ALL US CRAZY, BUT WHEN JULY TEMPERATURES did their annual climb into triple digits, Kit and I packed off on a road trip to explore a stretch of Oklahoma's Route 66. Over the years, we've traveled various legs of the historic highway's approximately two thousand four hundred miles of paved road. From the shore of Lake Michigan in Chicago to the Santa Monica pier in Los Angeles, where it ends at the Pacific Ocean, Route 66 passes through eight states—Illinois, Missouri, Kansas, Oklahoma, Texas, New Mexico, Arizona and California.

Begun in 1926 and built under several Federal Aid Highway Acts, U.S. Route 66 was one of the largest public works projects ever undertaken in the United States. Dorothea Lange's black-and-white Depression-era photographs, Woody Guthrie's edgy music and lyrics, and John Steinbeck's bleak novel, *The Grapes of Wrath,* captured the desperate flight west of Oklahoma migrant refugees during the Dust Bowl years along what Steinbeck called "the mother road."

> *Been on this road for a mighty long time,*
> *Ten million men like me,*
> *You drive us from yo' town, we ramble around,*
> *I got them 66 Highway Blues.*
>
> —Woody Guthrie

After the road's 1926 designation as a national highway from Chicago to Los Angeles through Tulsa, the number "66" was adopted by Frank Phillips, founder of Oklahoma's Phillips Petroleum to promote his gasoline and the idea of Route 66 as "the Main Street of America." Its heyday lasted from 1945, when World War II ended (and life for me began), until 1965. Neon signs advertising motels, restaurants, and novelty shops (the kitschier the better) marked the highway that saw its last stretch paved in 1937.

In 1946, bandleader Bobby Troup, wrote the hit song "Get Your Kicks on Route 66," later recorded by Nat King Cole and nearly two hundred other performers. In 1960, when I was a high school sophomore, the mother road was again immortalized when Troup's lyrics became the theme song for the enormously popular television series *Route 66*. Each week, my sisters and I watched the show's young stars, Martin Milner and George Maharis, intersect and navigate their way through moral dilemmas encountered while driving their blue Corvette convertible along Route 66.

To travel historians, aging bikers, car buffs, summer road trippers, Steinbeck literati, lovers of blue highways, and fried food diner fans, Route 66 remains a nostalgic destination more than eight decades after its initial length of Portland concrete was laid. For two geographers in love with the road, the stretch of the old Route 66 between Tulsa and Oklahoma City was also a mecca of classic diner road food.

In Red Fork near Sapulpa, OK, we dined at Ollie's Station where chicken fried steak smothered in gravy made from scratch comes with your choice of two sides—fried sweet potatoes, fried green tomatoes, fried okra, French fries, onion rings, or potatoes (mashed or baked).

In Stroud the following one-hundred-and-five-degree day, I ordered fish tacos at the Rock Cafe, passing up their famous Alligator Burgers and German Jagerschnitzel. Reopened in 2009 after a fire gutted the seventy-year old landmark, the restaurant is again attracting celebrity attention. Owner Dawn Longacre Welch (part Cherokee, Choctaw and Irish) was the inspiration for Sally Carrera— the blue Porsche in the animated 2006 Pixar film, *Cars*.

That evening, we turned off the highway in Acadia where an iconic sixty-six foot sculpture of a soda bottle and straw ringed with multi-colored LED lights illuminated Pops—an ultra modern, red-rock-and-steel truss diner offering over five hundred soft drinks. We shared onion rings and a cold wedge of iceberg lettuce and sipped Arnold Palmers (half iced tea, half lemonade). It was the perfect light meal after a delicious day of meandering along this sweet stretch of Route 66.

> *Nowhere is Route 66 more at home than in Oklahoma, where the pavement follows the contours of the land as though it had always been there. In Oklahoma, the West and East collide on Route 66, and the state becomes the crossroads for America's Main Street.*
> —Michael Wallis, *Route 66: The Mother Road*

(July 2010)

HERE IS MY NEW YORK

*D*URING A HOT SPELL in the summer of 1948, E.B. White—a writer for *The New Yorker* and, several years later, the author of the children's classic *Charlotte's Web*—checked into the Lafayette Hotel in Manhattan. While there, he wrote *Here is New York*—a small, 54-page treasure of a book, capturing Manhattan as he found it then: "its sounds and smells, its restless energy, its teeming population, its intimacy, its privacy, its inconveniences, its heady delights, its aching loneliness."

When the book was published in 1949, the Lafayette was gone, leading White to observe that "to bring New York down to date, a man would have to be published with the speed of light...and that it is the reader's, not the author's, duty to do so."

And so, taking on E.B. White's challenge, I spent four days exploring New York City this May with a dear friend, Chomsri Lewinter. Chomsri knew Manhattan very little. Recalling E. B. White's sense of the ever-changing nature of this unique city, I set about filling in the blank spaces in my friend's mental map—organizing explorations on foot, by subway, in taxis, and by ferry—in, around, and about the city.

To understand Manhattan, I explained, she and I needed to walk the length and breadth of its numbered and named streets and grand avenues; move at ground level through its diverse neighborhoods and distinctive districts; hear the United Nations of voices conversing on the city's bustling streets or on their cell phones with someone on the other side of the globe. Posted subway directives called "subtalk" are posted in English, Spanish, French, German, Italian, Chinese and Japanese.

More than a hundred million Americans can claim ancestors who came through Ellis Island. To see New York, the melting pot of America, as twelve million immigrants did, we took a ferry from Battery Park to the Statue of Liberty that poet Emma Lazarus described in 1883 as "the Mother of Exiles."

At nearby Ellis Island, a freestanding sculpture made from immigrant luggage—each parcel filled with the few precious possessions immigrants brought to begin life anew in America—greets visitors in the entrance lobby. Throughout the interior, large black and white photographs taken by an amateur photographer who worked there as a guard for years hang on the walls. The stunning black and white portraits afford visitors a glimpse back in time at families of arriving immigrants dressed in the costumes of their native countries.

On the return ferry ride from Ellis Island, Manhattan appeared to us as the island that it is, bordered by two rivers, and connected to neighboring boroughs by bridges. After disembarking from the Staten Island Ferry, we walked north from Battery Park through a palimpsest of centuries of city streets laid down first in cobblestones to fit the narrow, southernmost contours of Manhattan. This was the site of the city's earliest settlement—later widened in an orderly grid as development spread northward. The 1930s-era Empire State and Chrysler buildings, formerly dwarfed by the World Trade Center Towers, again dominate the Midtown Manhattan skyline.

Drawn to the site of the eerily absent towers, Chomsri and I followed Broadway past Wall Street, stopping at the Trinity Church cemetery. Entering this peaceful sanctuary in the heart of the Financial District, we touched and were touched by a red 9/11 sculpture created from the massive roots of a century-old sycamore tree uprooted by falling debris from the looming World Trade Towers that once cast shadows on the cemetery from just blocks away.

Arriving at the former World Trade Center site, now surrounded by walls of plywood and chain link fencing, silent crowds gather daily beneath a 9/11 timeline with images that mirror those already seared into our collective memory, recalling seconds and minutes and hours of that singularly clear September morning when the world as we knew it changed forever.

Still, as E. B. White observed on the passing of an earlier treasured landmark, "the essential fever of New York has not changed." Like other visitors afoot in the city, we were refreshed by Central Park—a great green urban lung breathing life into the heart of Manhattan. The Museum of Modern Art (MOMA), the Metropolitan Museum, and Frank Lloyd Wright's Guggenheim continue to draw crowds. On our forty-block walk to the Upper East Side, we delighted in newly discovered finds along the way—Payard's Patisserie, the tiny Bistro du Nord and Corner Bookstore on Madison Avenue, and Eli's wholesale foods emporium on 91st at 1st Avenue.

Our dining experiences in Manhattan ranged from high tea at the posh 1904 St. Regis Hotel to lowbrow take-out fare at Fluffy's Deli. In between, we sampled steaming baskets of dim sum in Chinatown, cappuccino-with-a-jolt gelato in Little Italy, and spicy Thai cuisine at Pongsri in the Theater District.

Here, then, is my New York. Here is a city where cultures intersect constantly, where Chomsri and I interacted with hotel employees from Dallas, France and Bangladesh; an artist from Inner Mongolia; a sales girl from Montana: a souvenir vendor from Tibet; an Indian jeweler in the Hasidic Jewish Diamond District; two Peace Corps colleagues from forty years ago in Thailand; and taxi drivers from virtually everywhere.

Such is the rich and colorful mosaic that is New York—the city E .B. White once described as "the greatest town in the world—the gaudiest, most beautiful…most heartbreaking city in all history."

(May 2007)

ON FOOT IN SAN FRANCISCO

OWARD THE END OF AUGUST 2006, Kit surprised me with a trip to San Francisco. It was utterly spontaneous—organized on a whim to afford us a breather before September's full calendar of fall activities got underway. We each packed one small carry-on bag and a shoulder bag large enough for a novel, camera, journal, and snack for the flight west. Simple and light—a metaphor for the moment.

Kit had earlier reminded me that we would be attending a conference at the Hilton Hotel near Union Square the following spring. I did a Google search of that area of San Francisco's downtown, found the Maxwell Hotel—a small, European-style hotel in the neighborhood—and booked reservations for our stay.

Once on the plane, I dug out my copy of T.C. Boyle's *The Tortilla Curtain*—the Daniel Boone Library's September 2006 One Read selection. When life is full, as it always seems to be, flying time is perfect reading time. San Francisco is a city of immigrants. California and illegal immigration are the setting and focus of Boyle's powerful book. And so the trip began. I read on a cushion of air as we flew west over the flatness that defines Kansas and the Great Plains; passed over the Rockies, dry patches of the Great Basin, and the Coastal Ranges; and finally set down in California's grand peninsular city bounded by two inland bays and the Pacific Ocean.

Once on the ground, we decided to train into the city. Following the crowd, we wheeled out suitcases along the airport's skywalk to the BART (Bay Area Rapid Transit) level, purchased two transit tickets, and rode to the Powell Street station constructed beneath a trendy, shopping center the size of a city block. Anchored by a Nordstrom's

Department store, the center's floors of commercial and café activity were connected by elegantly curving interior escalators and an open atrium that made us feel as though we had landed in the heart of a giant ocean liner.

Once out in the sunlight, we walked past the Powell Street Cable Car terminus, wheeling our luggage and selves past colorful shops, flower carts, vendors, restaurants, bars, and street personalities hustling their wares and services—all vying for attention in this fast-paced, eclectic city. The sky was blue, it felt great to stretch our legs, and it was easy walking distance to the Maxwell Hotel on Geary Street between Union Square and the Theater District.

We had left Boomerang Creek before dawn, driven two hours east to St. Louis to catch our late morning flight for the west coast, taken a train into the city from the San Francisco airport, and walked four blocks through a colorful sea of humanity and a world of languages with one singular goal in mind for our first evening in the city— dinner for two in a quiet little restaurant near our cozy hotel. From then on, the rest of the city was ours to explore, one day and one hill at a time.

Happily, we found the Maxwell Hotel to be wonderfully situated and our room on the tenth floor provided us with a broad, unimpeded view of urban rooftops from different eras, as well as the bay and all of its activities. In the next block, we noted the Curran Theater where *A Chorus Line* was in its final week of performances before heading to New York City for a Broadway run. We'd seen the musical, one of our favorites, in Los Angeles in the late 1970s when the show was preparing for its first Broadway debut. Within an hour of our arrival at our hotel, we managed to secure two fourth row center tickets for a matinee during our stay.

But first, we would traverse some of San Francisco on foot, one city block and neighborhood at a time—our favorite way to experience the geography of urban places. The following morning, we walked in the direction of Union Square and turned on Grant Avenue toward the ornate ceremonial gate that announces the commercial entrance to Chinatown. Street signage throughout this popular neighborhood is in both Chinese and English. After passing a stretch of Chinese restaurants and tourist shops, we turned off the beaten path and entered a residential stretch of Chinatown where laundry hangs on bamboo poles from apartment balconies and seniors in pods were actively engaged in outdoor exercises and card games in a small urban park.

This park, built atop a parking structure on a hill, lies in the shadow of the Transamerica building—the distinctive pyramid-shaped office building that has been an architectural icon on San Francisco's urban skyline since its construction in the 1960s. Looking skyward at the apex of this great urban glass and concrete pyramid, we marveled at where life has taken each of us since the building's arrival on San Francisco's Embarcadero.

Our goal was to traverse the northeast quadrant of the city from Union Square to Fisherman's Wharf. Walking north in San Francisco literally means walking uphill. Not one hill, but neighborhoods of hills. After our exploration of Chinatown and the city's landmark Transamerica Pyramid, we continued north with the docks of the Embarcadero all that separated us from San Francisco Bay.

With this giant pyramid as our compass directional, we continued walking uphill through the Telegraph Hill neighborhood. Telegraph Hill and Coit Tower stood out like mountain peaks up ahead. Each cross street was a milestone. Sidewalks and streets grew ever narrower. Quaint pastel-colored dwellings appeared to lean at a tilt from their foundations. Like seasoned trekkers, we fell into a single-file formation and conversation fell away. One over-riding question hung in the thinning air: How far before the downhill part of the walk begins?

Telegraph Hill, we observed, is tightly packed with narrow common wall two-and-three story residences with immaculate gardens and street trees. No space is wasted. Signs instruct drivers to park at a ninety-degree angle to the curb—prompted, no doubt, by more than a few cars with worn-out brakes that left their precariously angled parking spaces without drivers.

Near the summit of our climb we chanced upon the Fog Hill Market. A faded advertisement painted on the store's milky white exterior wall depicted grazing dairy cows on the Berkeley Hills Farm circa 1910. As if on cue, we slipped into the corner market world of Hanna Chedyak—a Lebanese-American small businessman from Beirut. After buying two bottles of mango juice and a basket of fresh figs, we sat outside at a small red table Mr. Chedyak carried out front for us.

For the next thirty minutes, we snacked and soaked in the late morning sun while being entertained by the theater-on-the-street taking place before us. It was a ballet of non-stop motion as trucks large and small maneuvered into the impossibly narrow delivery space in front of the market. In between deliveries, Mr. Chedyak talked about Beirut, about Lebanon's future, and about the region in the mountains outside of Beirut where his family once lived. While San Francisco is now his home, it was clear that the fate of the land of his father plays heavily on his mind.

Our urban walk was all downhill from there—first through the funky North Beach neighborhood with its retro secondhand clothing shops, then along a descending diagonal slice of Columbus Avenue busy with cable cars leaving or returning to their northern terminus on Taylor Street near Fisherman's Wharf. As our lungs filled with moist ocean air, our thoughts turned to lunch. It was a breezy, fish-and-chips kind of day. With little effort, we followed flocks of seagulls to the wharf, bought lunch, and parked ourselves at an outdoor table with a one-in-a-million view—ferry boats en route to Alcatraz, decommissioned World War II ships, and fishing boats. To the west, the Golden Gate Bridge stood out between the bay and the Pacific Ocean, a splendid visual landmark for tourists arriving at the northern terminus of the cable cars at Fisherman's Wharf.

For the return trip, we hopped on an open-air cable car that announced its arrival at every street corner with clanking bells and the manual shifting of heavy steel gears by our muscular driver. We were happy as clams to be on his shift, watching the city go by all the way back to Union Square—literally our jumping off point.

At Powell and Post Streets, we dropped by Williams-Sonoma, the company's four-story flagship store. For the next hour, we explored each layer of this visually delicious cake of a cooking store built around an open central atrium. From top of the line, restaurant quality, six burner stoves to shelves of delicious foodstuffs that include Williams-Sonoma's namesake line, *Grande Cuisine.*

Julia Child would have loved this store because it is a museum of every cooking utensil imaginable. Like Child, collecting and finding interesting uses for kitchen gadgets was a passion of Chuck Williams, the store's founder. Exhibits of William's lifetime collection of old kitchen gadgets line the walls, along with framed food sketches paired with his favorite recipes.

I was given a tour of level three by David Bolt who creates magical table settings with Provençal linens and the store's General Manager, Marisa Halvorson, who was engaged in her own lively conversation downstairs with Kit about the store's unusual layout. Satisfied that we had had a culinary museum experience of the finest caliber, we strolled back to our hotel to dress for our next adventure—dinner somewhere at one of the neighborhood restaurants Marisa Halvorson shared with us when I asked, "Where does Chuck Williams eat when he comes to visit the store?"

(September 2006)

No Turn Before the Shoreline

$\mathcal{I}$N LATE JANUARY, I ARRIVED at the Los Angeles International Airport for my five o'clock return flight to St. Louis—just ahead of the Monday morning L.A. freeway commuter traffic. After a surprisingly smooth passage through security, I picked up a tall caffe latte at Starbucks, purchased a box of Mrs. See's locally famous nuts and chews chocolates, and disappeared into Marianne Wiggins's luminescent, impossible to put down novel, *Evidence of Things Unseen*, until boarding time.

As the pilot turned our plane's nose west in preparation for takeoff, the sun popped up rosy as a Pasadena parade, washing the cold gray runway the warmest imaginable shade of dawn pink. Seconds before liftoff, I noticed a warning sign on the runway—*No turn before the shoreline!* Then suddenly, we ascended up and over the ocean, leaving behind the arching curve of the Pacific Coast Highway and L.A.'s transverse Santa Monica mountains. Silently, the landscape below disappeared into the clouds as we banked left and headed back toward the frozen Midwest.

I first arrived at this very edge of the Pacific in the summer of 1974, part of a caravan of two cars and a twenty-four-foot U-Haul van, accompanied by my sister Kim, my redheaded friend Pat Fennell, and our mutual desire to get out of Nebraska before another impossible winter froze our resolve. With Omaha behind us and no jobs or place to live as yet on the horizon, our roadmap was as simple as the signage on the LAX runway—*No turn before the shoreline!*

Within a year, Pat and I were both teaching at Audubon Junior High School in south central Los Angeles. In 1988, I left L.A. with

Kit to begin new chapters of life, first in Washington D.C., and for the past two decades in Missouri. Pat continued to teach English in L.A., retiring last year as a mentor teacher after a distinguished, thirty-four-year career.

My recent L.A. visit with Pat and her husband Gary—an eclectic inventor and holographer currently fascinated with hydroponic gardening—happened during episodic fits of rain, hail, sunshine and snow in the surrounding mountains. Undaunted, Pat and I donned raincoats and headed for an afternoon at the Getty Center, perched on a dramatic hilltop in the Santa Monica Mountains with breathtaking views of the Pacific to the west, and Century City and the downtown L.A. skyline off to the east.

Dodging intermittent showers, we explored the monumental granite pavilions that house the J. Paul Getty Museum—studying Van Gogh's irises, paintings by sixteenth-century Dutch Masters, and detailed etchings by Rembrandt and his students. Outdoors, we photographed skies as black as night that a minute later were filled with dazzling post-rain sunlight, illuminating the Getty's sculpted gardens and expansive marble courtyards.

Mornings began early in Pat and Gary's kitchen with lively conversation fueled by cups of Peet's high-octane coffee. Parked in front of their gas kitchen stove's open door, Gary warmed his backside while he and I carried on heated debates on politics and strategies for dealing with the war in Afghanistan.

For two glorious days, L.A. was a Chamber of Commerce picture-perfect postcard with snow-capped mountains above the downtown skyline, sixty-degree temperatures, and a true blue sky in which both the sun and moon were clearly visible overhead midday.

Sunday, we wandered through the Huntington Library and Botanical Garden grounds, past citrus trees filled with oranges and lemons, pomegranate trees, camellias in glorious bloom, and Shakespearian sonnets nested amongst herbs that inspired the poet to write about them. Supper that evening was at Lucques—celebrated

Los Angeles chef Suzanne Goin's Melrose Avenue restaurant.

Back home now where absolutely nothing is in bloom in our February garden, a jar of preserved lemons needed in Pat's recipe for Israeli couscous with butternut squash captures sunlight on our kitchen island. In a south-facing window, a tray of Gary's patent-pending, hydroponic garden wheatgrass has exploded with green shoots that would make my midwestern cats Fanny and Pooh deliriously happy in the middle of winter.

As snow falls on Boomerang Creek half a continent to the east, I allow my thoughts to revisit L.A. landscapes and dear friends now on my mind. Then, smiling, they (my thoughts) turn just beyond the shoreline, bank and fly home to this Missouri world where my heart now happily resides.

(February 2010)

Hot Dogs, Cappuccino, and Antifreeze

$\mathcal{O}$N MY WAY INTO ASHLAND one November past, I encountered a message on the Break Time gas station's marquee that still makes me smile to this day. At the four-way intersection on east Broadway, I read the following three-line advertisement—"Hot Dogs, Cappuccino, & Antifreeze." It was just too wonderful for words!

But since words are what writers are supposed to be about, here is the story of where those three seemingly disparate items for sale at the station's convenience store transported me that day.

First, I found myself revisiting the corner of 16th Street and M Street in Washington, D.C. Kit and I had just finished a lunch at Kramerbooks and Afterwords Café near Dupont Circle and had walked to the National Geographic Society's 16th Street office building. Food was not in the least on our minds when we stopped to visit with our old friend—a hot dog vendor from Ethiopia whose food stand has been a fixture at that intersection for as long as we can remember. During our days working for the Society in the 1980s and 1990s, this lady's husband hauled her portable food stand to this spot five mornings a week, year round. There, "Mrs. Ethiopia" as we called her, conducted a thriving business from within a space not much larger inside than the cab of my old Chevy pickup truck.

When she sees us, her face always lights up. Wiping her hands on her apron, she extends her arm through the window and takes my hand in hers. Hers are hands warmed by endless hours of working over a steamer filled with hot dogs that she dresses in chili, onions, cheese, and pickle relish before wrapping them in thin sheets of foil paper with the care of a chef working with filo dough. Before Kit took my picture with her, she replaced her plain white headscarf with one more ornately ceremonial. Then, as always, Mrs. Ethiopia prepared two hot dogs with the works, served with chips and sodas. We cannot imagine eating again, but do.

The word *Cappuccino* takes me to yet another intersection—a small hotel on the outskirts of the town of Concorrezo, a short train ride from Milan, Italy. I'd traveled there to attend the wedding of Mark and Cinzia—my former student and the Italian woman he'd fallen in love with while studying abroad. Each morning, I found my way to the hotel's breakfast room and ordered a pastry and cappuccino. The women behind the coffee bar produced tiny cups filled with industrial-strength espresso as well as oversized cups of cappuccino and latte from a formidable-looking machine that frothed with great ceremony and produced a frenzied spurting of steamy sounds.

A similar coffee ritual takes place each morning at Boomerang Creek with our Nespresso coffee machine and milk frother attachment. While the end product is not exactly cappuccino or Italian espresso, the ritual connects me to a place and friendship still as rich in my mind today as it was two decades ago.

Finally, the word *antifreeze* triggered memories of four winters spent in Nebraska in the early 1970s. Those were nights so freezing cold I that had to plug an oil heater into my elm-green Volkswagen bug to ensure the engine would start the next morning.

While stopped recently at the same Ashland intersection, I made a mental note to take my car in for servicing before Kit and I drive this summer to Buffalo, Wyoming for the fourth annual celebration of Longmire Days. While they're at it, I'll have them add coolant and antifreeze. Antifreeze in July? Absolutely! You never know what you'll run into while exploring the wild west. Boy howdy! I'm thinking that Buffalo, Wyoming—nestled in the foothills of the Big Horn Mountains— is just the kind of place where hot dogs, cappuccino and antifreeze make sense no matter what time of the year you head into town.

(July 2015)

Our Great American Family Road Trip

*I*N EVERYONE'S PERSONAL HISTORY, there should be at least one family road trip across America that shines in the collective memory of all who were along for the ride. In the summer of 1978, Kit and I decided it was time for just such a journey. Kit had a shiny new school-bus yellow Westphalia Volkswagen pop-top camper van and two elementary aged children—Hayden (eleven) and Heidi (nine). I was the newest addition to the family, having met and fallen head over heels in love with their father the prior summer. Over the course of the year that stretched between the two summers, we had all been getting to know each other and had begun to consider what a newly blended family unit might feel like were the four of us to move into a home together at the end of the summer. What better way to find out than to test ourselves on an extended six-thousand-mile road trip from the Pacific to the Atlantic and back?

Our Volkswagen camper van was akin to a jolly little yellow submarine on wheels. There was bunk space for the kids below and when the top was popped, a bunk for the two adults up above. It had a sink behind the driver's seat, and a small table that could be affixed to the floor behind the front passenger seat. Four cubicles in the back held the very modest selection of stuff we packed along. Three of the four cubbies were filled with the kids' tee shirts, shorts, swimsuits, books, and cards they'd brought along for entertainment. For the life of me, I can't remember what Kit and I took in the way of clothes, only that we kept it light and simple.

From day one, a routine fell into place. We sang a daily repertoire of Salter family oldies but goodies. They were lively, sing-along songs that every Salter seems to know from birth, songs passed down from when Kit and his sisters were children—"Ragtime Cowboy Joe," "By the Sea," and "It's Only a Shanty in Old Shantytown." On it went, mile after mile, state after state, from the west coast to New England, and back through the American Heartland and Southwest, and home to Los Angeles. I would never be a Salter unless I could belt them out with the best and the rest of them.

Kit was our able pilot and I was the navigator—mapping our way whenever I wasn't sharing the driving. This navigation required foldout state road maps and a voluminous Rand McNally Road Atlas long before GPS and cellphones did the work for you. I plotted each day's route, selecting campsites by rivers or hot springs where we were able to park our little yellow Volkswagen out in the open air and under the stars. If there wasn't a river or stream option, the edge of a cornfield would do for the night.

Once parked, we unloaded four collapsible chairs and set up camp. I'd gather wildflowers for a bouquet in an old Mason jar, Hayden and Heidi took a swim, and Kit set up the Coleman stove and hauled a bucket of water for washing up after dinner. Dishwashing was never a chore, but rather another opportunity for a chorus of singing that before long included entire Broadway musical scores—especially inspired when we were crossing Oklahoma on the return leg of the journey.

When the light finally faded and we did as well, Hayden and Heidi got into their sleeping bags spread across the lower bunk space. Kit and I then put a foot on the sink and hoisted ourselves aloft and into the upper bunk. Once we were all snug in our beds, we'd read our novels by flashlight until exactly ten o'clock—the magic hour when we all turned our flashlights off and listened as Kit invented nighttime stories in the fashion of Radio Mystery Theater. He was magic—never telling the same story twice, inventing new characters and plots with just enough of an edge to keep the kids hanging on his every word without scaring the heck out of me.

Thirty-seven years later and countless roads traveled along the way, that song-filled summer road trip remains for the four of us among our happiest family memories.

(June 2015)

Moved by Flight

Biographer David McCullough begins his marvelous biography
of the Wright Brothers with this quote—

No bird soars in a calm.

—Wilbur Wright

*W*ILBUR AND ORVILLE AVIDLY STUDIED BIRDLIFE—"eagles,
snow-white gannets, hawks, pigeons, turkey vultures, or buzzards,
as they were known on the North Carolina Outer Banks, with wing
spans of as much as six feet." The secret to the art of flight, their
investigations told them "was to be found in the arched or vaulted
wings of birds, by which they could ride the wind."

Recently, my friend Michael Long called and invited me to a
special guest appearance by McCullough that same evening at the
Kansas City Public Library. He'd reserved two tickets for the evening
talk. We needed to leave Columbia by two o'clock to get in the queue
ahead of nine hundred ninety-eight other people who were also
hoping to get in. So begins a story about a serendipitous flocking of
kindred spirits, all flying toward the same destination.

I was just coming off of a two-week stretch of wonderful
houseguests, patterns broken, and perpetually rainy days. The last
thing I had in mind after the taillights of our last visitors disappeared
down our gravel road was a two-hundred-and-eighty-two-mile
round trip to Kansas City. Then, Michael called.

While the perfect culture-filled evening for Michael would
be a conversation with McCullough followed by dinner, jazz and
ballroom dancing, I'd had in mind a quiet dinner at home followed

by an evening on the screened porch with Kit, our two cats, a glass of wine, and *All the Light We Cannot See*—the magnificent Pulitzer Prize winning novel by Anthony Doerr I was eager to resume reading. My conundrum was that I also love David McCullough's historical works documenting places, events and remarkable people who have shaped America—a monumental literary accomplishment that has earned him the Presidential Medal of Freedom Citation.

Of course, I went to KC with Michael that afternoon. A spur-of-the-moment flight with the Wright Brothers was exactly the lift I needed that day. Arriving early and joining the queue already forming, we passed ninety minutes in ninety-degree heat without wilting, by engaging in lively conversations with new acquaintances—Dan Cotton, who'd driven from Lincoln, Nebraska, and Clarence Stessman of Kansas City. Dan has academic connections with our friend Brady Deaton. Clarence once hosted acclaimed sculptor, Sabra Tull Meyer at Fort Osage, Missouri at the installing of her sculpture of Sacagawea following the Lewis & Clark Bicentennial. Small world, indeed.

We had come from disparate places to hear one of America's most distinguished and celebrated historians speak about the character of two men from Dayton, Ohio who believed, at a time when very few did, in the ability of humankind to master the art of flight. That evening, we all soared with Wilbur and Orville Wright as McCullough recounted one seemingly insurmountable obstacle after another in both their personal lives and their quest to fly.

I thought about my father, born the seventh of seven children and raised on a small dairy farm in Bedford, Pennsylvania. Before finishing his senior year at the University of West Virginia, he took a train from Pittsburgh—McCullough's hometown—to Sikeston, Missouri. There, he learned to fly from a makeshift runway that had earlier been a cotton field. As a cadet, Dad flew countless solo hours in open cockpit planes while earning his wings, soaring with the wind in his hair above American landscapes that until then had only been lines on maps and illustrations in geography books. Later, as a twenty-five-year-old B-29 commander, Dad flew long-range missions during World War II from Guam to Japan—an experience the Wright Brothers had yet to imagine.

Moved by flight, Michael and I had spent an unforgettable evening with David McCullough followed by dinner at the historic Majestic Restaurant and Jazz Club at 10th and Broadway. Recounting the day's magic moments as we turned eastward on Interstate 70 toward home, we caught a flyby glimpse of the Kansas City Royals' Kaufman Baseball stadium—lit up with night lights and sparkling like a crown of jewels under a glittering crescent moon in a cluster with Jupiter and Venus. Priceless!

(June 2015)

Chapter Seven
DATELINE INTERNATIONAL

Moving about town, there were daily interactions with taxi drivers and rides on Old City Istanbul trams packed like sardines with local Turks en route to school, market, and work. In public spaces, vendors dressed in smartly pressed, white pharmacy coats and black pants sell simit— ring-shaped bread covered with sesame seeds and eaten as a snack— from shiny red and gold-wheeled carts.

C.S. January 2014

THE AGELESS NATURE OF A TUSCAN VILLA

*I*N THE SPRING OF 2010, Kit and I arrived at a villa with twelfth-century roots in the Tuscan hills. After a seemingly endless day and night of airports and delays caused by a volcanic disruption of air travel over the Atlantic, we'd been gathered up and delivered in the dark of night to the Spannocchia estate where we would spend the coming week painting.

Heaven awaited us. Like Lotti Wilkins and Rose Arbuthnot in Elizabeth Van Armin's 1922 novel, *The Enchanted April*, we had arrived six hours late and dropped our bags after stepping through an arched wooden doorway solid enough to keep out an army should this former twelfth-century castle ever again be under siege.

Exhausted, we were directed to the dining room where an open wood fire burned warmly and dinner had been set out in anticipation of our late arrival. Penne pasta, roast pork, carrots seasoned with the estate's own olive oil and rosemary, hearty Tuscan bread and bottles of Spannocchia's own wines. This moment, we decided, deserved a toast—the first of many in the coming week—and a kiss.

Oh, how we slept the sleep of ages that first night. Roosters reportedly crowed at dawn, but we didn't hear them. Breakfast alone was our reason to rise and join the others for our first cup of dark Italian coffee, toasted Tuscan bread with butter and jam, yogurt and granola drizzled with local honey, hard-boiled eggs with orange yolks and brown shells still warm to the touch, and a huge bowl of fresh apples, oranges, kiwi fruit and grapes.

Returning to our upstairs room across from the villa's family library, I pushed the tall wooden shutters back and drank in the tranquil landscape beyond an old stone wall bordering the yard below. The low fog of earlier morning had lifted, revealing red-roofed stone farmhouses set in the distant hills, and neatly cultivated fields, olive groves, and vineyards set on terraced slopes.

The ankle-deep grass in the yard was flecked with tiny white and yellow wild flowers and an occasional red poppy. Four fruiting lemon trees in enormous terracotta clay pots sunned themselves like happy guests near the *limonaia*, a former carriage house where the citruses winter over. Tall dark green cypresses stand out like sentry guards against a blue sky billowing with white clouds. A mass of lavender wisteria fans out from a thick woody base across the gray limestone façade of the limonaia.

Within reach out our window, pale yellow Banksia roses climb in clusters across the wall. Along stonewalls and terrace balconies, rectangular terra cotta planters hold geraniums as red as the poppies that emerge with wild abandon in Tuscan fields every spring.

On a walk that first morning around the grounds, I discover a fig tree growing from the crevices in a high stonewall, rich with green fruit. Passing through a gated opening into a secluded nook in a nearby wood, I come upon an abandoned stone outbuilding and wade into a sea of knee-deep wildflowers in a shady glade. At its center is a keyhole pond kept hidden like a secret within its flowery fold. A rosemary bush wild with purple flowers spills over the stone rim of the pond, covered with algae the gray-green color of bronze oxidized by the ages. Mark Twain described a Tuscan villa in his 1917 autobiography as…

> …not an old house—from an Italian standpoint…. painted in light yellow and has green shutters. It stands in a commanding position on an artificial terrace of liberal dimensions which is walled around with strong masonry. From the walls the vineyards and olive orchards of the estate slant away toward the valley; the garden about the house is stocked with flowers and a convention of lemon bushes in great crockery tubs.

Such is the enduring spirit of place that I, too, experienced my first morning at our villa in Tuscany.

(April 2010)

THE MAGIC THAT IS FLORENCE

*F*OR THOSE WHO HAVE BEEN TO FLORENCE, just the mention of the city's name ignites an inner lamp of recognition and reverence, illuminating a pathway in the mind to a place of enlightenment. Florence—from the Latin *Florentia* (goddess of flowers and gardens), also known as Firenze (the Tuscan contraction from *Fiorenzia* seen on Renaissance frescos)—has been a destination for artists, sculptors, architects, writers, poets, thinkers, travelers, and innocents abroad for literally ages.

Centuries before the Italy of today existed, there was Tuscany—ancient home of the Etruscans. While the region's map fluctuated with each geopolitical shift in rulers, Tuscans managed to stubbornly hang on to not only their independence, but also their language—inspiring a literary richness that attracted intellectuals from across the European continent.

In his recently published 2013 biography, *Queen Bee of Tuscany: The Redoubtable Janet Ross*," Ben Downing sets the stage for England's great poet Geoffrey Chaucer's visit to Italy in 1372-73. "Virtually at a stroke, the melodious triumvirate of Dante, Petrarch, and Boccaccio put the local (Tuscan) vernacular in the front rank of European tongues, and set it on course to become the standard language of a nation."

Seven centuries later, Kit and I arrived by train from Rome—drawn by the wish to paint and write in the late autumn October sunlight of Tuscany. Florence was our first stop, and our hotel, chosen quite by serendipity, was the Hotel Boccaccio. Three enormous, red leather bound volumes of *The Decameron* rest on a table in the lobby, as if the fourteenth-century poet and author Giovanni Boccaccio—as familiar to Italian school children as Mark Twain's tales are in American literature—might stop by for an evening reading from his masterpiece that documents Tuscan life during the Middle Ages.

From the moment we walked into the hotel and met Stefano, the manager we had been corresponding with for the prior seven months as the Italian journey took shape, our Florentine education began. Boccaccio had espoused a humanistic approach to education—one that valued history, poetry, and a citizenry (including women) able to speak and write eloquently and with clarity. His stories have indeed survived the ages. The *New Yorker* (11/11/2013) featured a book review by Joan Acocella entitled "Renaissance Man: A new translation of Boccaccio's Decameron."

How better to immerse oneself in the culture and history of Florence than by exploring the city's stone streets and alleys on foot, uncovering tales of love and life lessons along the way? For if you truly listen, it is the language written on stones over the ages that speaks the loudest.

Strolling at sunset along the Arno River, light washed over us in a timeless embrace that pulled us in the direction of the Ponte Vecchio. Amidst the shops filled with gold jewelry and the crowd of shoppers, we stepped to the edge of an opening on the bridge where I photographed names on a stone wall and a chain of locks spilling over the side of the bridge—names of lovers whose lives were symbolically locked together when each lock's key was thrown away.

The following day, we wandered again through the city, stopping at cafes, visiting the Piazza del Duomo a second time, and visited the Münstermann apothecary shop (est. 1897) where I found Italian hair combs. Near our hotel, we befriended a Bangladeshi family of brothers along the Via dell'Albero near our hotel who sold us bottles of mango juice, lovely shawls, and a ring with a stone the color of Florentine spun gold.

Most memorable of all of our conversations with Florentines was at Sogni in Carta—a small, family-owned stationery and journal shop where leather crafting has been going on in this "laboratory" since 1926. We bought pens wrapped in Florentine paper and a journal with a tree etched in relief into its leather-bound cover. Within this handmade book, tales of the days that followed our arrival in Florence will be recorded by hand as they resurface in my memory, one story at a time.

(November 2013)

Spring on Two Continents

*I*N THE DAYS SINCE OUR RETURN from Spain, there has been little time to look back on all that happened over the course of our May 2008 week in Madrid. Kit and I returned late on a night filled with rain and lightning that bedazzled us during the final forty miles of our two-hour drive from the St. Louis Airport to Ashland, concluding our sixteen-hour travel marathon from Madrid to Boomerang Creek.

Our luggage never made it out of the back of the truck that night. We simply greeted our three yawning cats, washed our tired faces and fell into bed. The following morning, as the cats raced out into the morning air after a week of house arrest, I walked with coffee in hand to the meadow garden to check on the progress of my spring peas and last summer's newly planted crop of asparagus.

Throughout March and April, I'd eagerly awaited days warm and dry enough to get our garden in ahead of all that needed to be done before our departure for Spain. I'd managed to plant three rows of peas during a brief, three-day dry spell last month, only to have them drown in the cool rains that have local farmers still trying to get their corn crop planted. Now, with Spain behind us and June just ahead, all I have for my efforts are a few puny pea vines and ominously, only a single asparagus spear.

For the remainder of the day, all energies are focused on un-packing, preparing for a soon-to-arrive houseguest, sorting through a mountain of accumulated mail, and perusing a week's worth of newspapers. Kit mows the lush, rain-fed grass while I do loads of laundry and hang it all outside on our T-post clothesline to dry in a stiff May breeze.

Cathy Salter

Throughout this first day home, our thoughts remain a continent and ocean away. There our son Hayden is up early squeezing Valencia oranges and preparing scrambled eggs for the *niño* and *niñas*—our darling grandson Nicolas and granddaughters Ines and Catalina—before negotiating morning traffic and roundabouts to drop them at the Lycée Français de Madrid where all three attend school.

Mornings are hectic in their household, but somehow it works. The children arrive mostly on time, Hayden then begins his long 10:00 a.m. to 9:00 p.m. workday at the Madrid office of Spanish architect Jose Rafael Moneo, and our lovely daughter-in-law Ana retreats to her home computer where she works relatively undisturbed in the deafening quiet that fills the house until it's time to pick up the children in the afternoon. Amanda, a young Brazilian woman, arrives at ten in the morning to clean up the kitchen, do the laundry and bring the much-lived in house back to order.

Whenever we visit, Kit and I take the number 146 bus into central Madrid, stopping for a café con léche and pastry at the Café Belles Artes. For an hour, we savor the conversational nature of this grand Art Deco cultural center with its café window on morning street activity along Calle Alcalá. We pen postcard notes to friends and family, order a second cup of coffee with steamed milk and map out the day's explorations. At five, we're back at Hayden's home, setting off on foot with Ana, Nico, and their dog Remo to shop for the evening meal at a super *mercado* and several small specialty grocery shops along a bustling neighborhood market street.

One afternoon when school lets out at one o'clock, I accompany Ana and the two niñas, who are dressed in pink tights, leotards, and tutus to their weekly ballet class at Charlie Revelée Studio. The following evening when Ana leaves for a six o'clock meeting regarding her travel assignment at the Beijing Olympics, I bake a chicken rubbed with Spanish olive oil in a large pot with chopped potatoes, onions, and carrots. Kit intermittently plays with the grandchildren and updates me on world news from the *Sunday*

Telegraph, beginning with Tuesday's Democratic Primary results in North Carolina and Indiana. Then news of a devastating cyclone in Myanmar and a 7.8 earthquake in Szechwan, China. Finally, news much too close to home—tornado damage in parts of Oklahoma and southwest Missouri.

Around nine-thirty, Ana returns just as the family is called for dinner. Wine is poured, the children settle into their places at the table and I think back to when Hayden was Nico's age. During that precious time together around the dinner table three decades earlier, Kit and I shared news of the day with Hayden and his sister Heidi when they were young children. It is a tradition Hayden is hoping to continue, but it is not easy in his family's busy world of 24/7 internet communication, cell phones, carpooling in a busy European metropolis, Hayden's constant travel demands relating to international architectural projects (Beirut, Boston, Providence, New York City, Geneva) and Ana's expanding journalistic assignments.

On a particularly lovely Sunday afternoon, we set off together on a family outing to the Museo Sorolla. The prior night, while perusing my Madrid travel guide, I had been struck by a photograph of an artist's studio in a nineteenth-century mansion. The walls of the room were the color of sunbaked terra cotta. Brilliantly lit canvases with scenes of elegant women in long white dresses strolling the Mediterranean seaside with parasols and broad-brimmed straw hats covered the walls. Wooden curiosity cabinets stuffed with treasures, handsome benches, the artist's easels with colorful palettes and jars of brushes, Spanish tiles and Chinese porcelains, rich hardwood floors and oriental carpets inhabited the open, lived-in feeling of this grand room.

"We'll go tomorrow," Hayden said. "Museo Sorolla is a small, little know gem in the La Castellana neighborhood that was the studio and home of Valencian Impressionist painter Joaquín Sorolla from 1910 until the artist died in 1923." We arrived mid-afternoon and entered the Andalucian-style garden designed by Sorolla himself. It was a cool, shady mixture of potted shrubs, beds of ferns and flowers and graceful pools and fountains decorated with ceramic tiles from Valencia.

When we entered the house, it was as it had been during the artist's lifetime. Sorolla lived there with his wife and children and loved painting them inside the house as well as in his garden. The artist often took his family on outings to Mediterranean beaches where he painted plein air seascapes, capturing his wife and children on sun-filled canvases.

"How is it," I wondered aloud, "that I've never heard of this Spanish Impressionist who was a contemporary of the great portrait artist John Singer Sargent?" When I walked through room after canvas-filled room of Sorolla's home that afternoon, the answer quickly became clear. The majority of the artist's paintings are displayed in his home, not in museums. That realization, and the artist's world expressed in paintings that lined the walls of the grand room I was standing in, literally took my breath away.

That evening, I had another memorable experience when I sampled goose barnacles, known in Spain and Portugal as *percebes*, for the first time. When Hayden's father-in law, Marcos Martin, presented us with three large bags of barnacles, I did not immediately appreciate their value or know what one does with a barnacle. I've since learned that these strange looking, filter-feeding crustaceans attach themselves to rocky surfaces and have a muscular, gooseneck stalk attached to a hoof-like foot. These Galician delicacies, harvested by daring divers who rappel down cliffs along Spain's Atlantic coast, are the morels of Madrid.

"*Taste one*," Hayden said, demonstrating how to remove the foot and extract the edible meat from the stalk. "*It tastes like the sea.*" Hayden, Nico and I ate the barnacles raw. Next time in Madrid, we'll go to a restaurant near the Plaza de Toros that I'm told serves the best barnacles in Madrid—raw or steamed in their shells over stock or seasoned wine.

Another evening, we presented the grandchildren with a DVD of the movie *E.T. The Extra-Terrestrial.* Clad in our pajamas, we all piled on the couch with their white Scottish Highland terrier Remo at our feet. As the dialogue began, Ana laughed. "How funny. We're watching *E.T.* in Madrid, but they're speaking Mexican Spanish."

In hushed tones, Ana gave our granddaughters a brief explanation of "extra-terrestrial." And though she assured them that E.T. was "just a little lost alien with a gentle spirit who wanted to return home," the two girls stood on the couch the entire movie with their hands over their mouths and, occasionally, their eyes. For Ines and Catalina, *E.T.* was an unforgettable adventure that gave them goose bumps from beginning to end. Along with goose barnacles, it was indeed one of many memorable Madrid moments that I carried home at the end of our full-immersion window on the pulse and pace of family life in this bustling Spanish metropolis.

Home again at Boomerang Creek, the vegetable garden planted before our trip to Madrid is finally surfacing. Each day, I remind myself to I take a deep breath of spring air and recall an expression I learned forty years ago living in Thailand: *mai ben rai* (never mind). Things will get done eventually. With spring on two continents now behind us, my plan is to savor the memories and enjoy the coming summer, one day at a time.

(May 2008)

London's Multicultural Masala

*I*N THE COOKING OF THE PUNJAB REGION of northern India, the spice *garam masala* is an essential ingredient. *Masala* is any blend of spices and *garam* means hot. In New York City's Chelsea Market, Spice and Tease Company's garam masala is a blend of Moroccan coriander; cardamom from Tamil Nadu, India; bay leaves; Tellicherry pepper; cinnamon; caraway; Zanzibar cloves; China #1 ginger, and nutmeg.

Having just returned from a week in London, masala is the perfect way to describe the twenty-first century, multicultural face of London's population. Kit and I were part of a Salter family gathering that is its own special masala of cultures. Our California born son, his Spanish wife and their two daughters met us at the Chelsea cottage of Kit's niece—born in Pakistan, raised in Connecticut, married to a Swiss, resident in London, and mother of a lovely teenage daughter who, like our preteen granddaughters, speaks a potpourri of European languages as well as English.

Our week together as a blended family hailing from Madrid, London, and the American Heartland was made all the richer by the addition of our niece's English friend, Richard Adams—an honest to goodness, salt of the earth Brit from Essex. Thrown into the masala, Richard sailed along the shifting currents of conversation like the sailor that he truly is.

Conversations around the household were a rich babel of British and American English, French, Spanish, Swiss-German and teen speak. On the streets of London, on strolls through Kensington Gardens, at the Tate Britain Art Gallery, in Chelsea's Pig's Ear Pub, along Oxford's pulsing fashion street, and when minding the gap while riding London's underground trains, the musical mélange of languages is literally from all over the map.

Our driver from and back to Heathrow Airport was an Indian born in Uganda who has lived in London since his family sought safe haven there in the early 1970s. Wealthy Russians and Middle Easterners have moved to London, bought up prime real estate (including Harrods Department Store), but this is just the newest wave of immigration in a city where multiculturalism has long been a part of London's history.

According to the *Times* of London, the UK's capital is one of the world's most multicultural cities. "Roman soldiers, Huguenot silkweavers, Jamaican airmen, Bangladeshi sailors, and a host of other people from around the world have helped to shape its history and its future…. London is a city that has been going for so long that multiculturalism has become a habit."

The Irish literally built London, as stated in the *Times*, "from the docks through to the sewerage systems and the railways." As Britain built a colonial empire that spread worldwide, people came from the Asian subcontinent, from Africa, and from the Caribbean. Turkish, West African, Chinese and Thai, Portuguese and Moroccan shops and restaurants can be found throughout the city.

While in London, I had two fascinating intersections with Afghans. The first took place in the book section of Selfridges department store where I had a long conversation with a beautiful sales girl whose family emigrated from Kabul to London in the 1970s. A day later while strolling along the Portobello Road Market, one of the most famous street markets in the world, I chatted with a jewelry vendor who was also from Kabul. I shared my own memories of what Kabul was like when I first arrived there in the winter of 1970.

Before long, an etched silver band set with an oblong carnelian gemstone that seemed to have captured the unexpected fire of an Afghan sunset caught my eye. The ring fit perfectly. After some back and forth bargaining, I said that given my age and travel history in Kabul, I qualified to be his "other Afghan auntie." Amused, my Afghan "nephew" cut the price in half, and we were both happy to have had the chance to revisit this ancient country we've both known and loved forever.

On our final day in London, five of us (and two toy poodles) shared the cab of an older man whose reddish-tinted grey beard and clothing led me to ask if he was from Afghanistan. Proudly, he announced, "No. I'm from a most beautiful island surrounded by blue water—Mauritius." Another face added to the multicultural masala that is London today.

(October 2014)

IMAGES OF ISTANBUL

*A*LTHOUGH MY JOURNEY to Istanbul has just gotten underway, I've already been traveling there across centuries. This is the power of geography books and travel classics filled with maps and wonderful stories written by adventurers, poets, geographers, historians, journalists, and globe-trotters—men and women, young and old—who set out to explore strange and romantic lands.

As soon as travel dates were fixed on my January calendar, I disappeared into my studio and began searching through an eclectic collection of books for images of Istanbul over the ages. I was eager to revisit the palimpsest of empires that have controlled this strategic site that both links and divides the Orient and the Occident—the East and the West.

The geography of Istanbul is overwhelmingly one of waterways and peninsulas strategically situated at a crossroads of mainland routes between Europe and Asia, making it an ideal site to be the capital of great empires. In Philip Mansel's *Constantinople: City of the World's Desire 1453-1924*, he describes the city's location—

> Situated at the end of a triangular peninsula, it is surrounded by water on three sides. To the north lies a harbor a kilometer wide and six kilometers long, called the Golden Horn, probably because it turns golden in the rays of the setting sun; to the east the Bosporus, a narrow waterway separating Europe and Asia; to the south, the Sea of Marmara, a small inland sea connecting the Aegean to the Black Sea. The city was both a natural fortress and a matchless deep-water port, enjoying easy access by sea to Africa, the Mediterranean and the Black Sea…. Its site seemed to have been expressly created to receive the wealth of the four corners of the earth.

Founded as a Greek colony in the seventh century BCE, it was re-founded in 324 CE as Byzantium and served for a thousand years as the capital of the Roman Empire in the East. In the sixth century when Emperor Justinian built Hagia Sophia (Santa Sophia), he ruled an empire that stretched from the Euphrates River in the East to the Straits of Gibraltar in the West. When Christian Byzantium succumbed to Turkish and Arab armies from the East in 1453 A.D., the great cathedral became a mosque (Aya Sofya). In today's Turkish Republic, it is a secular museum.

Following in the footsteps of writers who have journeyed to this fabled city, I travel along with adventurer Richard Halliburton in his 1932 book, *The Flying Carpet*, fascinated by his foot-loose, spirited accounts of trips to Constantinople in the 1920s and 1930s. Halliburton arrived first in his plane, the *Flying Carpet*, and later aboard a steamer from the Black Sea. He had been fascinated as a child by images in geography books of the ruins of ancient Babylon, the Egyptian Pyramids, Indian marble towers, and great cathedrals— among them, Santa Sophia.

Twelve years after first seeing Santa Sophia, "Mother of all Churches," from the air and describing "*its dazzling lights and praying thousands*," Halliburton returned for a solo nighttime visit. He wrote,

> *In the darkness and the silence, with the moonbeams streaming down through the windows of that wide-spread dome, I felt, even more than on the first visit, that I beheld a temple too mighty, too soaring, to have been built by man.*

By now, my mind is filled with images from Lord Byron who swam the Hellespont, and Mark Twain who had opinions about everything from Turkish food to Istanbul's street dogs. I have crossed the Bosporus on a ferry with author Paul Theroux, explored the Spice Bazaar with travel writers Frances Mayes and with John Freely, and felt the melancholy nature of the city through the eyes of Turkey's literary Nobel laureate—Istanbul resident, Orhan Pamuk.

So it is that I feel ready to begin my own exploration of Istanbul, well armed with images from travelers who have walked the ancient city's cobbled streets, sailed along its waterways, or arrived by air at night and been bedazzled by its domed mosques, tall thin minarets, and mysterious harbor lights.

(January 2014)

Cathy Salter

THE MANY FACES OF ISTANBUL

*H*ISTORICALLY KNOWN AS BYZANTIUM and Constantinople, the city of Istanbul had a population of approximately a million people in 1945, the year I was born. By 2014 when I navigated the city's ancient cobblestone streets and explored its grand covered bazaars and bustling waterways, its population had grown to almost fourteen million. Istanbul is now the second largest metropolitan area in Europe in area and by population and the third largest metropolitan city proper in the world.

This fascinating crossroads of commerce and empires now inhabits my head like a movie I cannot leave. It's at once a tapestry of richly etched images washed with colors created from precious stones, fixed in wool threads woven into Turkish carpets and ancient tiles. Above all, it's the connections that I made to the city's warm and hospitable people, and the faces of people I will never forget.

Moving about town, there were daily interactions with taxi drivers and rides on Old City Istanbul trams packed like sardines with local Turks en route to school, market, and work. In public spaces, vendors dressed in smartly pressed white pharmacy coats and black pants sell simit—ring-shaped bread covered with sesame seeds and eaten as a snack—from shiny red and gold-wheeled carts. Just as popular are vendors selling fresh squeezed pomegranate juice, roasted chestnuts and roasted ears of corn. Nearby, men with portable brass shoeshine stands offer a shine with a two-year guarantee.

Between the Sultanahmet (Blue) Mosque and Hagia Sophia Museum, and within the walled Topkapi Palace, Muslim visitors dressed in an array of flowing robes and head scarves from Indonesia,

---

western China, the Middle East, North Africa and regions of eastern Europe strolled parks and visited mosques and monuments.

A real crush of humanity happens when you pass under one of the historic archways leading into the historic Grand Bazaar—a complex of sixty-one streets and over five thousand shops filled with a cacophony of hawkers selling oriental carpets, pashmina shawls and scarves, leather goods, copper, jewelry, and hand-painted ceramic plates and tiles. My own ankle-length sweater coat, colorfully patterned like an oriental rug, caught the attention of a wealthy Saudi/Jordanian woman exiting the Four Seasons Hotel in the Sultanahmet neighborhood, as well as rug sellers with henna-colored beards inside the Grand Bazaar.

A short walk from the Grand Bazaar toward the New Mosque overlooking the Golden Horn, the historic Egyptian Spice Bazaar is dense with local shoppers and tourists. Here shops offer an array of dried fruits, bins of dried rose and jasmine flowers, heaps of savory and pungent herbs, pomegranate and green apple cinnamon tea, Turkish Delight sweets, Black Sea caviar and jars of precious Iranian saffron—the most expensive spice on earth—along with varieties of saffron from Turkey, Kashmir and Spain.

You have not experienced Istanbul until you spend a morning dancing with a local rug merchant around a price for a genuine handmade Turkish double-knotted wool carpet. Bargaining for that magic figure is expected and can be a pleasurable journey for all. Green apple cinnamon tea arrives in a tulip shaped glass as a gesture of hospitality. Piles of rugs are unfurled on a large wooden floor, colors and origin are discussed, and finally when one is selected, the bargaining slowly begins.

The rug and shawl that I purchased are Kurdish dowry pieces from the eastern region of Turkey bordering Iraq. Both embody the rich burgundy, gold and teal colors that I'd experienced in the interior of the fourth-century A.D. Hagia Sophia Basilica—a massive open space filled with mystical light reflected from tiny specks of Byzantine gold imbedded in the mosaics covering its walls and dome.

At the Pera Palace Hotel, constructed in 1892 for passengers arriving from Paris aboard the Orient Express, you experience old world service and conversations with the concierge about the hotel's most famous guests—among them, Dame Agatha Christie, Ernest Hemingway, Ian Fleming, and Atatürk—"Father" of the modern Turkish Republic. There, hospitality and Istanbul's history come together seamlessly, making one's experience in Istanbul a true Turkish delight.

(January 2014)

The Power of Serendipity

This is the story of a Turkish carpet and the power of serendipity. For my trip to Istanbul in January 2014, I traveled with a single piece of carry-on luggage. This, I told my traveling companion and longtime friend Chomsri Lewinter, would make it easier to resist the seasoned carpet salesmen waiting to prey on us the minute we entered the Grand Bazaar. My resolve would be tested daily in this city where oriental carpets beckon at every turn.

During a small-group morning tour of Istanbul's Old City historic sites, we were unexpectedly driven to an upscale carpet and jewelry store. For an hour, men built like Turkish wrestlers hauled stacks of silk and wool carpets onto the grand wooden floor of the showroom. Weaving his web, the mustachioed owner of the establishment spoke of the art of Turkish wool dying and carpet weaving. The spell, however, was broken when he took a cell phone call from his wife who was in Paris shopping—our chance to slip out and head directly for the Grand Bazaar where we could lose ourselves in the crowds.

This is easy to do in this fantastical, maze-like crossroads of commerce that has been in constant operation for several thousand years. Overwhelmed at last by the crush of shoppers, the dizzying array of exotic textiles and spices, and the babel of hawkers at every stall, we finally exited through one of the bazaar's arching gates to clear the cacophony from our heads.

Blessed with unseasonably mild January temperatures, we opted for a peaceful afternoon on the Bosporus, cruising from Istanbul's Golden Horn north toward the Black Sea. Sochi—situated on the Black Sea's Russian coast—would experience similar spring-like temperatures during the 2014 Winter Olympic Games after I returned to the frozen American Heartland.

Our final morning in Istanbul, Chomsri and I walked past the ancient Roman Hippodrome where charioteers once competed like Olympic athletes. Near the Hagia Sophia, we wandered down slope along a narrow lane, emerging in a quiet neighborhood shared by the Four Seasons Hotel—a Tuscan yellow structure that was once a government prison—and discovered a street of family-owned carpet and ceramic shops.

"We haven't officially been to Turkey unless we return with a rug," Chomsri then announced, finally ready for the challenge. Before long, she'd out-bargained a carpet salesman, ending up with two carpets while I still had none, though not for long. Leaving the store, I had an unexpected, serendipitous, magic carpet moment of my own.

Like a ship pulled by some magnetic force toward the coast of Serendip—the Arab name for the island of Ceylon (later Sri Lanka)—I was drawn into the Pilavci Carpet emporium, in business since 1972. There I learned first hand that this Ottoman family with roots in Kayseri—a city recognized worldwide for the quality of its carpets—holds trust, honesty and friendship in the highest regard.

As if expecting me, Osmand, middle son of the owner, greeted me with a cup of hot green apple tea and offered to select carpets for me to consider.

"That won't be necessary," I said, pointing to a rug under a stack of Kurdish tribal dowry carpets. "These are the three colors I'm looking for."

Unfurled against honey-toned, hardwood flooring, the carpet was magic. Deep and rich in tone, the vegetable-dyed colors of the carpet's double-knotted wool yarn mirrored the ancient Byzantine colors within the Hagia Sophia's domed interior.

"*It is time,*" I told Osmand, "*for the dance to begin.*" We then slowly began circling toward a fair and mutually agreeable price. Excusing himself twice, Oz conferred with his father who remained off stage until the dance was done.

A guarantee of origin certificate signed by Israfil Pilavci was then presented to me, followed by ceremonial pictures of Oz's father seated next to me, as if a family wedding had just taken place.

Recently, Osmond emailed, asking about the carpet and my journey home. This story, a weave of serendipity and friendship, is my reply.

(January 2014)

Cathy Salter

Chapter Eight
The World From a Distance

"In the quiet of my own morning exercise, I noted the brilliance of rose hips on a scraggily wild rose bush and the emergence of bluish berries on the junipers. Our neighbor's three horses grazed in the lush pasture beyond our shared fence line. All was still until a distant hunter's rifle broke the silence. Caution took hold. The horses looked toward the sound, and I suddenly found myself attuned to the realities that define Afghanistan these days."

C.S. July 2006

The Conundrum of Afghanistan

THANKSGIVING WEEK BEGAN WITH THE PROMISE of sixty-degree temperatures that by mealtime Thursday would plummet into the thirties. Monday morning was clearly the time to get in some laps on the mown pathway around our meadow.

Upon setting out, I was reminded of another place worlds away in distance and time, as well as of the fascinating accounts of travelers who've been there. Walking toward the spot on the southeastern horizon where the sun now rises at Boomerang Creek, I recalled Jason Elliott's initial reaction after arriving in Afghanistan in the late 1980s. "From the beginning," he noted in *An Unexpected Light: Travels in Afghanistan*, "we became captives of an unexpected light. Even as we stepped into its unaccustomed brightness that first morning (in Kabul), it seemed probable we had entered a world in some way enchanted, for which we lacked the proper measure."

The pristine November morning of my walk, I'd been captured by a sunrise the color of a sun-ripened apricot that I simply couldn't ignore. Halfway around the meadow, my thoughts bumped headlong into another traveler, Rory Stewart, who trekked six hundred miles across Afghanistan in the winter of 2002, two weeks after the fall of the Taliban.

Stewart, a seasoned traveler and scholar of the region, had already walked across Iran, Pakistan, India and Nepal, but had been denied permission to cross Afghanistan by the Taliban. Determined to complete the Afghan leg of his journey, he set out that January crossing the places in between—from Herat near the Iranian border, through the desert and mountains of central Afghanistan, to the capital of Kabul.

In his terrific 2006 book, *The Places In Between*, Stewart described his early morning departure from Herat—"The sun had come up casting a harsh clear light as I looked east toward the desert and mountains I was undertaking to cross alone."

Near the end of the first quarter-mile lap of my walk, I recalled Stewart's initial resolve to get his personal journey underway. "I adjusted the straps of my pack…and felt the familiar unevenness in the inner sole of my left foot, stretched my toes, and paced out." Feeling a twinge of discomfort in my own left foot, I followed Stewart's advice, and did the same.

In the quiet of my own morning exercise, I noted the brilliance of rose hips on a scraggily wild rose bush and the emergence of bluish berries on the junipers. Our neighbor's three horses grazed in the lush pasture beyond our shared fence line. All was still until a distant hunter's rifle broke the silence. Caution took hold. The horses looked toward the sound, and I suddenly found myself attuned to the realities that define Afghanistan these days.

My thoughts then took a detour to the road Stewart chose not to follow linking Herat to Kandahar, long a Taliban stronghold and the country's former capital. Pomegranates, an ancient plant that probably originated in northern Persia, are grown near Kandahar. There, former National Public Radio reporter Sarah Chayes is making a difference in a small but significant way.

Her Arghand micro-cooperative employs thirteen men and women representing nine different tribes and ethnic groups—a mix that is no small miracle of cooperation in Afghanistan today. Their soaps are handmade from the oils of pomegranates, almonds and local botanicals and offer a viable alternative to opium production for local farmers. [www.arghand.org]

Chayes's cooperative, she feels, is a microcosm of what needs to happen in Afghanistan today. The legendary pomegranate, with its interior chambers filled with sweet red juice, has quenched the thirst of desert travelers since before the days of Alexander the Great. Perhaps, with cooperation and increased support, their production will help solve the conundrum that is Afghanistan today.

(April 2014)

Traveling With Pomegranates

*T*EN FRIENDS HAVE GATHERED around a luncheon table at Columbia's Wine Cellar & Bistro to exchange thoughts on Sue Monk Kidd and Ann Kidd Taylor's memoir *Traveling with Pomegranates*. We are travelers ourselves, with a mutual passion that has brought us together in a fall class at Osher Lifelong Learning, a journey of sorts of our own that continues to sustain us these cold January days.

The mother and daughter memoir we are discussing has taken us on a journey to the sacred places of Greece, Turkey and France visited by its co-authors between 1998 and 2000—a time when each was on a quest to redefine herself and rediscover the other. "*Ann,*" her mother Sue writes, "*was struggling to figure out the beginning of being a woman, and I, the beginning of the end of it.*"

While traveling in Greece, their own mother and daughter journey intersects the ancient myth of Demeter and Persephone. Hades, lord of the dead, abducts Persephone into the underworld. Persephone's mother Demeter—goddess of grain, harvest, and fertility—searches for her and falls into despair, leaving the crops to wither and the earth to become a wasteland. Zeus demands that Hades release Persephone, but while leaving, she eats the seeds of a pomegranate, thus ensuring her return to the underworld for a third of each year.

It is appropriate that we have gathered in winter to explore the myth of Demeter and Persephone symbolizing both death and life. I pass around a pomegranate I've brought so that each of us can feel its leathery skin. This chambered, apple-like fruit looks as ancient as its origins around the semiarid Mediterranean and throughout the Arabian Peninsula where pomegranates thrive as a deciduous tree or large shrub, producing delicious fruit.

But what do most of us really know about pomegranates today beyond their vitamin-rich, anti-oxidant powers? Romans believed the best pomegranates came from Carthage. The Spanish named the fruit *granada* and placed its image on the city of Granada's official seal. Commercially produced pomegranate syrup is called grenadine. These days, pomegranates are commonly found in salads, balsamic dressings, and health beverages, valued for their life-enhancing vitamin C and dietary fiber.

Holding up the pomegranate, I take my fellow travelers on yet another journey. Like the ancient death and life myth of Demeter and Persephone in *Traveling with Pomegranates*, there is a modern-day myth as well that relates to a darker truth. A pomegranate bursts when dropped on a hard surface, sending seeds from its chambered fruit everywhere. This, it is thought, inspired the French military to borrow the modern French name for the pomegranate when naming the deadly hand-tossed explosive, the *grenade*.

Recently I read a *TIME* magazine article by Joe Klein that outlined his thoughts on the endgame in the war in Afghanistan. What is needed to finish the war in Afghanistan, Klein believes, is "security, development and a stable Pakistan." In a *shura* council attended by American Ambassador Karl Eikenberry, Afghan elders and absentee landholders from Kandahar City told the ambassador that what was needed most was more "paved roads, electricity, and cold-storage facilities for their crops."

Back in Washington, Klein posed what he calls "the cold storage" question to senior military, diplomatic and White House officials. One military official explained that pomegranates are being shipped now from Kandahar airfield and refrigeration is needed to store them before shipping.

"*Afghan pomegranates,*" Klein explains, "*have assumed an almost mythic value among U.S. officials, since they are the most valuable cash crop after opium poppies and a suitable replacement for them.*"

The late Richard Holbrook, Obama's special envoy for Afghanistan and Pakistan, was obsessed with them."

My mind now travels with pomegranates to Afghanistan, where I see an unexpected light emerging from the underworld. Spring returns, and pomegranates once again thrive in orchards, replacing deadly grenades that for too long have rendered this ancient world a hopeless wasteland.

(January 2011)

A Hot Topic Warranting Global Attention

*M*IDWAY THROUGH THE Association of American Geographers 2010 annual meeting this spring in Washington, D.C., an Icelandic volcano with an impossible name became a hot topic of conversation among the eight thousand geographers from around the globe in attendance.

On April 14, Iceland's Eyjafjallajökull (pronounced *Ey*-ya-fyat-lah-*yoh*-kuht) volcano—meaning "island mountain glacier"—started spewing ash as it had a month earlier before temporarily quieting. Then again on April 14, a second eruption caused by magma that had been building under pressure exploded through a glacial icecap, sending forth a seven-mile-high ash plume filled with fragmented silica (glassy particles)—formed when cold water from the melted ice quickly chilled the hot lava.

Acting on the side of caution, airports across more than twenty European countries shut down. For the next five days, the normally busy airspace over the North Atlantic was devoid of jets and their telltale trails, filled only with an eerie silence and ashen clouds that drifted over the European continent.

Eleanor Rawling, an energetic British educator based at the University of Oxford's Department of Education, found herself stranded, along with thousands of other air travelers on both sides of the Atlantic. Kit and I shared a wonderful lunch and engaging conversation with Eleanor and a longtime, mutual friend at the National Geographic Society with whom Eleanor was able to stay during this period of air travel disruption. A week later, Eleanor was home again in the UK, having smartly navigated her way through what one news source cited as "the worst breakdown in civil aviation in Europe since World War II."

If asked to explain the geological conditions that created Iceland's high concentration of active volcanoes (about one hundred thirty volcanic mountains, with eighteen recorded eruptions since the country was settled in 874 A.D.), Eleanor would most likely draw an outline map of Iceland surrounded by the Atlantic Ocean. To that outline, this bright geographer would then sketch the Mid-Atlantic Ridge running beneath the island from southwest to northeast like a vein pulsing through its living heart—setting Iceland squarely astride the submarine boundary between the Eurasian and North American Tectonic Plates.

Eleanor might also add that Iceland's geography includes wholly submerged volcanoes and the newly formed volcanic islands of Surtsey and Jólnir. Half of Iceland (the second-largest island in Europe) consists of mountainous lava desert and other wasteland. Twenty percent of the land is used for grazing, and only one percent is cultivated.

Being a world traveler, Eleanor might then shift half a world away to the Pacific—a watery world of more than twenty-five thousand volcanic islands, coral atolls, reefs and twenty-one seas scattered across sixty-three million, eight hundred thousand square miles. It is the liquid blue basin within the earth's Ring of Fire, so vast that it stretches from Antarctica to the Arctic Ocean, and halfway around the world at its widest point near the Equator. Nothing in the world is bigger or deeper than the Pacific Ocean.

Within this watery basin lies Oceania—a world made up of the Pacific's island jewels. Like the pearly layers that form around a grain of sand in an oyster shell, submarine volcanoes build up from lava that escapes from cracks in the ocean floor. Gradually, lava builds upon itself until it finally breaks the water's surface and a new cone-shaped island is born. Each volcanic island becomes a black pearl in the matchless string of islands that bejewel the Pacific Ocean.

Nothing under the Atlantic or Pacific remains the same forever. Like any living thing, birth is eventually followed by death. Over eons of geologic time, the earth's tectonic plates shift and bump into each other. In the Pacific, older islands become disconnected from the "hot spots" from which they were born, and the now-extinct volcanic islands become atolls that gradually sink back into the sea.

Closer to home, ash spewing from Iceland's Eyjafjallajökull volcano—two thousand six hundred ten miles from New York City and five hundred thirty four miles from Scotland—reminded the world that volcanoes are indeed an awesome force of nature that we are powerless to control. Just ask Eleanor.

(April 2010)

Timbuktu in Peril

$\mathcal{F}$OLLOWING A LATE JANUARY RAIN, I set off walking around our meadow pathway and ended up in Timbuktu. The northern leg of the footpath was too muddy to negotiate, setting me off course through meadow grasses where I discovered a complex network of beaten pathways.

Like Gulliver, I stood high over the routes of field mice, rabbits, possums, raccoons, and deer. But to my mind's eye, the paths were those of desert nomads crisscrossing the African Sahel. Determined to follow them, I found myself on an ancient caravan route that took me from Boomerang Creek to Timbuktu. Located in the central region of Mali—a West African country slightly less than twice the size of Texas—this legendary city is as remarkable as it is remote.

For most of the world, the word "Timbuktu" has long evoked a place that is as far as you can go from wherever you happen to be. Why then, you might be wondering, is Mali suddenly making international headlines today? Backtrack to the 1960s, when France granted independence to its colonies in West Africa and the Mali Federation was created. Ruled by a dictator until 1991 when a coup ushered in a democratic government, Mali—ninety percent Muslim—held its first democratic presidential election in 1992.

Tourists, historians and religious scholars regularly journeyed "to the middle of nowhere" to see first hand the architectural and scholarly treasures of Timbuktu, a UNESCO World Heritage Site.

Timbuktu's collection of documents, many written in ornate calligraphy, form a compendium of geography, Islamic history, politics, astrology, medicine, law, and science. A manuscript

Cathy Salter

discussing slavery in West Africa during the seventeenth century notes "the fundamental and original nature of humanity is that individuals are free." For some scholars, such manuscripts serve as proof that Africa had a written history at least as old as—if not older than—the European Renaissance.

But tragic events at the U.S. Consulate in Benghazi, Libya in 2012 and an attack on an Algerian oil refinery (1/20/2013)—resulting in the deaths of Americans and foreign workers—have affected tourism in the region, and caused France, Britain and the United States to expand counter-terrorist activities in the region. Mali, landlocked and with sixty-five percent of its land area desert or semi-desert, is particularly vulnerable to political winds and radical factions that increasingly blow across its vast desert borders with Algeria, Mauritania, Niger, and as far away as Libya.

February 4, 2013, TIME introduced the term "Africanistan" to the region's political lexicon. Following the overthrow of Libya's Muammar Gaddafi in October 2011, a vast arsenal of weapons fell into the hands of rebel forces, fleeing mercenaries, and al Qaeda-linked militants who disappeared with the speed of a sandstorm into the desert.

April 2012, well-armed Tuareg rebels seized control of Timbuktu and claimed northern Mali as their homeland, prompting over four hundred thousand Malians to flee southward. Radical Islamists then imposed harsh Sharia rule. Like the Taliban in Afghanistan, they targeted historic sites revered by Sufis, a mystical school of popular Islam, digging up burial sites of Sufi saints and destroying half of Timbuktu's sixteen ornate Sufi shrines and earthen mausoleums.

With Timbuktu's treasures clearly in grave peril and a multi-national African force slow to come to Mali's aid, French troops came to the rescue—bombing rebel Islamist outposts and racing with Malian troops to retake Timbuktu. Out of retribution, fleeing jihadi militants set fire to one of the greatest libraries of Islamic manuscripts in the world—Timbuktu's Ahmed Baba Institute, housing forty thousand fragile scholarly documents, many passed through families from generation to generation for centuries.

As the battle for northern Mali escalates, three hundred thousand additional manuscripts are at risk, many are in the care of nomadic ethnic Tuareg who "have been custodians of Timbuktu's old literary tradition, dating back to the time of the Renaissance, when the city was a major crossroads for gold traders. Bound in weathered goatskin covers, they have survived countless perils along the way." (*TIME* 2/04/13)

Pray it is not too late to protect Timbuktu's jeopardized treasures from the ignorance of those who would destroy chapters of West Africa's priceless cultural heritage.

(January 2013)

OMAN AFTER THE SULTAN

*I*N MARCH 27, 2015, STUDENTS from grades four through eight in all fifty states and the U.S. Territories will be competing in state-level National Geographic Bees. The competition will test their knowledge of world geopolitics. Should you like to try and compete with these sharp young geographers, let me offer this question. Where is Oman and why should Americans care about this country's future?

For much of the twentieth century, Oman—the second largest country on the Arabian Peninsula—was cloaked in obscurity. A tradition of seafaring and trading went back centuries. Its merchants supplied copper and frankincense to the ancient world, pioneering sea routes to China as early as the eighth century. Until it lost its empire late in the nineteenth century, Oman ruled a medieval empire with colonial and revenue interests in Africa and Asia, was a major maritime power, and was the first Arab nation to send an ambassador to the United States.

Until just forty-five years ago, Oman was one of the most repressed societies in the world. There was no television; radios were banned as the work of the devil. There were no Omani diplomats abroad, and the sultan kept his country in almost complete isolation.

When oil was discovered in Oman in 1964, its ruler Sultan Sa'id ibn Taimur remained slow to modernize or help his people. At that time, Oman's capital city, Muscat, was situated among rocky hills in the desert, literally surrounded by a fortress wall with city gates. It was a virtually bankrupt, rigidly centralized, medieval monarchy rife with poverty, illiteracy, and internal conflicts. Thousands of disaffected Omanis had fled the country to work and study abroad.

Then, in 1970, the sultan's British-educated son Qaboos bin Sa'id overthrew his father and transformed Oman from a backwater with only three primary schools (boys only), one private hospital and 6.2 miles of paved road into a prosperous state with generous social programs.

In today's highly unstable Middle East region, Oman is a key U.S. ally, commanding the western shores of the Strait of Hormuz—the strategic gateway to Arabian Gulf oil. Over the past forty-five years, Oman's enlightened leader has peacefully introduced modern reforms including universal education and health care. It is now a contemporary country with highways, sleek new airports, satellite TV dishes and a range of public and private universities. Children start studying English and computers in the first grade. Boys and girls are expected to finish high school at least.

During the Arab Spring uprisings that began in Tunisia in December 2010 and spread to Egypt and Bahrain, protesters accused autocratic rulers of growing out of touch. In Oman, the sultan had kept in touch with his people and remained popular.

An absolute monarch, Sultan Qaboos is seen by most of his 4.1 million people and the West as a visionary who has not only unified, but modernized his country. It is remarkable that in today's volatile Arabian Peninsula and Middle East region, Oman's ruler has managed to avoid the spread of fundamentalism, terrorism, civil unrest and the omnipresent creeping threat of Al-Qaeda and ISIS forces in his country.

But this could change. The seventy-four-year-old sultan who has never married, and has no heir or designated successor, is feared to be in declining health. *The Economist* (12/6/14) noted "For almost six months, the sultan has been under the care of doctors in Germany with what is said to be colon cancer." Also, some young Omanis are impatient with the pace of social and political reforms.

Add to these worries the declining geopolitical stability of Yemen—Oman's wreck of a neighbor to the immediate west—that recently forced the evacuation of American Embassy personnel from Yemen's capital. Omanis and the West are understandably concerned about Oman's future and wondering, "After the sultan, how long will this peaceful and prosperous nation stay that way?" It is a geography question we should all be asking.

(March 2015)

Seven Lives That Mattered

*D*AWN VIEWED THROUGH A FILTER of falling snow turns white into blue. Snowflakes dance with a passion driven by urgency. Individually, each snowflake is a unique and beautiful creation, fully formed though short-lived. In the blue dawn, their efforts mount into winter's first measurable snow. Their brilliance captures our attention, and offers us pause to reflect.

In today's globally wired, tuned in 24/7 world, moments of quiet reflection are rare. Social media bombards us with horrific images of evil acts against humanity that leave the civilized world heavy of spirit. Exhausted by seemingly endless global conflicts, the world has watched the brutal forces of ISIS spread like a black plague across a region weakened by political and sectarian turmoil.

Numbed and outraged by nightly reports of senseless, murderous acts, we should pause to remember seven Americans who simply couldn't ignore suffering taking place at home and abroad. Their lives made a difference. Their actions, here briefly chronicled, mattered greatly to the lives they intersected and touched. Four were kidnapped and killed in Syria by Islamic State groups. Three were apparently murdered in Chapel Hill, North Carolina by a hateful neighbor. They were all exceptional Americans.

James Foley, forty, grew up in New Hampshire. He was an instructor for the Teach for America program before becoming a journalist on the front lines of conflict in the Middle East. Foley was kidnapped in November 2012 near the Syria-Turkey border. He was beheaded in August 2014.

Steven Scotloff, thirty-one, was a freelance journalist who strove to show the personal stories of people affected in areas of conflict. Scotloff was beheaded in September 2014.

Peter Kassig, twenty-six, was a former U.S. Army Ranger who served in Iraq in 2007. He founded a not-for-profit humanitarian organization, SERA (Special Emergency Response and Assistance), to provide refugees in Syria and Lebanon with medical supplies, clothing, food, and propane fuel tanks. Kassig was beheaded in November 2014.

Kayla Mueller, twenty-six, of Arizona received the Gold Presidential Volunteer Award as a teenager for her work with multiple service groups. She later helped homeless women and HIV patients in Arizona. In 2010, Kayla spent five months with a humanitarian group in India, volunteered at an Israeli camp for African refugees, and volunteered with a group in the Palestinian West Bank. In 2012, Kayla traveled to the Turkish-Syrian border to support Syrian refugees. Kidnapped in August 2013 after leaving a Doctors Without Borders hospital clinic in Aleppo, Mueller died in Syria in February 2015 while a captive of ISIS.

Three Muslim-American UNC-Chapel Hill students had dreams and plans. Deah Shaddy Barakat, twenty-three, second year dental student; his wife Yusor Mohammad Abu-Salha, twenty-one, about to enter dental school; and Yusor's nineteen-year-old sister Raza who was studying architecture at North Carolina State in Raleigh, provided free dental supplies and food for the homeless. Barakat and Yusor, married a month ago, planned to go to Turkey this summer as advocates of global dental health to treat Syrian refugees. February 10, 2015 all three were shot in the head execution style by a Chapel Hill neighbor—a self-described supporter of the online group "Atheists for Equality." The FBI is investigating their murders as a possible "hate crime."

These seven Americans seemed to share the belief that suffering should never be seen as normal. At home in the world, aiding the suffering became the direction and purpose of their lives. President

Obama said upon learning of Mueller's death, "Kayla represents what is best about America." The same is true of James, Steven, Peter, Deah, Yusor, and Raza. Their lives mattered; and how they lived their lives should always be remembered.

In a statement on Friday February 13, offering condolences for the Chapel Hill killings, President Obama said, *"Whenever anyone is taken from us before their time, we remember how they lived their lives—and the words of one of the victims should inspire the way we live ours. 'Growing up in America has been such a blessing,' Yusor said recently. 'It doesn't matter where you come from. There are so many different people from so many different places, of different backgrounds and religions—but here, we are all one.'"*

(February 2015)

HALFWAY HOME

*I*N A JOURNEY THAT HAS TAKEN HIM to another planet, our friend Dr. Shakir Hamoodi is on his way home. It has been twenty-eight long months since his period of solitary travail began. Most days he walked the grounds of the Leavenworth satellite compound where he was imprisoned, comforted only by the herd of buffalo grazing just beyond the prison fence. He shared their joy when a baby buffalo was born not long ago, and contemplated the birth of his own grandson five months after he arrived at this foreign place and became a number. Overhead, flocks of geese from the east were a sign that family and friends at home remained constant in their efforts to gain his release and tell his story.

The second week of December, unseasonably warm breezes settled in across the Midwest. Birds returned to our feeders in flocks after an unusual absence. Moles were freely digging tunnels in the soft earth of our meadow, and bright red cardinals alighted in the trees at the edge of our woods, looking like living Christmas ornaments. It was as if some profound change was underway.

Indeed, it was. Without ceremony, our friend Shakir was placed on a Greyhound bus headed for Columbia. Emerging from the fenced compound in which he has been detained since August 28, 2012, he nodded at the buffalo that have been spiritual companions on this spare piece of Kansas prairie just west of the Missouri River. Arriving alone at the Midway Travel Center Greyhound station west of town, he took a taxi as instructed to the Reality Halfway House— his assigned interim residence.

While there, he would be required to apply for work in the community, though he will not be allowed to work at the family's World Harvest Market—the international food emporium he opened in Columbia a decade ago. Once that hurdle was cleared, he would live under house arrest in his own home for the remainder of his sentence, and be eligible for parole April 7, 2015.

On my walk around our meadow the day of Shakir's release, I thought back over the past twenty-eight months to the day when Kit and I watched with his wife, children, and a small circle of friends as this incredibly courageous man disappeared through a doorway into Leavenworth Federal Penitentiary's massive limestone face. Our collective angst on the drive back to Columbia mirrored what he must have been feeling not knowing what awaited him on the inside.

I also recalled visits to the prison and his selfless efforts to keep our spirits and hopes alive. I am forever grateful for the steadfast efforts of friends and supporters who prepared Shakir's legal request for a commutation of his sentence, donated to a trust fund to help support his family and store in his absence, wrote newspaper articles, and sent personal letters to our elected officials, the U.S. Office of Pardons, and to the one person with the power to pardon Shakir or commute his sentence—the President of the United States.

I thought about Chinese artist Ai WeiWei and his political meditation on dissent. Not allowed to travel outside of China, this political activist takes his message to the world through art. In an art exhibition installed at Alcatraz Prison, assistants of the artist assembled Lego portraits of one hundred seventy-six dissidents imprisoned in countries around the world. Dr. Shakir Hamoodi is one of six Americans represented in the exhibit. He received over five hundred postcards while at Leavenworth Satellite Prison with messages handwritten from visitors from around the world who have come to Alcatraz to see and experience the exhibit firsthand.

Shakir's journey has been a weight on our spirits that now is lifting. Though halfway home, he was still not free. His Columbia family and friends—Christian, Muslim, Jewish, Arab, and people of all faiths—have welcomed his return to Columbia. Shakir is a true humanitarian whose faith has taught him to act with charity and compassion. Though innocent, he does not dwell on the past twenty-eight months he spent in prison—an injustice he cannot change. Rather, his message to the younger generation is to let go of anger and violence. Instead, live today with goodness and happiness as your goal. Then focus on what you can do tomorrow to help make this a more peaceful and just world.

(December 2014)

Ai Weiwei At Large on Alcatraz

A decade ago, Cheryl Haines established the FOR-SITE foundation dedicated to the creation, preservation and understanding of art about place. The place in focus was San Francisco, and her mission was to use art to inspire fresh thinking and dialogues about the city's natural and cultural environments. Early art exhibitions celebrated the natural habitats of San Francisco's Presidio—a one thousand, four-hundred ninety-one acre national park site and former army post—and the Golden Gate Bridge on the seventy-fifth anniversary of its construction.

In 2012, Haines began focusing her foundation's energies on Alcatraz, the island known as "the Rock" in San Francisco Bay. Studies revealed the island's complex history—one with roots as a military fortification and prison in the Civil War era and during World War I, its period as a federal penitentiary (1933-63), its occupation by Native Americans (1969-71), and finally its conversion to a national historic landmark and park (1972).

Haines has collaborated with many international artists on various FOR-SITE projects, including Chinese artist and activist Ai Weiwei. In 2011, Ai was detained for eighty-one days by Chinese authorities as a result of his outspoken opposition to China's policies regarding Tibet and other human rights abuses. After his release, Haines visited Ai in Beijing and promised to bring his ideas to a broader audience through art. Here, she realized, was an opportunity to use art and Alcatraz to tell the story of Ai Weiwei, who survived the Cultural Revolution, and those of dissidents around the world detained by their governments and denied basic civil rights as a result of their beliefs.

Working with the National Park Conservancy and National Park Service, the current @Large Ai Weiwei on Alcatraz project then fell into place. Alcatraz as an ecological site and former prison is viewed in a new light. Because Ai is still not allowed to travel abroad, the collaboration involved countless email exchanges and volunteer artists to assemble seven art installations. What made it possible was Ai's understanding of architectural space in a prison—having been an inmate himself.

In early April, Kit and I took a boat to Alcatraz with our daughter Heidi who lives in the Bay Area. Nothing quite describes the feeling one gets as you arrive on the Rock and look up at the cell house where prisoners spent years locked up across the bay from San Francisco.

We had traveled from the tranquility of the Heartland to this isolated site to experience first hand Ai WeiWei's *Trace* artwork— one hundred eighty-one portraits of prisoners of conscience, each face created out of Lego building blocks. Working with Amnesty International, the artist selected individuals from thirty-one countries around the globe. Says FOR-SITE Executive Director Cheryl Haines, "They present a human face through which the basic tenets of this exhibition are presented, calling our attention to pressing societal and political issues."

Walking around the vast floor of the New Industries Building where former prisoners worked while being observed from above by guards on a protected catwalk, I stopped at the Lego portrait of our friend Shakir Hamoodi. In a notebook identifying each dissident, it reads—

United States: Shakir Hamoodi (released Dec 2014)

Pled guilty to engaging in a conspiracy to violate the International Economic Emergency Powers Act. Hamoodi is an Iraqi American nuclear engineer. He sent money to family and friends in Iraq for humanitarian purposes during US sanctions. In 2002 he criticized the Bush administration's plan to attack Iraq. In 2012 he was sentenced to three years in prison and three years probation. His crime is no longer illegal.

Haines and Ai Weiwei hope that visitors to @Large leave Alcatraz thinking differently about the concept of freedom and gain an understanding of the purpose of art, which is to fight for freedom. To quote Ai Weiwei—*"Only art can reveal the deep inner voice of every individual with no concern for political borders, nationality, race or religion. This exhibition could not come at a better time."*

(April 2015)

IMAGES THE WORLD CANNOT FORGET

$\mathscr{P}$HAN THI KIM PHÚC. SHARBAT GULA. Aylan Kurdi. Over time and because of language differences, we forget names. But there are images we never forget. Some haunting photographs become icons that evoke an entire nation's pain. Some remain etched in our minds as clearly as if printed on contact paper.

Each image is a window into a larger human tragedy. The terrified Vietnamese girl running naked after napalm burned her little body. Three New York City firemen raising the American flag at Ground Zero. The Afghan refugee girl whose haunting eyes captured the attention of the world after her image appeared on the cover of *National Geographic* magazine. The lifeless Syrian child photographed when his body washed ashore after a boat carrying his migrant family capsized en route to Kos, Greece.

On June 8, 1972, South Vietnamese planes dropped napalm bombs on the village of Trang Bang. Then a South Vietnamese Air Force pilot bombed fleeing villagers he mistook for enemy soldiers—killing several and badly burning Kim Phúc. Associated Press photographer, Nick Ut's photograph of a crying girl running after tearing off her burning clothes was featured on the front page of the *New York Times* the next day. The image later earned a Pulitzer Prize, and was chosen as the World Press Photo of the Year for 1972.

During the course of the Afghan-Soviet conflict (1979-89), *National Geographic* photographer, Steve McCurry visited orthopedic hospitals and refugee settlements in Northwest Pakistan where he found the most visible sign of the war's effect on Afghanistan's people. By June 1984, more than a quarter of Afghanistan's pre-war population of fifteen million lived in exile in neighboring Pakistan and Iran. There they were given asylum in the Muslim tradition of hospitality in refugee settlements made up of tents or mud-and-straw dwellings. With the war at a stalemate, McCurry sensed that Pakistan's capacity to accommodate the world's largest refugee population had reached the saturation point.

Nonetheless, Pakistan provided daily rations of wheat, oil, skim milk, sugar and tea as well as a kerosene allotment to incoming refugees. Afghan girls in the camps had an opportunity to go to school, some for the first time in their lives. On assignment along Pakistan's Northeastern Frontier in 1984, McCurry visited Kachaghari camp where he photographed Zarghuna Ghumkhor who had studied science at Kabul University teaching a class of little girls seated at her feet in an earthen-floored classroom.

It was in such a makeshift classroom in another refugee camp that McCurry gained permission to photograph a young girl perhaps twelve or thirteen years old during a five-minute session. Not until he was back in Washington developing his film did the photographer realize what he had captured that day with his camera.

The June 1985 *National Geographic* carried a story about life along Afghanistan's war-torn frontier, illustrated by McCurry's photographs. On the cover was Sharbat Gula—an Afghan refugee girl with green eyes staring out from under a tattered red headscarf. This single photograph captured the plight of Afghan refugees after a decade of war. It is one of the most well-known images of the twentieth century and is now considered *National Geographic*'s most famous cover.

On September 3, 2015, a toddler's lifeless body was photographed face down in the surf where it had washed ashore near Bodrum, Turkey. The tragic image of three-year-old Aylan Kurdi, a tiny Syrian child wearing tennis shoes, sent shockwaves around the world and focused attention on a humanitarian crisis too long ignored—the wrenching plight of tens of thousands of families traumatized by chaos, crossing into Europe on foot, by boat, train, or bus in hopes of finding safety and asylum. Headlines in the Turkish newspaper *Milliyet* reacting to the image read: "Be Ashamed World."

The heartbreaking image of Aylan Kurdi is now the human face of the massive migrant crisis facing the richer countries of Europe today. What should and what is the world willing to do?

(September 2015)

Part Two

A Year at Boomerang Creek

On my mental calendar, the year begins in September, the month when our life in Missouri began both at Breakfast Creek and sixteen years later at Boomerang Creek. Indian summer is my favorite time of the year, just ahead of autumn's brilliant arrival on the landscape in and around Boone County.

Tomatoes are on the vine and there are red and golden raspberries ripe for fall picking. Sugar maples and oaks have begun to change color, and apricot sunsets wash daily across newly harvested cornfields all across the county.

Herbs in the *potager*, (kitchen garden) have matured over the summer months in their terra cotta pots at the edge of the porch. Soon I will cut sprigs of rosemary and lemon thyme and set them to dry in the sun before they are stored in glass jars for use in savory winter meals. For surely winter will come again as it always does.

On a cold December morning, I will walk under gray skies that speak of change in the air. Before long, the first tiny flakes of snow will appear, one falling on my face—its icy kiss whispering "winter." In the shade garden, giant hostas yellow and melt like brie back into the ground. Only the hellebore retains its dark green color in winter's garden where frogs and cicadae sleep and silence abounds.

By March when cold winds send my hair flying wildly, the garden and I wait for warmth to return to the soil. In our orchard I check for signs of life to emerge in early spring. At last, a balmy weekend, and returning robins busily root for worms in soil mushy from April showers. Spring peepers make joyful noises heard through windows now open again to the glorious night air.

In summer, fruit and vegetables pile up in the kitchen. As fruit ripens on trees in the orchard, I peruse cookbooks for favorite chutney recipes and can pears for the pantry. Chilled summer soups with tomatoes, peppers, chopped avocado, cucumber and cilantro are followed by hearty Mulligatawny soup and pots of chili in late fall when once again, Kit begins to bring in, split, load, haul, and stack wood for winter fires in the Buck Stove. As one year at Boomerang Creek is recalled in four seasons, a new year is about to get underway.

(June 2015)

Chapter Nine
Time and Nature Across the Seasons

The unseasonable temperatures have awakened plants and humans alike, causing a collective stretch, an awakening from a winter's sleep. It won't last, of course.

C.S. February 2015

Peach Blossoms and Fig Leaves in Winter

On a frigid January day, I head out to the orchard and prune the dickens out of the fruit trees. I'd first brushed up on the subject by watching a YouTube demonstration by Stark Bros' Nursery tree expert, Elmer Kidd. Before long, each fruit tree had its own pile of spindly suckers and inward growing limbs that I reckoned Elmer would have thinned out had he been in our orchard with me that afternoon.

Before calling it an afternoon, I gathered a generous armful of peach twigs, each dotted with small buds that would never become peaches. They just might bloom if arranged in a tall vase of water and left to soak up sunshine in a south-facing window. The perfect spot was near two Meyer lemon trees, a dwarf olive, and assorted herbs that cheer my gardening spirits in winter. This is the time when spring's arrival seems a distant dream and there is more darkness in the days than light.

Then, February arrived on surprisingly warm breezes alive with migrating backyard birds. A friendly wren landed momentarily on a porch bench and peered in through a window as if to say, "Reserve the wren house on that south wall for me. I'll be back when spring is here to stay."

Squirrels are simply everywhere, springing from the clothesline T-post onto a bird feeder where they dangle by a single back foot like acrobats while stuffing their cheeks with birdseed. On the ground below, cardinals, blue jays, nuthatches, black-capped chickadees, doves, and sparrows vie for the seeds that drop to the ground.

Between the birds and the warm breezes that draw me out to the winter garden, nature's unbound energy can be felt all around me. The unseasonable temperatures have awakened plants and humans alike, causing a collective stretch, an awakening from a winter's sleep. It won't last, of course. It's simply too early for spring. But try and tell that to the peach branches that bloomed the first week of February, rosy pink with the promise of life still alive in their pruned branches.

In my studio across the glade, a similar miracle greeted me the same week. Three years ago while visiting Albuquerque, I bought a New Mexico fig tree small enough that it came home with me wrapped in newspaper in a carry-on tote bag. Over spring, summer and fall, the potted fig lives outdoors near the herb garden. However, in winter, it prefers the warmth of my studio near a sunny window. After dropping its giant fig leaves from the prior season, it rests bare-branched in sunlight that pours through a sliding glass door, content as a tree frog in a state of hibernation.

Since its arrival in Missouri, the fig has grown as tall as me. Like me, when it is consumed with a thought, it has a hard time remaining silent. *"Spring,"* the fig must have thought that warm February week, when the green tips of its branches began to swell and brighten. Soon, perfectly formed fig leaves unfurled like flags at the end of every branch.

How extraordinary that peach blossoms and fig leaves visited me in winter, precisely when I was in need of rethinking the direction that my own writing had been taking. Like a constant gardener, I needed to prune away dead wood and give shape to words and ideas that will bear fruit in the months ahead.

There are still weeks of winter ahead and perhaps a snowstorm or two. But inside my studio, I'm happily writing with a new sense of direction, just across the room from a fig tree with spring green leaves that wave and cheer me on. Back on track and focused on my writer's task, it will be spring soon enough.

(February 2015)

WHERE THE LIGHT FALLS

I AWAKE AT MY USUAL EARLY HOUR to find the sky still dark. Sunrise is yet an hour away. The clocks have all been turned ahead to save light in anticipation of spring's arrival. The March lion that roared with bluster just weeks ago has morphed into a gamboling lamb, eager to nibble on the sweet, green grass emerging from under February's snow cover in the meadow at Boomerang Creek.

When temperatures reached the sixties recently, accompanied by two days of warm rains, the white landscape melted before our eyes. Gardens, lawns, glades and meadows were soon waterlogged with snowmelt. Run-off not absorbed by the soggy ground rushed into creeks, ravines, and ditches with a force. The natural slope of our meadow sent a flood of snowmelt to a narrow drainage channel between the shade garden and our south woods.

Drawn outside into the spring-like elements, Kit and I each grabbed a steel-tined rake and set about evacuating clumps of soggy leaves that were clogging sections of the three hundred-foot long drainage channel, hindering the flow of rushing water to a drainage culvert at the end of our gravel driveway. In an hour's time, water was racing unimpeded through the culvert to the boomerang-shaped creek that gives its name to our five-acre property in the country.

Invigorated by the exercise and the surprisingly balmy air, we then tackled large cedar branches snapped off by the weight of late February's heavy, wet snowfall. Positioning myself like a horse pulling a load, I muscled branches to a distant corner of the meadow along our northern woods. After having battled a cold virus that flattened me for almost two weeks, I felt back in the world of the living at long last.

Signs of seasonal change are emerging everywhere. Spring peepers are peeping. Cheerful choruses of birdsong fill the air. Jonquils, hyacinths and hellebore Lenten roses have pushed up above last year's brown cover of decaying hosta leaves. With the slightest encouragement, buds stand ready to burst forth in flower signaling spring's arrival on the March calendar. Already the urge to garden is in the air. Stores are filled with assorted bulbs and seed packets. Unable to resist, I now have fifty strawberry plants ready for planting in our raised strawberry bed. When that is done, fresh straw will be added to retain moisture during the growing season.

Evenings are now spent on the screened porch where we sit with Pooh and Fanny, our two cats, mesmerized by the sound of water rushing again in the creek below. Hours are filled with reading, a welcome evening activity throughout the winter months. With a workshop for painters and writers in Tuscany on our fall calendar, I recently found myself captured by a new novel by Katherine Keenum, *Where the Light Falls*.

Set in the 1870s amid the bohemian neighborhoods and teaching studios of Belle Époque Paris, the novel is awash in light and color. Jeanette Palmer, a young American woman studying art in the City of Light, takes a walk along a boulevard in Paris and observes "where the light falls and where the shadows lie."

> Jeanette walked past flower vendors with pushcarts loaded with buckets of roses and bronze chrysanthemums, while across the street lavender shadows played against mellow stone. A few blocks away, the harsh white glare of the electric light…would soon come to bleach and harden everything in sight.

Looking out my window, the harsh glare of February's stark white glaze that earlier had blurred the line between sky and earth has been softened by rain and warm breezes. Spirits are high. Hope is in the air. Where the light falls, the world is once again filled with the promise of spring.

(March 2013)

Eternal Summer in the Grateful Heart

$\mathcal{R}$ain fell early this morning, its presence felt in the thick heaviness of the air an hour before its arrival. Across the eastern meadow, a shelf of flat, gray clouds engaged the sun in a wrestling match, intent on pressing the dawn light back down into night. Happily rooted on its own stage, a ballet troupe of pink belladonna amaryllis dance across the shade garden. Naked ladies up at dawn dance with sweet abandon in the shade of our August garden.

All around the region, farmers give thanks for this year's bountiful crops, now tall from a spring and summer of generous rains. After last summer's stressful drought, the small orchard at Boomerang Creek is having its best year ever. My battle with our pear-thieving, bushy-tailed critter population appears to have been won.

The solution was simple. I punched a hole in a dozen aluminum pie tins and hung them like giant tinsel ornaments from the lower branches of the pear trees to dissuade our army of pesky squirrels from harvesting the delicious fruit. Banging and clanking in the warm summer breezes, the pie-tin rouse has kept the hungry hordes at a distance. One red-tailed squirrel makes an occasional dash for the pear tree, but Kit is quick to shout out a warning that sends him high-tailing it back to the nearby woods.

To date we've filled a large wooden fruit basket with ripe peaches, boxed up some to be shared with friends, and we are eating our way through what remains. Some have been chopped up for muffins and cakes made from recipes in my 1974 spiral-bound copy of Stephenson's Old Apple Farm Restaurant recipes, then called "receipts." Their famous green rice casserole, peach chutney, banana bread and apple fritters made the restaurant—located east of Kansas City at Highway 40 and Lee's Summit Road—a dining destination for sixty-one years before it closed in 2007.

I treasure this humble, down-home family cookbook that has moved with me from my first tiny kitchen in Omaha, to kitchens Kit and I have shared in Los Angeles, Washington D.C., at Breakfast Creek, in Albuquerque, and now at Boomerang Creek. As before, it maintains an honored spot in my rather eclectic kitchen cookbook library.

These summer days when fruit and vegetables are piling up in kitchens around the county, abundant recipes from local restaurants as well as variations on classic recipes are available online, in food magazines, on TV food shows, and every Tuesday in Marcia Vanderlip and Nina Furstenau's Tuesday Food columns in the *Columbia Daily Tribune*. A cook has a virtual library of delicious recipes at hand 24/7.

In the August 2013 issue of *Bon Appétit*, I discovered a fascinating variation on gazpacho—classic Spanish summer soup—called "Chilled Tomato and Stone Fruit Soup." Blend two pounds of tomatoes, a cup of cherries (frozen or fresh), an English cucumber, sweet red or jalapeno pepper, a peach, a garlic clove and white balsamic or Sherry vinegar. Drizzle with olive oil and season with kosher salt and ground black pepper.

Served chilled in a cup with chopped avocado, cucumber or cilantro, it is heavenly, and I'm now eager to share it with my daughter-in-law, Ana Martin Salter. A gifted chef herself, Ana is just the one to introduce this unexpectedly sweet and cherry-colored gazpacho recipe to Madrid's restaurants and mercados.

Back at the Creek, my thoughts turn to the dead oak tree we reluctantly had cut down a few weeks ago, just before our grandson Nick arrived for a visit. It has now been split, loaded, hauled and stacked on firewood racks with his help and that of several friends. A rain-tamped earthen circle is all that visibly remains of the grand old oak's former footprint.

As I step into the circle's center, a message wells forth from the tree's still buried roots, mirroring my reflections. *"There shall be eternal summer in the grateful heart."* Indeed, it is so.

(August 2013)

Cathy Salter

Come Dry Autumn, Dust Happens

*A*S AUTUMN APPROACHES on the calendar, days pass with little moisture to revive the gardens. A creeping lethargy sets in, preying on animals, plants, and people alike. Like a great spider, heat holds the living in its web, sucking the energy from us a little more each day until we can hardly move. We try to remember the sound and feeling of rain. Then, finally, all is dust.

Dust happens. Life emerges from parched earth with rain and returns to dust without it. It is a part of life and a metaphor for how we sometimes deal with the flow of our days. How to deal with it in the short term is one of life's most persistent challenges.

A friend in Manhattan began a letter on the nineteenth of July but did not complete and mail it until the sixteenth of August. At the end of the first page, she came to the heart of why she had been remiss in writing—

> *an incredible lethargy has descended upon me as the weather has become oppressive—like we live in a gray, thick cloud of heat and bad air. I scuttle between air-conditioned place to air-conditioned place, slow and beaten by the air around me.*

As the dog days of September drag on, little bothers accumulate and confound us. Deadlines loom on the horizon. Invasive weeds and voracious grasshoppers invade our summer gardens. Each day, the grass turns a shade browner and black walnuts fall like bomblets from drooping trees. As the autumnal equinox approaches without rain, the grass stops growing, and the hum of sit-down mowers is eerily absent.

Tired of battling the heat, a farmer friend goes home mid-morning after working and takes an uncustomary breather. Dust from one of his grain bins has momentarily stolen his wind. In those few minutes of broken pattern, his thoughts revisit a favorite fishing spot. He is able to wash away the dust by lying down with dreams of fly-fishing in a cool mountain stream, miles from the relentless chores of his dawn-to-dusk workday.

Perhaps we have periodic droughts in life because they force us to slow down and think about what we are doing with our lives. They are spiritual droughts that leave us stranded from our creative selves, struggling to get through work that we no longer seem to have the heart to finish. When our creative side gets out of balance, life is a lumpy ride indeed.

My own close encounter with dust happened last weekend. There comes a time when you simply can't hide it any longer. It gets in your face and demands your attention. By summer's end, the porches at Boomerang Creek are home to friendly spiders and attract a gray assortment of fuzz and foot traffic debris like magnets. Orb spiders weave complex webs between porch posts and nearby trees, only to retrieve them like spent parachutes the following dawn. Walking face first into one of these webs sets arms to flailing and leads to fuming over the fact you were caught in the very same web just the night before.

One step in dealing with life's figurative dust is to begin clearing the piles that build up around one's workspace. There is something very satisfying and therapeutic about being able to suddenly see the surface of your desk for the first time in weeks. It is a chance to begin again, to get out from under the weight of paper that seems to pile up like a river approaching flood stage no matter how you try to contain it.

In mid-September, some folks fuss while others dream of fly-fishing. I attack the piles around me, weed the strawberry bed, prepare batches of basil pesto, and dream of October in Tuscany. Face it. Dust happens. Our challenge is to learn how to deal with it when it does, or simply ignore it.

(August 2013)

THE AUDIBLE HUM OF HARVEST IN THE HEARTLAND

*W*ALKING BETWEEN THE HOUSE AND STUDIO at Boomerang Creek, I took a detour off the mulch pathway to collect persimmons that have begun to fall from one of the native trees in our mixed woods. Under a black walnut tree, multitudes of husky green, ankle-twisting outer-shell globes made walking a challenge. Shagbark hickory shells lay in split-open-quarters, exposing a smooth brown nut to be harvested by our busy squirrel population. Brushing nuts and leaves aside, I found my own treasures, filling the bowl I'd brought along with wizen-faced, fallen persimmon fruit.

In this time of national economic uncertainty, there is a fever of harvesting activities going on all across the Heartland where change can be felt and heard in the autumn air. Canada geese honk overhead, dry leaves crunch underfoot and fat grasshoppers noisily nibble in what remains of the vegetable garden. With the arrival of October, nighttime temperatures dip into the forties and daytime highs have me searching my closet for a sweater before heading outside.

This year, in this season of corn harvests and pumpkin festivals, I find myself pummeled by the non-stop coverage of the 2008 presidential campaign and in mental overload trying to understand all of the nuances of the economic crisis gripping the nation. So when our friend Orion Beckmeyer called to say he had checked the sugar content of his Chambourcin grapes and pickers were needed that weekend, I happily agreed to join their annual autumn grape harvest.

When Saturday arrived, I rose early, dressed and walked outdoors into the still dark yard with my morning coffee. To the east, a faint circle of light traced a suggestion of a waning moon moving from its last quarter to new moon stage. I felt connected to the same vast night sky our daughter Heidi and Kit had studied hours earlier from their campsite in a lone corner of Nevada where they've gone on a father-daughter road trip. By six-thirty, I was dipping in and out of patches of low-hanging fog as I drove the country roads that connect Boomerang Creek to the Beckmeyer Vineyard off Route A in the Hartsburg Hills.

I arrived to find a generous supply of white plastic buckets evenly distributed along each row of vines. Sleepy-eyed pickers began to arrive shortly after seven, and hot coffee and clippers were available for anyone who had not brought their own. By day's end, two flatbed trailers loaded with twelve and a half tons of deep purple grape clusters had departed for Rocheport's Les Bourgeois Vineyards at its spectacular bluff top site above the Missouri River.

Once home again, I apologized to our three miffed cats for having kept them inside on such a glorious late September day. I then showered from head to toe and scrubbed everything I'd managed to stain with purple juice over the course of the day's picking. On the radio, I learned that Paul Newman—the politically independent, blue-eyed actor, salad dressing entrepreneur, racecar enthusiast, and philanthropist—had died at the age of eighty-three. After going through the mail and massaging my aching arches and bruised heels, I fell into bed and didn't wake until the phone rang at 6:44 the following morning.

"Good morning," Orion sang through the phone like a camp counselor attempting to rouse his reluctant charges. There were six more rows of Chambourcins to be picked, and would I come as soon as possible, pretty please? Over the past fifteen years, Orion has taught me everything I know and have subsequently written about on the subject of farming. He and his wife Barbara are undeniably wonderful, salt of the earth people. Any thoughts I might have had of a leisurely wake up coffee and the Sunday morning paper were suddenly toast.

By early afternoon, the weekend's grape harvest and lunch were over, giving me just enough time to go home to freshen up before returning to drive with the Beckmeyers for an evening harvest celebration at Terry and Mary Neuner's vineyard on the Maries River near Westphalia. The Beckmeyers and Neuners both grow Norton/Cynthiana grapes, slated for harvest in early October. In 2003, the Norton/Cynthiana grape variety was designated as the "Missouri State Grape" by Governor Bob Holden, and Westphalia Vineyards was the Gold Medal Winner of the National Norton Festival Wine Competition in 2006.

Recently, *TIME* food critic Joel Stein fell in love with this late-ripening, dark purple Missouri native while tasting wines from all fifty states for a magazine article. Stein described it as "the Midwest's big, tannic Norton." That evening at the Westphalia Vineyard, guests sampled Terry Neuner's 2007 Norton, Cabernet Franc, Riesling and new Riesling-based Rosé. Tasty hors d'oeuvres were served al fresco, followed by a bodacious indoor buffet of barbequed ribs and chicken, baked beans, deviled eggs, brownies, and Central Dairy ice cream in cones. Inside the winery barn, the hum of fermentation was clearly audible above the crowd.

This October and over the winter months to come, I will sleep better knowing that in this beautiful part of our country, the Beckmeyer and Neuner 2008 Norton grape harvests have been blended and are now aging happily in white oak barrels at the Westphalia Winery.

(October 2008)

The Magic of October

*S*TARS HAVE A WAY OF CONNECTING US to other places. They are my map back to Tuscany when I recall my last star-filled night in Italy. They are my route back to a desert oasis in western China where I once rode a camel under a full moon. They are, in fact, a connection to every place in the world where I have ever tilted my head back and gazed up into the heavens.

Over Boomerang Creek, the stars are a road map on clear nights when Kit and I stroll out into our open meadow. Change can be felt in the cool October night air as we gaze up at the stars and reflect on events of the day. The same Big Dipper and North Star that Alaskans have captured on their flag serve as our compass to true north and help us keep our direction as we chart our course for the coming days.

October has been surprisingly colorful this year. An extremely dry summer led to a bountiful grape harvest at local vineyards and a second spring blossoming for fruit trees. Only once has there been a hint of frost on the October pumpkins sprinkled across the Hartsburg bottoms.

Indian summer temperatures warm up the days, but nighttime temperatures hint of the season soon to come. October days are a riot of ostentatious oranges, golden yellows, and sassafras reds. At the end of each day, sunsets go down in a breathtaking blaze of rosy peach against lavender horizons.

Anticipating colder days ahead, Kit has been splitting and stacking firewood with the help of friends Greg Busacker and Dale Coble. The rain gutters have been cleared of leaves and tender potted ferns and herbs brought inside where they will live throughout the winter season.

Cathy Salter

Roses love the mixture of sunlight and coolness that come with October. As plants so often do, late in the season roses take on the colors of fall, blooming in shades that mimic autumn's reds and golds. On late afternoon trips to the meadow rose bed, I've been rewarded with gorgeous shades of peach and magenta roses, tall spikes of purple meadow sage and basil flowers, and wild goldenrod I gather for indoor bouquets.

By the middle of October, it seems that the whole world is ready to celebrate the season. For two days, Hartsburg becomes everyone's hometown. Indian corn, pumpkins and squash, jars of locally canned apple butter, and the anticipation of spending a day visiting a small local river town once again brought thousands to Hartsburg for its twenty-first annual Pumpkin Festival despite threatening clouds and an afternoon of persistent rain.

Vendors arrive Friday, set up, swap stories, and camp overnight. Cars filled with festival-goers are moving into town at a steady crawl by eight on Saturday morning, and are guided out into the bottoms where parking extends by now for more than a mile. At nine, festivities begin with a spirited parade as all-American as it gets. At the head of the parade, four Hartsburg American Legion flag bearers march past the crowds on Main and along First Street. Behind them, the Southern Boone County High School band fills the street, followed by walking battalions of politicians and elected officials eager to meet and greet their public.

After the parade, visitors walk comfortably through this community of families who have farmed the bottomlands for more than a century. Parents push baby strollers and pull toy wagons filled with pumpkins the size of their babies. Children have their faces decorated with dragons and glitter or paint images of Casper the Friendly Ghost on miniature pumpkins the size of their tiny hands.

I marvel at the numerous varieties of pumpkins and squash on display in Norland, Jo and Holly Hackman's front yard. I've brought along pictures clipped from an October issue of *Country*

Living magazine to share with the family. It features heritage squash and pumpkins grown by the Condill-McDonald family in Arthur, Illinois—an effort to preserve heirloom vegetables and educate backyard squash gardeners. Jo points out a number of the unusual pumpkins in the article that are sold at the Hackman farm and by other Hartsburg farmers.

Their beautiful names and colorful descriptions instantly transport me on a geographic journey. Rouge Vif d'Etampes (French) pumpkin; Tennessee Spinning gourd, Xmehen Ku'um (Chinese), yellow and green striped Southern Miner, white Lower Salmon River, Salvadorean Ayote, speckled Hopi Orange, Guatemalan Blue Banana, and Yokohama acorn squash; blue-green Jarrandale and tan Thai large pumpkin; Italian Stripetti squash; and a French Galeux d/ Eysines pink pumpkin with peanut-like warts.

Wandering over to Second Street and Main, the old becomes new again. A former general store that once had an upstairs stage and theater became a bicycle repair shop catering to cyclists on the KATY Trail before closing a few years ago. Late this September, remodeled and reinvented as the Hartsburg Grand Restaurant, it re-opened and began serving lunch and dinner every Thursday through Sunday. For the Hartsburg community, it represents a piece of the town's past once lost, now given a second life.

From pumpkins to people to politics, the festival is a celebration of diversity in small town America. For two days, the mix of races and backgrounds in the crowds that fill Hartsburg's streets is as rich as the varieties of squash and pumpkins now grown in this area.

Across America, we gather throughout October at festivals like the one in Hartsburg to celebrate the harvest and the farmers who make the land productive. It is a time to share traditions of the season with friends and family. The position of the stars, the cycle of the seasons, the phases that our own lives pass through—all are ever-changing. All come round again. Full circle. That is the joy of life. And sharing life is always a cause for celebration.

(October 2012)

A Glorious Season of Thanksgiving

*T*HE WEEKEND BEFORE THANKSGIVING, our daughter Heidi and her partner called from northern California. "Sugie and I are preparing to pack for our flight to Missouri," she said. "Any truth to rumors we've heard about nine-degree temperatures in your neck of the woods?"

"Dear hearts," I assured them both. "Your father and I have been outdoors all afternoon removing summer screens and giving windows in every room a Windex shine inside and out. It will be dark when you arrive Wednesday evening, so we'll have the porch light glowing. When you wake up Thanksgiving morning and prepare your first cup of green tea, you'll see clearly the beauty of the wooded world that surrounds Boomerang Creek."

I went on to say that we were dressed in jeans and light sweaters. Kit had spent the afternoon clearing a ton of dried oak leaves that had obscured the narrow gravel driveway where it curves and descends over our creek and exits the property. We didn't want Dave, our super-friendly UPS driver, to plunge his big brown, earth-shaking, dust-disturbing, holiday-package-laden delivery truck down in our creek. What if a Thanksgiving turkey or ham were in one of those boxes? Our neighbors would never forgive us.

"But *exactly how cold is* the temperature?" Heidi asked emphatically, still not assured by my meandering response to her earlier query. I assuaged her worries by relaying the Thanksgiving week forecast for Boone County—*partially sunny days with temperatures in the mid fifties during the days and low thirties at night.* "Sounds a lot like Bay area temperatures to me," I added. After I assured her that I have plenty of cozy robes, sweaters and jackets they could wear, we moved on to the Thanksgiving menu.

Heidi has been a vegetarian since her early teens when she learned that lactose intolerance was the cause of her allergies. Milk and cheese products were immediately eliminated. Then chicken and meat. Finally, as she grew increasingly fond of vegetarian and vegan fare, "anything with a mother" was safe in her kitchen. Given the fact that turkey—Ben Franklin's choice for America's national bird—is the centerpiece in ninety-nine percent of American households on Thanksgiving,you might be thinking this would be a problem for me as I plan our daughter's holiday meal.

But, no. Having recently seen TV footage of Alaska's governor pardoning a big Tom at a turkey farm, while in the background, other less fortunate birds in the flock met their grisly demise, I'm seriously ready for a turkey-free Thanksgiving. Especially since Heidi has emailed a list of food items that she and Sugie will need for their contribution to the holiday dinner.

Heidi's list included bunches of carrots and yellow onions, parsnips, both green and red cabbage, plus one green apple for a salad, kale or collard greens, Silk soymilk, ground oats (not instant), and finally, a kabocha squash. I had all the ingredients except for the exotic-sounding squash with a name that sounded like a tractor. What, I asked myself—a lover of the beauty and flavors of heritage and common squash varieties alike—is a *kabocha* squash?

I thought about calling our friend Dan Kuebler, a local organic grower and member of the Columbia Farmers Market. Instead, I did a Google search and instantly had more information on the subject than one mind can imagine. Here is some of what I learned—

The *kabocha* (pronounced *ka BOW cha*) is a variety of winter squash commonly called Japanese pumpkin in Australia, New Zealand and Southeast Asia, and kabocha squash in North America. It is popular for its strong yet exceptionally sweet flavor like butternut squash or pumpkin and sweet potato combined. Its moist texture is

Cathy Salter

like chestnuts. An average kabocha weighs two to three pounds.

This squash variety is described as "hard, has knobby-looking skin, shaped like a squatty pumpkin, and has a dull colored deep green skin with some celadon-to-white colored stripes and an intense yellow-orange color on the inside." Reading the description, I realized to my delight that I actually had the very *cucurbita maxima*—otherwise know as kabocha squash—sitting in our kitchen vegetable bin. By chance, I had purchased it at our own local Farmers Market in Ashland.

Next, I searched for the perfect kabocha recipe. Heidi and Sugie prefer theirs simply roasted with a touch of salt. Kit and I will have ours roasted sweet and spicy with brown sugar, cayenne pepper, cumin, cinnamon, nutmeg, salt, soy sauce, and pumpkin seed oil for drizzling. Other Thanksgiving meal sides will include humble root vegetables pan-roasted with olive oil and rosemary, pureed garden green peas and mint, old-fashioned mashed potatoes, Salter family creamed corn, cranberry and orange relish, stuffed celery hearts, and buttery crescent rolls.

The two main courses will be pumpkin gnocchi with sage toasted in browned butter and quinoa pie with butternut squash. For dessert, traditional Riggs family pecan and pumpkin pies with homemade whipped cream will be served. At Sugie's request, a Missouri persimmon pie has been added to the dessert menu. What could be more delicious than a blending of traditional family favorites and new world possibilities this particularly glorious season of thanksgiving?

(November 2008)

WINTER PRESENT AND WINTER PAST

"*T*HE AMOUNT OF BROWN ON THE WOOLLY BEAR (that part in the middle) foretells the severity of the coming winter." So wrote Eric Sloane, a noted weather expert and painter as he collected bits of American folklore at Weather Hill Farm—his aptly named home in Cornwall Bridge, Connecticut. How exactly, I wondered, would I check a wooly bear's middle if one suddenly lumbered under our birdfeeder to pillage the oily sunflower seeds that keep our local flocks singing in temperatures that have plummeted to near zero?

Weather folklore also suggests that if turkey feathers are unusually thick by Thanksgiving, look for a hard winter. Another notes that a dark breastbone in a Thanksgiving Day turkey indicates a hardy winter to come. However the jury is still out on these theories and predictions, because this November turned out to be our first totally vegetarian Thanksgiving. Our menu was built instead around heirloom squashes, exotic grains, garden green peas, cranberries and pies filled with glorious pureed pumpkin meat and fat pecans. No flocks of wild turkeys visited our woods to inspect for feathery thickness. Thus, there was no breastbone to analyze and then simmer in a soup pot.

Lacking the presence of a wooly bear or a flock of wild Missouri turkeys to gauge the hardness of winter present, I turn instead to the wily squirrels that rule the lofty heights of the oaks, walnuts, cedars, ash, persimmons, and shagbark hickory trees that shelter our house. Last winter, there were no nuts or berries to speak of because of a late frost the prior spring. Hungry birds were in constant competition with lean squirrels and foraging deer for the rich mixture of seeds we supplied in the feeders throughout the long and spare winter months.

This year, following a spring abundant with rain, heavy nut-laden trees dropped buckets of acorns and walnuts throughout autumn. So fat they were a hazard for anyone negotiating our gravel driveway, these billiard ball-sized black walnuts were raked to the edges of the woods. Acorns aplenty were squirreled away soon after they hit the ground. As a consequence, not a single squirrel has tampered with the green metal squirrel guard suspended above our bird feeders. Boomerang Creek's squirrel population is fat and content in leafy nests easily detected these cold days in the bare upper reaches of our tallest trees. I imagine these scattered families of high-flying acrobats snugly bedded down in their insulated aerie abodes, rocked into cozy sleep by the wintry winds that have blasted the Midwest this December.

Snug in my writer's nest in my studio, I explore virtual weather patterns from one coast to the other and learn that "heavy weather" is pounding much of the northern United States. As cities from the Midwest to New England clean up after a major winter storm, the Northwest is braced for blizzards. Spokane, Washington records seventeen inches of snow. But what really catches my attention is news that ice-coated roads have led to school closings in Seattle, where two charter buses collided and skidded off a road.

News of buses traveling on ice-coated roads triggers images of an icy experience of my own four decades ago. That winter, the Greyhound bus on which I was traveling from New York City to Omaha, Nebraska drove directly into the center of an Iowa blizzard. Like Jonah entering the mouth of a great whale, the storm swallowed our bus and the road along with it. Windows frosted over from our anxious breathing as each passenger stared outward in an effort to discern anything at all—cattle huddled in a circle against the wind, a passing car, the distant lights of a lone farmhouse or small town or, we hoped, an exit sign to somewhere.

Without taking a vote, my fellow travelers and I shared a collective sense of confidence in our undaunted and incredibly brave driver—a man we had never actually met—literally entrusting him with our lives and fortunes, small as they were, for why otherwise would we have been thrown together on a Greyhound bus in the dead of winter, headed across Iowa in a raging snowstorm?

When I listen now to reports of freezing rain in these final days of December, I recall the collective sigh of relief as our bus driver geared down and exited Interstate 80 that brutal winter now long past, finally pulling to a stop at a hotel in an Iowa town whose name I've since forgotten. There were no vacancies when we arrived, but we were welcomed into the warm, dry lobby. There, gathering into pods here and there around the lobby's benches and open spaces, we weathered the storm as snug as the squirrels nesting in the trees at Boomerang Creek these frosty winter nights.

(December 2008)

AN ICE STORM CAME CALLING

J AM NOT CERTAIN WHAT WOKE ME early Sunday morning—
the thunderous crashing sounds echoing from the woods or an
awareness of being in total darkness. The ceiling fan over our bed
was motionless. The ambient green face of our digital clock radio had
gone dark. Another reverberating crash in the woods evoked images
of rival bucks clashing like cymbals, their massive antlers locked in
head-to-head combat.

The battle of nature that had begun in the night was in fact a
drama of Wagnerian proportions. Warm air flowing up from the
south had clashed with cold air descending from the north, resulting
in a destructive band of sleet and freezing rain that coated a wide
swath of Missouri in ice. Area-wide power outages resulted when tall,
dense trees sagged under the weight of ice-encrusted branches. In
random, rifle-like reports, crystalline limbs snapped like brittle bones,
shattering in explosive cascades onto roads, driveways, sidewalks,
rooftops, and power lines.

Adjusting to the darkness, I moved by memory toward the
kitchen, locating a flashlight, then a box of matches before heading
into the living room. The pine mantle above our hearth was decked
with holiday candles in hurricane lanterns. Before long, the room
glowed with soft yellow candlelight, and Kit had a fire crackling in
the Buck stove.

We later learned that the power had gone out around 5:30 a.m.—
the time I normally get up, head for the kitchen, and push the start
button on the coffee machine. Problem was, our entire house—kitchen
appliances, cordless phones, furnace, TV, radios, garage doors—is

powered by electricity. That Sunday morning and erratically over the two days following, the only power we had was of our own making.

Before doing battle with the elements, I was determined we would have hot coffee. The logical solution was to set up our Coleman stove. The problem was we were out of propane canisters. Undaunted, I searched through a storage unit in the basement, discovering my mother's copper chafing dish and stand. She used it to keep her spicy cheese dip hot when she and Dad entertained in the 1950s and 1960s. Recently, she gave it to me, along with two tins of Sterno canned-heat cooking fuel that must have been half a century old.

Back in the kitchen, I perched an aluminum stovetop coffee pot on the copper stand, pried open the Sterno lid, held a match to the surface and *violà*! Canned heat! Patiently we watched a delicate blue flame dance across the clear, jelly-like petroleum fuel, eager for the bubbling sound of hot water rising through coffee grounds like oil gushing up a well, announcing the magic of coffee. "This is like camping," Kit said as we warmed ourselves by the fire and sipped our hard-earned cups of coffee.

For breakfast that morning, Kit fired up the outdoor charcoal grill, made toast and cooked a fine ham and cheese omelet in my father's old cast iron skillet. Wanting to make use of the bed of hot coals, I cut up stew meat, dipped it in seasoned flour, and browned the meat before adding chopped onion, assorted root vegetables and broth. While we enjoyed our camp breakfast *al fresco*, the stew simmered under the grill's hood to a tender and delicious richness.

Later that morning, our daughter Heidi called from California to thank us for the cozy memories she has from thirty years ago in Los Angeles when we were a newly configured family of four. For ten years, we lived in an eight hundred square foot urban canyon cottage that radiated love and provided Heidi and her brother Hayden with memories they are now recreating for their own families.

Heidi's priceless call was received on a corded landline phone in the kitchen—our only functional phone during a power outage. Bits of news came in from friends and family throughout the day. When there was still no power by late afternoon, I searched for and finally located my father's old portable weather band radio. Powered by four fresh AA-batteries, the radio came to life with updates on the weather situation and a forecast of more of the same just as sleet and waning daylight began to fall.

That evening, Kit and I talked while watching the fire with our three cats curled up next to us, lost in their own state of feline bliss. In the background, Christmas songs on a country radio station could be heard on Dad's little black weather radio, interrupted by occasional announcements of school cancellations across the listening area. We read our novels aided by two flashlights and noted with awe that Jane Austen and the Brontë sisters created their timeless literary masterpieces without ever experiencing the wonder of electricity.

At the close of the day, still without power, we recalled the ways my parents' two gifts had aided us that day. Finally, we gave thanks for the Boone Electric and Ameren linemen who would be working on through the icy nights and days ahead, restoring power to rural customers like us while their own families eagerly awaited their safe return.

The next day, we learned of widespread ice damage to venerable trees in the Ashland area. A Boone Electric crew repairing a power line down Liberty Lane told Kit that Hartsburg looked like a tornado had hit the town. Our friends Jane and Dick Flink had trees and branches fall on their house at Lake Champetra and reported that one of their neighbors was tragically killed when an ice-encrusted tree fell on him.

Two friends who live in a heavily wooded area ten miles north of Ashland never lost power while some thirty thousand customers in Jefferson City reported they experienced power outages by Wednesday afternoon. Monday, our own power came on, and promptly went off again. I reported the outage to Susan at Boone Electric who hadn't seen her husband—a lineman for the cooperative—since the ice began wreaking havoc. Two Boone Electric linemen who were already in the area soon arrived, got us back on the grid, and happily accepted apples, two ham and cheese sandwiches and a can of Pringles as they left to help their next customer. Two hours later, a major line break undid their heroic efforts, this time affecting an even wider area.

Not knowing how long we could count on power once it came on again, Kit set off for Columbia to stock up on emergency supplies. Propane for the camp stove and Sterno were high on the list. We have a Coleman stove, but until this storm, Kit's charcoal grill had served all of our outdoor cooking needs. It hadn't occurred to us when the weathercasters warned of ice and freezing rain late Saturday that a prolonged power outage might be headed our way.

Fortunately, we had plenty of flashlight batteries, matches and boxes of utility candles on hand. What we needed was more ice melt and a few grocery items. Otherwise, I figured we could eat from our pantry for some time. Before leaving, Kit threw several densely packed tubes of sand in the truck bed for additional ballast.

While the power was still on, I put a whole chicken and assorted root vegetables in the oven to roast. Then, slipping into boots secured with Yak Trax ice grippers, I headed outside with my camera to capture images of ice. Every limb, leaf, object and blade of grass that I focused on was encased in solid ice. The flag at the end of our covered porch hung frozen stiff on its pole. As I reached to take it down, the crunching of footsteps on ice announced a visitor emerging from our woods.

I looked up to find it was our self-reliant neighbor, Fran, rosy-cheeked and fully geared for the weather. She needed to borrow power. While ours had returned that morning, she and her husband Frank were still without electricity. A fireplace kept their house warm enough, but their four-week old litter of eleven puppies was not at all happy about being in a dark garage. Moved by Fran's positive "can do" spirit, I located three outdoor extension cords; then the two of us secured the first of them in an exterior outlet. Mission accomplished,

Fran trekked off through the woods with hundreds of feet of makeshift power lifeline trailing like an orange snake behind her.

Kit returned with supplies and news that main roads were mostly clear, but gravel side roads were a solid sheet of ice. Late that afternoon, Roger—a neighbor from farther down our road—was on his way home from Moser's, where he works in the meat department. A passing trailer swung wide to avoid him and ended up sideways at the end of our driveway. Another neighbor, Rick Richardson, just home from two non-stop days with a crew clearing airport runways, spent an hour and a half helping Roger clear our road.

We called Fran and Frank who still had no power and invited them to join us for a roast chicken dinner and conversation by the fire. They arrived with a bottle of homemade rum eggnog and reported that a Boone Electric crew was at that very moment working in the icy dark woods behind their house in an effort to replace their downed power pole.

The four of us gave thanks that evening for the efforts and sacrifices of the power crews and volunteers across the region. Neighbors help neighbors, friends stay in touch, and emergency crews brave the elements. Such is the blessed nature of life in the country when an ice storm comes calling.

(December 2007)

Part Three

TALES FROM NEAR AND FAR

*W*HEN YOU LIVE IN THE COUNTRY, tales sometimes begin on a simple errand into town. And more often than not, they have to do with a pickup truck. As in life, there are bumps in the road that caution us to slow down, and occasional slow leaks and flats that need fixing. We learn from each experience, all the better for having dealt with adversity square on. And soon, we are back on the road again, and the detour along the way becomes a tale worthy of telling.

C.S. June 2015

Chapter Ten
LOCAL STORIES

Mr. Forsee's pickup truck probably moved though most of its first two and a half decades unnoticed and unheralded by anyone except its owner, until I saw it for the first time the morning I took my truck to Rice's Garage for its annual inspection. I was late, but needn't have worried. Time, along with the overhead ceiling fan in Rice's office and waiting room seemed to have ground to a stop. It was 1967 again in the service bay.

C.S. June 1997

PICKUP STORIES

*I*N UNPACKING THE BOXES FROM OUR MOVE from Albuquerque back to southern Boone County in the fall of 2005, I came across a *Ralph Lauren Country Home* 1995 fall catalogue. The catalogue was open to a picture of a 1948 Chevy half-ton pickup truck parked next to a weathered barn lined with rambling black raspberry canes. In the lower right-hand corner of the page, I read the particulars. "3100 series. Six-cylinder engine. All original parts, restored from the ground up. Deluxe cab, rear-corner windows, fat fenders, chrome grill, running boards, original color (burgundy), $16,500.00."

The American truck seems to have a language of its own. The two men in flannel shirts pictured sitting in the parked pickup each have an elbow resting outside the rolled down door windows. Above them on the page are lines in bold black suggesting their thoughts.

I have owned three pickup trucks since moving to the country seventeen years ago. The first was a 1991 Chevy S-10 Durango that I bought in Jefferson City, Missouri on a blizzardy Friday in late December when Kit convinced me the dealership would be eager to move inventory at a bargain price because no one in their right mind would be out shopping for a new car or truck on such a miserable day. My pickup was cherry red, and I loved driving it with the windows down and Willie Nelson in the tape deck along for the ride.

Over the years the color mellowed and rust ate its way into the truck's doors and underbelly, but it never failed to garner nods of approval and half-waves from the steering hand of other pickup drivers in passing. A few years back Rob Sherman re-painted the S-10's body and retarded the creeping rust. Jimmy Nichols never stopped asking if I wanted to sell it.

It made the drive to New Mexico in March 2005, but like me was never happy there. For the move, we put a camper top on its previously open bed that had carried endless bales of straw; deconstructed logs from an 1860s cabin from Rich Fountain, Missouri that Larry Hall helped us reconstruct in the pasture at Breakfast Creek; and countless pieces of history acquired at local auctions over the years. In Albuquerque, it sat idle most of the time in a relic driveway in front of an old garage used for storage. Parts began to fail, the radio went silent, and its once free spirit faded in the high desert sun.

While my S-10 appeared cherry on the outside, corrosive road salt over fourteen Missouri winters had done their damage to the undercarriage. We traded her in for a 2002 Toyota Tacoma pickup that was rust-free when we decided to pack it up and move back to Boone County. Within days of our arrival, the Tacoma was registered and the B-CREEK plates that I'd kept from the old S-10 were in place. If trucks could talk, mine would say that our new property, Boomerang Creek, has felt like home from that day on.

While Kit and I were living in Albuquerque, we drove up to Santa Fe for the day from time to time when friends and family visited. Without fail, we visited a tiny gallery owned by Barbara Boyles who calls herself a "pickup artist." Her gallery walls are covered with colorful photographs printed on linen paper of old rusted pickup trucks. Truck details are captured at close range. To her artist's eye, a Chevy grill becomes a totem; an old NM license plate edged with fading colors captures the Land of Enchantment's earth and sky at sunset. Each image becomes a work of art.

Boomerang Creek came with its own yard art installation—a 1950 Ford Street Rod half-ton pickup with an Arizona Grand Canyon State license plate that reads "1 Bad 50." The property's prior owners put the Rod out to pasture years ago and generously left it for us. Since moving in, I've had at least five men offer to "get rid of that old piece of junk" for me and each time I've told them the same thing that I used to say when Jimmy Nichols would try to get me to sell my red Chevy Durango.

"Not a chance, Jimmy. I'm keeping it forever."

Only this time, I will. The Street Rod has a sapling growing up through a missing floorboard and back out the passenger window. Like me, it has put down roots after an earlier life along highways distant from this quiet place off a two-lane country road. Being of almost the same vintage, the Rod and I both feel at home here and have no plans to drive off into the sunset anytime soon.

(January 2006)

SLOW LEAKS AND FLATS

*I*T WAS A SIMPLE ERRAND. Drive into Ashland. Fill up the truck at Casey's. Make a quick stop at Moser's for milk and a loaf of rye bread, deposit a check at the bank and stop at the Post Office on the return drive through town. Then it was home for a bite of lunch in our freshly painted creamy white kitchen. That was all that needed to be done before meeting Kit in Columbia later that evening.

Driving a ribbon of two-lane country road into town, I listened to the soundtrack from *Brokeback Mountain*, a film based on a short story by Annie Proulx who lives and writes in Wyoming. I have just re-read the story in her book *Close Range* and am eager to see director Ang Lee's film adaptation of the story. Like Proulx's sparse prose, the music evokes stark, wind-blown landscapes and the lonesome, hard-scrabble stories of those who play out their lives where, as one Wyoming rancher put it, "reality's never been of much use out here."

While in town, I filled up the truck and noticed that prices were back up and the truck was sorely ready for a trip to the car wash. Normally I'd have worn my daily uniform—a worn-in pair of jeans and a barn jacket—but on this particular day I had a dinner date with Kit who was headed home from a four-day trip to the East coast. The mud on the driver's side of the truck made me wish that I'd left the brown velvet skirt and white jacket in the closet and dressed in my jeans that never look the worse for wear after a little brush with mud or grime.

After carefully hoisting up my skirt and stepping onto the gravel dust encrusted running board, I managed to make a clean landing in the driver's seat and headed out east Broadway to Moser's Grocery

Store. Chicken breasts, Farmland Lower Sodium bacon and milk joined the rye bread in my basket along with chicken broth for the risotto dish I was planning for the following evening. No time for my usual chat with Fox in the meat department or a leisurely perusal of the aisles. I still had two more errands in town and needed to head for home.

But I soon learned that I wasn't going anywhere anytime soon. My beautiful black pickup's thick-walled, treaded-for-rough-wear, back right rear tire was flat out of air. All I could think of at the time was "this was a stupid day to have worn a skirt into town."

My only prior problem with tires was in May of 1995 when I'd picked up a nail driving out to help in a sandbagging effort in Hartsburg. It developed into a slow, annoying leak that I dealt with by simply adding more air when it looked low. After putting off the inevitable, I finally drove it to the old Rice's Garage in Ashland to have the hole patched. The slow leak, I remember thinking, was a message to slow down, deal with what needs fixing, learn from the experience, and get on with life.

This time, however, I was dealing with more than a slow leak. The rim was on the pavement. I would have to call AAA, I thought. But that is not what happened. A kind friend emerged from Moser's, drove to Wren's garage in Ashland to get an air tank, drove back, and pumped up the tire so it was drivable. I was soon on my way to Wren's garage to get the now inflated tire looked at and hopefully repaired.

I was in luck. In no time my truck was in one of Wren's service bays where the tire was quickly removed, freed of its rim, and dunked in a water tank until a bubble led us to the problem that had me there in the first place.

While the hole was patched and the repaired tire switched with a brand new spare, I walked to the bank and post office. It was a crisp, clear day and the cold air felt wonderful on my face. I was thankful for the help from my friend in the parking lot at Moser's, for Wren's efficient service on a minute's notice, and glad not to be alone on

Cathy Salter

some desolate road out in the middle of nowhere in one of Annie Proulx's Wyoming stories—flat out and friendless.

There are bumps in the road, I thought as I climbed up into my truck after my hour-long detour, and this year has certainly had its share. But as with slow leaks and flats, if we deal with them square on, we can get back on the road again and more critically, find our way home.

(January 2006)

CELEBRATING THE QUILTERS OF TWO RIVER TOWNS

*O*BSERVED OVER TIME, a river can be seen as having a life of its own. After flowing in an historically described channel, waters erode, change course, create oxbows and islands of isolation, intermittently dry up and periodically flood its banks. River towns and bottomland are enriched some years and devastated others. Rivers define both the places and the people whose lot it is to live out their lives nearby. Generations of quilters from Hartsburg, Missouri, and Gee's Bend, Alabama, will tell you this is so.

In 1994, I researched and edited a centennial history of Hartsburg's Peace Church—founded in 1894 as *Friedens Evangelische Gemeinde* by German farmers who felt a strong desire for a church in which they could worship in their language and according to their customs. In the process, I learned of the central role that quilting has played in the life of Peace Church for more than a century.

Almost from the beginning, the women of the church organized a benevolent society around the art of quilting. Piecing quilt tops and quilting became a method for women at Peace Church (today called the Circle) to earn money to send to orphanages and missions in Missouri and other states as well. Following the example of earlier women's organizations at Peace Church, the Circle earns money for its benevolent activities by making quilts on consignment for members of the community. The Circle also funds numerous activities that help maintain the church and support disaster relief victims in the area. When friends and relatives are ill, the Circle women donate a lap-sized prayer quilt to speed their recovery.

While researching the Peace Church history, I interviewed

Dorothy Bockhorst—a venerable Circle member by then—who had attended early Benevolent Society meetings with her grandmother and learned by watching her quilt. Carmen Hughes, who had never quilted before moving with her family to Hartsburg in the mid 1970s, has been a Circle regular ever since. Newcomers are welcome to join Circle members as they share lunch and commune around the quilting frame in the church basement on the second Thursday of each month.

For the past two decades, Kit and I have hung quilts as works of art and slept under others in the cold months of winter. In addition to locally made traditional quilts, we came to admire the artistry of classic Amish quilts—those conceived and stitched by women of Lancaster County, Pennsylvania from 1870 to 1950. Their geometric patterns—homemade creations of practicality and simplicity—also reflected the essence of Amish principles. For their bold colors and purity of design, they have been recognized as true works of American art.

But it was only when our October 2007 issue of *Smithsonian Magazine* arrived that we discovered the artistry of the quilters of Gee's Bend. In the article, "Fabric of our Lives," *New York Times* art critic Michael Kimmelman describes the "eye-poppingly gorgeous Gee's Bend" quilts as "some of the most miraculous works of modern art America has produced. Imagine Matisse and Klee arising not from rarefied Europe, but from the caramel soil of the rural South."

These novel quilters are all African-American descendants of former slaves from Gee's Bend—a community established in 1816 by Joseph Gee as a cotton plantation on an almost completely isolated, island-like bend in the Alabama River. Following the Civil War came years of hardscrabble life for this population as tenant farmers. Meager government support dissipated and cotton farming continued to decline in the 1920s and 1930s.

During this period, Gee's Bend residents faced starvation and grew increasingly cut off from social and economic development in the rest of the country. Ultimately, the government purchased the land in Gee's Bend from white owners, sold it back to the African-American farmers at a dollar an acre, and built new homes to replace existing log cabins. Over time, the town's struggles and the story of its survival were passed on in songs sung by the women of Gee's Bend and in the recycled fabrics that found new life in their quilts.

That same fall, Kit and I visited our friends Judith McCandless and Grady Clay in Louisville, KY, when the Gee's Bend quilt exhibition was featured at the Speed Art Museum. The exhibition features seventy quilts created by more than fifty women spanning four generations. Early quilts were made of blocks and strips of worn denim, cotton, and corduroy work clothes as their function was keeping families warm in the winter months and comfortable the rest of the year. From 1945 to the present, bold combinations of broad, abstract patterning and vibrant colors are found in quilts now being seen as masterpieces of contemporary American art, not just functional decorations.

Quilts are the histories of individuals and times captured in materials and forms from the past and present. In Hartsburg and Gee's Bend, two towns that have survived time and the power of nearby rivers, the art of quilting—still vibrantly alive and unifying—is transforming the way many people think about art.

(June 2008)

NORTON GRAPE HARVEST AT BECKMEYER VINEYARD

*W*HEN KIT AND I MOVED to Southern Boone County in the fall of 1988, we were surprised to learn that by 1866, Missouri was the second largest wine growing state in the Union. On a road trip to Hermann, we visited Stone Hill Winery, established in 1843, just four decades after William Clark—co-leader of the 1804-1806 Lewis and Clark Expedition—noted *the abundance of ripe summer grapes along the lower stretches of the Missouri* while passing through the territory. By the turn of the century, Hermann's Stone Hill Winery was the third largest winery in the world.

Over the past two decades, the explosion of the wine industry worldwide has reshaped our mental map of where grapes are and can be grown. Today, a trip to the wine section of your local grocery store is a rich geography lesson featuring excellent wines from Southern Hemisphere vineyards in Australia and Chile, as well as award-winning local Missouri wines from grapes grown in Rocheport, Westphalia and Hartsburg.

In June 2012, Kit and I took the Osher Lifelong Learning wine class we were teaching on a tour and wine tasting at the Beckmeyer vineyard in Hartsburg. Thirteen years earlier, our farmer friends Orion and Barbara Beckmeyer spent the summer clearing four acres of sloping pastureland of scrubby thorn brush and dared to imagine a vineyard where cattle had previously grazed. Massive Osage orange posts were sunk as anchors at either end of each wine row and support wires were stretched taut. Finally two thousand, four hundred sticklike vines were planted along the rows—three acres of white Chardonel grapes and one acre of Missouri's prized red Norton grape.

In 2002, summer's harvest provided a modest crush of Beckmeyer grapes bottled by Thornhill Winery—a Hartsburg business operated at the time by Diane and Bob Holland, the Beckmeyer's neighbors. A year later, plentiful spring rains followed by weeks of hot, dry weather blessed the fledgling vineyard with near perfect conditions. By the end of July 2003, vines reached over our heads, forming a cool canopy of broad grape leaves that sheltered tight clusters of luscious grapes from the relentless sun of late August.

During the first week of September 2003, John Held from Stone Hill Winery drove over from Hermann to sample the Beckmeyer's grapes himself. Impressed with their quality, he sent two flatbed trucks, each carrying deep bins to contain the harvested grapes and stacks of yellow plastic baskets for the picking crew. To do a crush, Stone Hill required a minimum of ten tons of Chardonel grapes picked in a single day.

On a brilliant September Sunday morning that year, fifty-one volunteers—fellow farmers, students, retired friends, Hartsburg neighbors, local church members, sons, daughters, and grandchildren—gathered at eight o'clock for a moment of prayer before filtering out into the vineyard to bring in the harvest.

We came with gardening shears, bottles of water, broad-brimmed hats and baseball caps, sun block and insect repellant, sunglasses, and boundless optimism. Our instructions were to cut double clusters at their wishbone joint, and dig out any moldy grapes before tossing the bunches into the plastic baskets. Periodically, an ATV (All Terrain Vehicle) pulling a small trailer would drive down the rows collecting full containers of grapes that were then dumped into the bins lined up on Stone Hill's flat bed trailers.

By late afternoon, the harvesting motion had become rhythmical. Sunlight turned sunburned grapes high on the vines into transparent globes of hot liquid ready to explode with sweetness. Eyes strained in the bright white brilliance of a cloudless sky, and bees hovering under broad leaves joined in the cacophony of buzzing conversations that hummed up and down each row. By dark, eleven tons of grapes had been picked and lay resting in their bins, ready for a dawn delivery to Stone Hill Winery where they would be cooled and crushed.

Nearly a decade later, volunteers gathered on Labor Day 2012 to pick the crop of Beckmeyer Vineyard Norton grapes. The exceptionally dry summer and Orion's attention to irrigating his acres of grapes produced a harvest of nearly perfect Norton clusters of deep bluish-purple grapes that filled thirteen enormous bins by the end of the day.

Beckmeyer Nortons are now happily fermenting and being prepared for blending with Terry Neuner's Nortons, picked the same day at the Westphalia Vineyard. "A miracle," those who picked grapes at both vineyards that day would say.

"God's plan," Orion, the Beckmeyer vinedresser, will tell you.

"Amen," Terry Neuner would echo, "Amen."

(October 2012)

CELEBRATING LIFE WITH LOUISE

*T*HE FINAL WEEK OF JUNE, LOUISE DUSENBERY, a friend and neighbor since our move to Missouri in 1988, turned ninety. For the sixteen years that we lived at Breakfast Creek, Louise was our source of information about country life at the southern end of Boone County. When Kit and I moved to Boomerang Creek a decade ago, Louise sold her country home of forty years, and without a blink bought a home in Ashland two miles from ours. There, she stays busy planting trees, creating gazing ball gardens and mowing her yard just as soon as the last snow of winter has come and gone.

Did I mention that at ninety, Louise still mows her own yard with a red Craftsman sit-down mower—a job that took two days at her former ten-acre spread on Westbrook Drive? That expansive yard was golf course gorgeous, leading us to joke about bringing in a tour bus of golfers and turning them loose with their putters. We also thought about taping lawnmower sounds during the summer to play under her bedroom window in the dead of winter.

On Louise's birthday, we invited the old gang—Louise, Larry Hall and Diana Hallett—for dinner to swap tall tales from our shared adventures while neighbors on Westbrook Drive. Kit had shined and waxed his spiffy red Craftsman mower and parked it near the porch hoping for a birthday photo-op of Louise in the driver's seat at ninety. Not to be outdone by my Aunt Lou who recently rode a horse on her one hundredth birthday, Louise rose to the challenge, swung her leg effortlessly over the seat, posed with a red felt cowgirl hat on her head, and looked like she hadn't aged a day since we first met.

Recalling that birthday night, I am enormously thankful for all that I've learned from Louise about life in the country, hedge apples, seed ticks, dividing irises, local lore, and living life to the fullest. "You may think my life has been dull," she said when we asked her to talk about reaching ninety, "but it hasn't been." Not for a minute, you can be sure. And for me, life with Louise as our neighbor and wise country sage has been an adventure from the get go.

Not one to sit still, Louise has traveled to nearly every state, taken a cruise on the St. Lawrence River, seen the tall ships in New York Harbor, explored Washington D.C., and helped stuff ten thousand four hundred seventy roses into an award-winning float for the Pasadena Rose Parade. When elected President of the Ashland Garden Club a few years back, she asked me what she should try to accomplish. "Plant street trees," I said. "Ashland needs some eyebrows."

She never got City Hall to buy the idea, but under her square-shouldered leadership, she and her amazing club members created perennial flower gardens up and down Broadway. In 1993, they won the top individual award for civic development from the National Council of State Garden Clubs. Louise and club member Carl Henry drove to Asheville, North Carolina to accept the national award.

"I'm slowing down a bit now," Louise conceded after dinner. But knowing Louise, I am guessing not much. So far, she's had thirty-seven friends call to sing *Happy Birthday* to her. She has a new mega puzzle to assemble, and she keeps busy with weekly card games when she's not playing pool at the Senior Center or out walking her cocker spaniel.

Walking with Louise to her car, I said, "The next time you drive down to your hometown of Van Buren, I want to ride shotgun." No doubt we will try to change each other's politics as we have done to no avail for the past quarter of a century, and she will suggest that we stop for a "POP" dinner—pizza, Oreos and Pepsi. What can I say? Life with Louise is a trip, one that I love sharing as her longtime neighbor and pal.

(June 2014)

CHERRY PICKING TIME

*I*T WAS AT ERNA BECKMEYER'S INVITATION that I tasted my first, fresh-off-the-tree, Montmorency cherry. Al and Erna's cherry trees—the largest being more than half a century old—were laden that June with a bumper crop of sour cherries. I'm guessing it was planted after the couple bought land along Route A and moved from their original farmhouse in the Hartsburg Bottoms following the third summer of flooding down there in the 1940s.

Like the Chardonel, Norton, and Chambourcin wine grapes grown by their son Orion and his wife Barbara Beckmeyer on their adjacent farm, these "cherry pie" cherries have to be harvested at the moment of peak ripeness. When that moment arrives, word goes out to neighbors inviting them to come pick as soon as possible—before eager birds impatient to feast on the tempting red fruit stripped the branches clean.

That year, I picked cherries off branches so heavy with fruit that they touched the ground, and I climbed ladders to reach the sun-kissed, reddest, sweetest cherries at the top of the tree. Pickers had already stripped two small trees the day before, but the old parent tree stood waiting for anyone with the gumption to climb a tall ladder and time to spare. Orion set up the ladders, and then left me to my morning's meditation. For the next two hours, I was alone with the birds and the bees while the morning sun warmed my freckled shoulders and an occasional breeze cooled the sweat beading along my brow.

From atop a tall ladder, I had a bird's-eye view of the shiny corrugated Beckmeyer Farm grain bins just across the road. Beyond

Cathy Salter

them, hills roll gently toward the Missouri River as it winds its way toward Jefferson City. Three of the bins had been deconstructed and trucked up from the Hartsburg Bottoms after the flood of 1993 knocked them catawampus. Then, on a night I will always remember, a dance took place under a full August moon on the giant circles of concrete flooring that had been poured as foundations for the soon-to-be relocated bins.

When I finished picking, I stopped in to visit with Erna and shared a bowl of broccoli soup her daughter Janet had made the day before. Then, I drove home with four or five large Central Dairy ice cream containers filled with juicy pie cherries nested in the bed of my cherry red Chevy pick up.

For anyone familiar with this heartland summer tradition, picking is just the first step in the labor-intensive journey one must be willing to undertake before cherries can be canned as a jam or preserve, boiled and reduced to a bounce, or baked and latticed into a pie. Pitting—an arduous, time-consuming, one-cherry-at-a-time, hand-eye coordination-challenging, juice-all-over-the-place operation—comes next.

My base of operation was the kitchen sink where I positioned one bowl of cherries, a dish for the pits, and a large measuring cup to receive the pitted cherries. My cherry pitter is a handheld, scissor-like tool into which you insert a single cherry. When the handle is closed, a spike drives the pit out of the cherry and through a small opening at the base.

After two hours of pie-pitting labor, I had a pile of cherry pits and approximately eight cups of pitted cherries—enough for two small pies or one and a half deep-dish pies. During that repetitive process, I listened to two audiobook discs of *Pride and Prejudice*, practiced ballet in place (*pliés* in third position while facing the sink), and meditated on a singular moment that morning when reaching up for a cluster of red cherries through green leaves, I was struck by the true blueness of the June Missouri sky.

Kit and I recently added a Montmorency cherry tree to the orchard at Boomerang Creek, and friend David Allen has given me a super duper, top-of-the-line cherry pitter. The Beckmeyers parent Montmorency cherry tree is no longer standing, but at age one hundred, Erna continues to enjoy life one day at a time.

(August 2014)

Chapter Eleven
A World of Gardens

There is too much working in my own head this morning to just sit. I will write about it instead. Imagine it. Capture it in words, and in that way, be able to share the moment with others. Maybe they will have the time and the patience to witness one of spring's unfurlings in their own backyard.

C.S. May 1994

The Urgency of Spring

*G*ARDENS TAKE ROOT IN THE IMAGINATION. Some are simple, contained in pots conveniently arranged on a porch. Others are over the moon. Whatever the size and scale, when spring arrives with the urgency that it has this year, there is little else on a gardener's mind than gardening. For me, no matter how full the calendar or hectic the pace, a day finally arrives when I simply can no longer resist the urge to tackle the task of readying the gardens at Boomerang Creek for spring.

This year, with March one of the warmest on record and a week of soft, intermittent rain, spring exploded onto the scene all at once. Every fruit tree in the orchard is in bloom. Trees are leafing out. Purple redbud blossoms spill randomly through the woods as if nature had flicked her artist's brush with abandon across the landscape, transforming the season as if by magic from winter to spring.

Grass greened overnight. Hellebore plants, green all winter, sent forth new leaves and produced Lenten roses in perfect sync with the calendar they follow religiously every spring. Impatient daffodils trumpeted their arrival a full month before Easter. Not to be left behind, the perennial footprint of hostas, peonies, bleeding hearts, oriental lilies, ancient native ferns, astilbes, irises and cosmos began pushing up against the thick bed of dry leaves still blanketing the shade garden.

Not for another day could my inner gardener ignore the signs of spring's urgent arrival. Fanny, our stealthy vole hunter, blends in perfectly with the dry leaves. Of late, she'd been delivering victims to me caught after patiently watching their ever-so-slight movements under the garden's dry leaf cover. She is not happy with my decision to clean out the shade garden, thus exposing her hunting ground to the light. "Forget the voles and focus on the moles," I urged. "They are a real problem this year. A can of tuna will be your reward."

With a shade garden as expansive as ours, I divide my tasks like slices of a pie. One segment at a time, I rake away leaves, then remove by hand the pungent smelling, invasive groundcover that has already insinuated itself throughout the garden. With leaves and groundcover gone, the footprint of emerging perennials is fixed. Leaf piles along the edge of the garden are then collected in a barrow and wheeled into the woods where they will decompose and feed the trees. Finally, seasoned mulch generously shared with us last fall by Boone Electric Cooperative during tree trimming season is broadcast throughout the garden, dressing it beautifully for the dance of the flowers to come.

Gardening is a bit like writing. Lost in the task at hand, the mind wanders about, grabbing hold of thoughts that float like aerie dandelion seeds set sail by a passing breeze. I make a mental inventory of gardening chores that will still not be done at day's end. The meadow garden and rose beds need cleaning out. Dead asparagus ferns have been cut back, but the bed itself needs weeding and mulching before the first green spears push up.

Cathy Salter

Then there is the perennial question of what this year's meadow garden will be. Tilled, it can once again be a high maintenance vegetable bed. But I've been adding berry bushes and may add a few blueberry bushes this spring. Cilantro, bronze fennel and lavender grow wild in this bed, require almost no care, and reward us from spring through fall with little work or attention. And then, the Ashland's Farmers Market and the Southern Boone Learning Garden are always eager to supply what our garden has not.

Nurture and maintain the gardens we already have, I decide. Then my thoughts follow other passions, writing and painting, that are pulling at me these days. Finally, hours later, I come in from the garden, aching and smelling of dirt. As writer Margaret Atwood once noted on the subject of spring gardening, that is precisely as it should be.

(March 2012)

Equinoctial Musings

*T*HE FARMERS WHO LIVE ON WHITE FLOWER FARM in Litchfield, Connecticut have been plantsmen since 1950. That same year, barely five years old, I watched my father pull a carrot from our backyard vegetable plot in Roswell, New Mexico. From that magic instant on, I was a gardener at heart.

Recently, a spring catalog arrived from White Flower Farm with some equinoctial musings penned by Amos Pettingill, a character invented by the nursery's founders who recounts interesting things about plants and the seasons. *"Dear Friends,"* Amos begins, before noting that March 21 was the date that the sun's daily path crossed the equator to the north, marking the arrival of longer days and shorter nights.

Winter from Amos's Northeast corner at White Flower Farm has been *"stunningly long, cold, and deep, with patterns of temperatures and snowfall the region has not seen since the 1970s."* Now with spring officially on the calendar, the threat to gardens, Pettingill warns, is no longer the heaving and drying caused by a rugged winter or low temperatures, but rather...

> *...an equally threatening element is the over-enthusiastic gardener, the kind who seizes upon the first warm day to begin grubbing around in the ground, disturbing the soil, displacing the mulch, and man-handling plants which may look dead but are often merely dormant.*

Duly warned, I still could not resist getting out into the gardens last week ahead of a cold front predicted to drop March temperatures back into the twenties for three nights. Our friend, Greg Busacker dropped off four bags of compressed ProMix—each 3.5 cubic feet in size and like lifting a small calf in heft. Kit then arranged for Crazy Dick, owner of Ashland's local landscape garden shop, to deliver a truckload of cedar mulch that I wanted for dressing our gardens, shrubs, and fruit trees.

Taken together, the tasks ahead of me seemed indomitable, like learning to identify the world of birdsong in a single afternoon. "One bird at a time," my friend Pat Fennell reminded me recently when she called from Los Angeles. Taking her advice, that is exactly how the job of preparing our gardens for spring was accomplished. The cold frame was weeded and refreshed with ProMix for the salad greens soon to be sown. Asparagus and raspberry beds, blueberry plants and fruit trees all had shovels full of ProMix applied and a deep ring of mulch added at the base.

Hosta beds next to the porch have been raked, fertilized and mulched ahead of their annual spring reawakening and the unfurling of their massive elephantine leaves. Raised peony and strawberry beds, rows of crepe myrtle shrubs, lavender mounds, rows of golden fennel and perennial cilantro, butterfly bushes and hibiscus have all been attended to.

In the course of three days, all four bags of ProMix were dispersed and a second truckload of cedar mulch had been ordered. Working with wheelbarrow, pitchfork, and gloved hands, the dead-looking meadow garden, raised beds, and hosta border along the porch were dressed for spring—one load of ProMix and honey-colored cedar mulch at a time.

On the final sunny afternoon before temperatures plunged, roses in a circular bed in the meadow were cut back and mulched. Time will tell how many have survived winter's harsh temperature fluctuations. Should we lose a few, Amos Pettingill recommends pairing a buttery gold Julia Child rose with the fragrance of licorice and cloves with White Flower Farm's dusky, deep purple Ebb Tide Floribunda. Together, the roses evoke the exotic colors woven into the carpet that I purchased in Istanbul this past January.

Amazingly, Istanbul was experiencing spring temperatures that week. The 2014 Winter Olympics were about to get underway in Sochi, and the Crimean Peninsula was still a part of the Ukraine. Flowers were in bloom in gardens and parks in Istanbul's Old City. How sad that, as spring is at last unfolding at Boomerang Creek, this strategic region bordering the Black Sea is now facing a chillingly uncertain spring of discontent.

(March 2014)

America's Edible Schoolyard Gardens

*S*IX MONTHS AGO, FIRST LADY MICHELLE OBAMA and students from D.C.'s Bancroft Elementary School broke ground for the first White House Kitchen Garden since Eleanor Roosevelt championed Victory Gardens during the Second World War. The event landed Mrs. Obama's initiative on the front page of both *the Washington Post* and *the New York Times,* and made international news. This effort to teach children better eating habits by helping them understand where food comes from is not a new idea, but it has struck a chord with food-conscious Americans concerned about the spiking growth rate in obesity and juvenile diabetes.

In late September at the opening of the new Farmers Market by the White House, Mrs. Obama spoke of the White House Kitchen Garden as "one of the greatest things I've done in my life so far." Whenever she travels overseas, "the garden is the first thing that prime ministers, kings and queens ask about." (Queen Elizabeth has in fact added a vegetable garden at Buckingham Palace.) At the Pittsburgh Summit 2009, G-20 spouses received a porcelain tea set and vase filled with honey harvested from the White House apiary's beehives. The kitchen garden provides food for the White House as well a Washington, D.C. social services agency called Miriam's Kitchen. Most importantly, it is helping to change the way Americans think about food, cooking and agriculture.

Alice Waters, a revolutionary natural-foods chef, couldn't be happier. Thirty-eight years ago she began her own organic Chez Panisse Restaurant in Berkeley, California and has been influencing the way America eats ever since. Fifteen years ago, Alice drove past Berkeley's run-down Martin Luther King Middle School and envisioned converting the school's acre of blacktop into an edible schoolyard garden. Last Fall, she published *Edible Schoolyard: A Universal Idea*, chronicling the story of her collaboration with MLK School's principal, the PTA, teachers, students, and parents.

In the fall of 2009, eighty elementary students applied to participate in the Southern Boone Learning Garden's after school program, now in its third year. Already, primary classes have made clay toad houses. After school, young Learning Gardeners are constructing imaginative scarecrows. In the garden just west of Ashland's primary and elementary schools, children can harvest cherry and plum tomatoes, pick basil and parsley, arrange vibrant red and purple zinnias, explore a cattle panel tunnel where enormous gourds hang down overhead, and look up into the faces of giant sunflowers planted months ago.

Like Ashland's Coyote Farmers Market that began with a dream and is now in its second successful year of operation, the Southern Boone Learning Garden has captured the hearts of the community. Kim Ponder, the local PTA President, has submitted a grant application to the National PTA's Healthy Lifestyles program centered on a community workday to build a greenhouse at the current garden location. Dan Nelson, a Moberly area farmer who sells produce at the Columbia and Coyote Farmers Markets, is also an active member of the Learning Garden's steering committee. Dan has enrolled the Learning Garden in the National Farm to School program—a program in at least seventeen states working to support their agricultural economy and their school children's health.

At a recent kindergarten-college level geography conference in Puerto Rico, I attended a presentation by Meredith Beilfuss, a Butler University geography professor, on Edible Schoolyards. She has put me in touch with the College School in St. Louis—a creative learning school with a theme-based, experiential curriculum. This independent, adventurous school has an active garden and greenhouse program for students from pre-school through the eighth grade. As part of their experiential education, students learn about the importance of healthy food, where it comes from, the natural connections between plants and animals, and the importance of biodiversity.

During this year's Pumpkin Festival in Hartsburg, the Learning Garden will have an information booth at the old General Store on Second Street with a donation jar and flyers about the program. Festival attendees are encouraged to stop by, sign up as a volunteer, and learn just what's cooking in Ashland's edible schoolyard learning garden. In the meantime, I am busy writing to the First Lady in hopes that she will find a way to visit our incredible Southern Boone Learning Garden. On my next trip to Washington, you can bet I'll be looking for a way to visit the White House kitchen garden.

(September 2009)

SHARING THOUGHTS ON WILD ASPARAGUS

*I*N 1962, EUELL GIBBONS OFFERED SOME THOUGHTS on wild food. In *Stalking the Wild Asparagus*—his best-selling book that is still a classic on the subject—Gibbons wasn't talking about strange doughnuts made with golden beets and ginger or the latest extreme culinary craze. He wrote about taking a walk on the wild side at a time when Americans were living in urban apartments or split-level suburban homes with manicured lawns. The world as he saw it when I was a teenager had become a vast and complex place.

Growing up poor in New Mexico, he learned early on to forage for food to feed his family. Later, when he published his thoughts on the benefits of wild food, he realized most Americans don't go into the woods or up to the mountains or virgin forestlands to search for wild food plants unless they are on a camping trip.

Interestingly, he pointed out that these were actually among the poorest places to look. The best foraging sites, he wrote are "abandoned farmsteads, old fields, fence rows, burned-off areas, roadsides, along streams, woodlots, around farm ponds, swampy areas, and even vacant lots."

Fast forward half a century to a world where two people who live in Missouri, but have never actually met, begin a Facebook conversation on the subject of wild asparagus. It goes like this:

May 5, 8:46 a.m.: *"During a serendipitous moment at the farm, I stumbled onto some stalks surrounded by grass and weeds. There had once been an old asparagus bed in the area and I think I've found it!! It tastes like asparagus. I'm going to give it some tender, loving care and see what happens."* Jean C.

May 5, 12:06 p.m.: "*That is how I found an old bed of asparagus near a split log fence when living at Breakfast Creek. The stalk you found is on its way to developing into a fern. If you clear the area carefully and slowly, you might discover more asparagus spear tips emerging. Keep us posted.*" Cathy S.

May 5, 12:15 p.m.: "*Cathy, are you referring to wild asparagus? Would the same be true of this mowed over asparagus bed that was planted decades ago?*" Jean C.

May 5, 12:22 p.m.: "*The relic bed I found some years ago did indeed get cleared and, come May the next year, I was ready with a paring knife in hand to harvest asparagus spears. At our present home, Boomerang Creek, we planted an asparagus bed eight years ago and are now harvesting spears like mad. Give it a try. Good luck.*" Cathy S.

Another Facebook friend wrote:

May 5, 12:30 p.m.: "*Before my dad started his own asparagus bed, he would drive the country roads and look for asparagus growing in ditches near old farmsteads. We jokingly called the asparagus he found "ditch weed." He now has a huge bed. To date this season he's harvested over eighty pounds!*"

Jean C. logged off with this final thought on the subject of wild asparagus: "*Thank you both for the encouraging comments. I'll keep you posted on what happens with the asparagus patch.*"

I shared this exchange with my longtime friend Suzanne Dunaway who is a fabulous cook, artist and cookbook writer. She and her husband Don live in southern France and also keep an apartment in Rome. Wherever they are, they are accompanied by Loulou, a black-and-white feline that has her own website blog: livingwithloulou.com.

On the subject of asparagus, Suzanne wrote:

"Here in my French garden I have wild asparagus, which I took from the hills and replanted so that I don't have to go out in the rain to find the wild ones each year. We have enough for a small omelette at least. Next year, more to come."

While sharing thoughts on asparagus found on a Missouri farm called Serendipity, Jean C., Suzanne and I have taken a virtual walk on the wild side that would make Euell Gibbon feel right proud.

(May 2015)

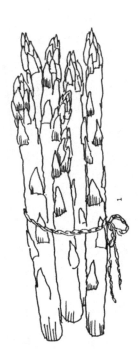

TRACING THE ORIGINS OF TULIPS AND QUINCES

*T*HERE IS MUCH ABOUT GARDENS that can be learned from a visit to Turkey. Why, one might ask, are tulips woven into a massive wool prayer rug in Istanbul's Blue Mosque and so frequently depicted in handmade tiles sold in this historic city's Grand Bazaar? What is the source of the delicious quince marmalade served for breakfast at Istanbul's elegant Pera Palace Hotel—built in 1892 for passengers arriving from Europe aboard the Orient Express Railway?

Searching for answers, I begin leafing through botanical volumes in my library. In *The Gardener's Atlas*, I learned that Ogier Ghiselin dee Busbecq, Ambassador from the Holy Roman Empire to the Ottoman Empire, noticed some fine flowers growing in Turkish gardens in Constantinople in the early spring of 1554. Among them were "those which the Turks call *tulipam*...admired for their beauty and variety of their colors."

Busbecq sent bulbs to the famous French horticulturist Carolus Clusius, Imperial Gardner in Vienna. Clusius then distributed bulbs to friends throughout Europe, marking the beginning of the Dutch tulip bulb industry. Dutch horticulturists in Amsterdam supplied London and the world with tulips, daffodils and hyacinths, while Dutch artists portrayed tulips in masterworks of art.

That mystery solved, I'm now on the trail of quince—a fruit commonly grown in America in colonial times but rarely found in contemporary backyard gardens. While in Istanbul, I was so taken with the delightful flavor of the fruit that I brought home a small jar of Quince (Ayva) Marmalade, produced by Soteks, Ltd, Türkiye. The label illustration is of a yellow, pear-shaped fruit and pinkish coral-colored blossoms.

Easter week, Kit and I spotted several well-established flowering quince bushes while driving Route A to Hartsburg—each filled with brilliant blood-orange colored, camellia-shaped blossoms. By afternoon, Kit had purchased one as an Easter surprise that has since been planted at the edge of the orchard near a dwarf Asian pear tree.

But what about quince trees, still common in rural America's backyards in the late nineteenth century? Perusing the *Encyclopedia of Cooking*, I learn that this hard, dry-textured fruit of a tree belonging to the apple family is native to temperate regions of Asia (Turkey being one location). The fruit ripens in September when quinces become golden yellow and resemble apples or pears.

After an online search of Stark Bro's Nursery in Louisiana, Missouri, an order is placed for a dwarf orange quince tree, a semi-dwarf Montmorency pie cherry tree, and a Brown Turkey fig tree. Established soon after James Hart Stark arrived from Kentucky in 1816 with apple scions from his family orchard, Stark Bro's is still family-owned and has the largest online, direct-to-customer nursery in the country.

Anticipating their arrival, I pour through old cookbooks in search of quince recipes. In *The Shaker Cook Book*—found years ago while visiting Shakertown at Pleasant Hill near Lexington, Kentucky—I find a recipe for Amelia's Quince Pudding. A beautifully illustrated copy of *Crabtree & Evelyn Cookbook* suggests a light menu of Tomato and Celery Soup, Glazed Pork Loin with Garlic Potatoes, and Brussels Sprouts in Brown Butter, followed by Apple-Quince Bread Pudding for dessert.

Having traced the quince fruit back to its Asian origins, I check Claudia Rodin's *The New Book of Middle Eastern Food* and find numerous contemporary recipes for this ancient fruit—quince(s) with fish; poached in syrup; preserves; with roast duck; stuffed; with tangine of lamb; and in couscous with tomatoes and fish.

Finally, I pull out James Beard's 1972 classic tome, *American Cookery,* and I'm delighted to read his take on this largely forgotten fruit, once common in America's backyard gardens:

> *Few people know the delicacy and flavor of cooked quince, and they are brilliant in bouquet both cooked and raw. When peeled, cut into sections and baked, they make a nice change from other fruit dishes. Cool the baked quince, and serve with heavy cream or sour cream.*

What's not to love about that old recipe?

(May 2014)

August in Transition

*A*s August slides quietly into September, change is already in the air. In a walk around the outer reaches of our tall grass meadow, I follow the mown pathway Kit maintains on his sit-down mower. Along the fence line separating our property from a farm it was once part of, I hear the sounds of our neighbor's goats and chickens and watch as their three horses trot over to see if I have a carrot or apple slices in my pocket. As I pass the bluebird house that was occupied earlier in the spring, a small head that had been sticking out of the opening quickly pulls back inside.

Rounding the final leg of the quarter mile mown pathway, I stop at the raised strawberry bed for some bending and weeding exercise. That done, I make a mental note to trim any raggedy edges around the rest of the flowerbeds with our push mower, another great exercise for strengthening and toning the body I remind myself. But the question is, *when?*

It has been a busy July and August. Regular routines become less routine when houseguests arrive and local road trips and activities suddenly take over the calendar of life. That is when the yard goes on automatic pilot and frequent thundershowers negate the necessity for time-consuming early morning or late afternoon waterings in the gardens and orchard.

As September arrives, I'm pleased to still find white blossoms on the Tuscan blue hostas in our shade garden. Native ferns on delicate black stems thrive in the coolness provided by our glade of shade trees even when temperatures reach into the 90s. In our meadow vegetable garden, asparagus ferns wave in the wind, mimicking the

Cathy Salter

native grasses that have grown tall with purple tops over the course of the summer.

In the vegetable bed next to the asparagus plants, giant green leaves on creeping vines have gone completely free range, filling the bed with egg-yolk yellow blossoms that open daily. By late August, spent blossoms have begun to morph into small bulb-shaped globes, hinting at an autumn harvest of pumpkins and squash.

Moles had their way with the yard this August, creating tiny areas here and there that look like sand traps on a golf course. The sudden appearance of a soft brown mound of dirt is a magnet for our cats. Draping his body over the pile of loose earth, Scribbles rubs and rolls around, oblivious of how silly he appears. Fanny, our stealthy, alpha Manx, hones in on the little subterranean critters and waits patiently for a mole to emerge.

When moles do not come out and play, Fanny eventually heads for the creek to gig for frogs. After her hapless hostages are proudly displayed in the yard, the fortunate ones are rescued by the resident gardener and released in the woods beyond the shade garden. Undaunted, Fanny then spends the rest of the afternoon stretched out in the coolness of the garden, on guard for the slightest sign of movement under the hostas.

Nearby, a Thai spirit house rests atop a cut elm that serves as its living post. Over the summer, a wren built her nest in this small wooden structure made by one of my Peace Corps friends from four decades ago. The wren brought her nesting twigs in through a diamond-shaped opening in the back wall of the house. A stone figurine of an Egyptian cat sits in the center looking out past a large pink artificial orchid and two life-like plastic lizards that guard the entrance.

Indeed, there is life in this little spirit house and throughout our gardens as August transitions into September. Each morning, the two plastic lizards are on the ground below, as if they've been exploring the garden in the night. Perhaps they are the culprits that feasted on my ripe tomatoes last week. Better harvest the pears before they too are discovered.

(August 2009)

The Moon, Mars and a Few Earthly Matters

$\mathscr{T}$HE RADIO CLICKS ON AT FIVE O'CLOCK in the morning within arm's reach of where I am drifting in and out of sleep. Although the volume is turned down low and just barely audible, news from around the world still manages to creep into my head, pushing me finally to roll onto my side, swing my legs over the side of the bed, and find my slippers by feel and habit. It is dark outside, save for a brilliant full moon and dazzling planet Mars visible through a west-facing bedroom window.

After letting the cats out, I walk with them across the damp grass in case a fox is waiting somewhere in the dark. We all look up at the moon and Mars and declare them to be the brightest part of the morning thus far, much superior to the gloom-and-doom radio reports of the latest car bombings in Iraq, the sluggish state of the economy, and the rants of polarized political ideologues in the shadow of the Lincoln Memorial on the Washington Mall.

Somehow in the noise of politics, no one hears anyone but themselves. The cats and I agree that this is no way to have a civil conversation. It is certainly not the way to achieve compromise and allow necessary and needed changes to take place. Here in the peacefulness of early morning, I can see and hear that change is going on all around me. In the peace that this garden allows me, I reflect on what has taken place in the final days of August.

For starters, daytime temperatures dropped from tiresome, triple-digit readings to chilly nighttime lows in the upper fifties. Daytime highs that remained in the low eighties were a most pleasant relief. Windows and doors were thrown open and the air conditioning

---

turned off. In its place, ceiling fans kept indoor air wafting and outdoor breezes did their sweet dance throughout every room in the house. Pooh, Fanny and Scribbles catnapped in the delicious coolness on the porch, then dashed about in the garden chasing grasshoppers that have begun to sense the seasonal changes now in the air.

In the meadow garden, cucumbers grow like champs whether they are watered or not. Tall tomato cage super-structures support monster squash and pumpkin vines filled with giant yellow blossoms that are now morphing into a cornucopia of autumn gourds. Dead center in the rose bed, a volunteer pumpkin vine has emerged from compost and threatens to encircle the entire ring of rose bushes. Seeking compromise so that all flowers and vegetables concerned can find common ground at the foot of our Mr. Lincoln red rose bush, a towering tomato cage has been installed amongst the roses. Happy to have a place in the sun, two large green pumpkins hang by tenacious tendrils from the cage's ladder-like sides, and soon others will emerge.

Near the studio, potted hibiscus plants that have not flowered for two summers are suddenly filled with buds. The first showy red blossom opened as if trumpeting the arrival of spring. But it is almost September elsewhere in the garden, and time to carry a ladder out to the orchard to finish harvesting our bounty of pears.

As the final weekend of August approached, a call came from the Beckmeyer vineyard to help pick grapes. For those who volunteered, there were barbequed pulled pork sandwiches with sides of Barbara's homemade applesauce, pickles, brownies and peach cobbler, and grape juice from their own vines.

September thus far has been hot and dry. Because our energy levels have a tendency to wilt in the warm post-lunch hour, catnaps are encouraged for all residents at Boomerang Creek pretty much every day. And as long as the mosquitoes remain active, you'll find us on the screened porch in the evenings—the perfect place to relax and reflect in the twilight hour when the sun slides into the Missouri River just five miles on down the road.

(September 2010)

December News from the Garden

*D*ECEMBER SEEMS AN ODD TIME of the year to write about gardens, but in fact the weather this morning has me doing just that. At dawn, the sun rose in a sky filled with clouds that resembled a crisscrossing of high-flying jet contrails. As if not wanting to be outdone, flocks of honking geese passed over our meadow in a perfectly orchestrated V-formation.

After a morning walk, Kit filled two five-gallon corrugated watering cans and lugged them over to the old 1950 Street Rod truck that lives on blocks at the edge of our meadow. Affectionately known as our "yard art installation," the solid-as-a-fortress shell of its former self has been given a new *raison d'etre*. Just exactly what, you are possibly wondering, could an old truck put out to pasture three decades ago, possible be remade into? In this age of magic thinking, Kit had the answer. Here is the story.

Late in November when a string of hard-freeze temperatures was predicted, we got busy and put the garden to bed. Hoses, save for one, were spread out to drain, then rolled into neat bundles and stored in the garage. Potted mums were hauled in a wheelbarrow to one of the kitchen compost piles, holes dug, and inserted, pot and all. There they will winter over, blanketed with rich soil that smells of decomposing onions skins and orange peels. Shelves in sunny south-facing windows in the dining room and kitchen were readied and quickly filled with potted begonias and culinary herbs to enhance winter soups, roasts and vegetables.

Our next focus was the potager herb garden on the porch that had grown large by summer's end, along with the plants within the pots.

An olive tree, Hawaiian plumeria, and fig tree found their way to a sunny window in my studio where they will give the room a sunny wall of greenery and feed my spirit through the gray days of February and March. An enormous Tuscan blue rosemary plant will winter over in my the studio as well—a reminder of the warm light of Italy where Kit and I will once again paint and write a year from now.

Pots of Spanish lavender, assorted mint varieties, lemon thyme and parsley, two large hydrangeas and a miniature orange tree—all requiring winter protection—still remained. But where would we store them? This is where our conversation began the morning the gardens were put to bed. I remarked near the end of our labors that I needed a small greenhouse. Kit looked at the old truck and said, "There it is," pointing to the truck. And with that, we had our green house without having spent a penny.

Soon our packed-to-the-gunnels, ready-to-go, clean-energy, "truck garden" greenhouse was filled with new purpose and life. The cab of the truck had long ago seen its passenger seat removed. In quick fashion, Kit had retrofitted the empty cab shell with floor boards (literally) spread to form a makeshift pallet upon which plants were then arranged. In no time, the cab was filled with a potpourri of fellow tropicals, happy to remain resident outside for winter. After a final watering, we left them humming as one harmonious chorus, prepared to witness the passage of winter from within their cozy, sun-filled glass enclosure.

Over the following week, temperatures dropped into the teens, cold enough to have a cozy fire in our Buck stove most evenings. Outside in the meadow, the happy humming continued as the windshield of the old truck iced over, giving the illusion that it had snowed. But the cold didn't last. The next day arrived with a record seventy-eight-degree forecast, so we once again found ourselves in the garden, filling the water cans to give our truck garden inhabitants one more winter watering.

Should the roses bloom in the meadow again this December, I won't be surprised. Our garden, even in winter, just keeps trucking along.

(December 2012)

Chapter Twelve
EDIBLE ADVENTURES

Days are lighter longer now, and that light somehow appears to be brighter and warmer. It pulls us outside each day to check on the peas and lettuce planted half a month ago. This daily regime in the early spring garden is wonderful exercise for both body and mind.

C.S. May 1994

FROM COWPOKE BEANS TO CASSOULETS

BEANS DON'T ALWAYS GET GREAT PRESS, but being my father's daughter, our kitchen is never without them. Pinto, dark kidney, cannellini, garbanzo, navy, black, and refried beans are stacked two cans high and three deep in the pantry. Bags of dried adzuki, fava, flageolet, lentil, and great white northern beans are nearby. Baby lima beans and *edamame* (soy beans) are staples in the freezer vegetable bin.

Recently I found a recipe for Cowpoke Beans that my father gave me twenty-five years ago. Stained and aged to the color of onionskin, it was lovingly typed on a three-by-five-inch index card—ingredients listed on one side and preparation instructions on the other. A cowboy quote speaks to the task ahead. *"You've got to treat these little pinto beans the same way you would a newborn colt—with a lot of love and attention."*

In the film *Brokeback Mountain*, cowboys Ennis del Mar and

Jack Twist eat beans straight from cans heated over a high altitude Wyoming camp fire. My dad simmered his pinto beans in a heavy Dutch oven after soaking them overnight in cold water. Only then did he stir in salt pork, a chopped onion, garlic, red chili peppers, tomato paste, salt, chili powder, cumin seed, and marjoram. After simmering another three hours, Dad's tender cowpoke beans were always served with a pan of Mom's made-from-scratch cornbread and hot maple syrup.

My own Dutch oven with glass lid has done venerable service in every kitchen Kit and I have inhabited for nearly thirty years; but we recently added a heavy French cast-iron Le Creuset roaster that has inspired me to move into territory beyond chili and Dad's cowpoke beans.

We are now talking about chickens, not just beans, and a Sunday dinner prepared in a pot for a hungry crowd. The dish is cassoulet, a tradition that goes back to the sixteenth century and to King Henry IV who saw chickens as a symbol of prosperity in France. To wit, according to Lydie Marshall in, *A Passion for My Provence: Home Cooking from the South of France,* Henry IV decreed that every French household should have a chicken cooking in a pot every Sunday.

Determined to recreate this classic country dinner, I turned to my collection of French cookbooks. Julia Child, co-author of the classic *Mastering the Art of French Cooking,* found cassoulet "a rich combination of beans baked with meats (pork, lamb, and homemade sausage), as much a part of southwestern France as Boston baked beans are of New England."

Next I searched through *The French Menu Cookbook,* by Richard Olney—an American culinary writer who lived in Paris for ten years, then moved permanently to Provence after falling in love with its light, its landscape and its odors. Olney believed there were as many cassoulets as there are cooks, and chose to define the dish as:

> ...a slow-cooked gratin made up of two or more separate preparations, one of which is always pork and bean stew, the others

of which may be chosen among preserved duck or goose, braised lamb or mutton, and roast or braised partridge."

Nostalgically, Olney added a footnote on the subject.
The gentle, sweet odor of broom (grass) which, in the past, was burned to heat the bread ovens in which cassoulets were cooked, lent, no doubt, a dimension to the dish that we shall never know.

Georgeanne Brennan in *Savorying France writes,*
...cassoulet is a defining dish in the Languedoc region of Provence, stretching from the cities of Toulouse, to Carcassonne, to Castelnaudary. While each city, village and family there may have its own version of the dish, it is, in essence layers of white beans that have been slowly cooked with herbs, and interspersed with layers of different cooked meats, thoroughly moistened with the cooking juices of both, topped with a final layer of bread crumbs, and then baked until a thick crust forms and the juices begin to bubble underneath.

I eliminated goose and duck as possible meats, having raised both at Breakfast Creek, where I named my flocks one and all. Chicken, pork, lamb, and sausage would have to do. The great white northerns were treated as Dad had advised me, *"as lovingly as newborn colts."* While the beans simmered, the chicken and pork roasted. Lamb and sausage were browned with onions and garlic, and then simmered to a savory sauce with tomatoes, parsley, white wine and thyme. After a morning of preparation, the cooked beans, meats and sauces were layered, layered again, covered, and baked together a final two hours.

Chefs agree that cassoulet is time-consuming and requires hearty eaters. But I was happy to cook for our invited friends Orion and Beckmeyer and Sally and Hugh Sprague who arrived with hearty appetites. Dessert was Tarte Tatin (French upside-down apple tart) baked cowboy style in an iron skillet. It was a delicious ending to a country supper of baked beans prepared French style in a pot at Boomerang Creek. Dad would have loved every bite.

(February 2006)

You Never Know What You'll Find

$\mathcal{D}$URING A JANUARY ICE STORM when Kit and I were housebound for several days, I curled up on the couch with a stack of unread magazines and began poring over them. While perusing the November 2007 *Country Living*, I paused to read the "Home Comforts" page—perfect reading matter, I thought to myself, for a day when our Buck stove was the only thing keeping us warm.

From the get-go, the page pulled me in. The article's title, "Bonnie Slotnick Cookbooks," announces the subject in a delicious Montmorency cherry red ink, followed by this inviting line—"On a quiet street in New York's Greenwich Village, Bonnie Slotnick runs a bustling business in vintage cookbooks." The owner, wearing a rose floral shawl over her shoulders, is pictured holding a stack of books from the shop that she opened in October 1997 after careers as a freelance artist and a cookbook editor.

Next to Ms. Slotnick's picture is a business profile. Business: shop and source for out-of-print and antiquarian cookbooks. Location: New York City. Inspiration: personal cookbook collections. Then the line that led me into the shop: "You never know what you'll find."

At that moment, I mentally entered the bookshop pictured in the article. The deep, narrow room pictured is lined from floor to ceiling with well-stocked bookshelves painted a creamy white. Along one side, a wooden kitchen table with a blue and white enamel top is piled with cookbooks, an aluminum flour sifter filled with autumn leaves, and a red pomegranate or apple resting atop a porcelain gravy boat. An antique enamel stove with a high backsplash just below the rear landing offers additional surface space for small books, vintage mixing bowls, and illustrated recipe booklets.

Cathy Salter

Kit and I love exploring the jumble of neighborhoods that stretch from the Battery in lower Manhattan north through Central Park into Harlem. Ever the archivist, I keep a file on places to explore on our next trip to NYC. But before I had time to file the cookbook shop article, I had reason to pick it up again. When my January 2008 *Gourmet* arrived, I checked the contents page and was intrigued by the synopsis of the issue's feature article:

> A granddaughter of freed slaves, the late Edna Lewis left home when she was just sixteen-years old and went on to become a renowned chef at Manhattan's star-studded Café Nicholson. Her books have spread the gospel of genuine southern cuisine and inspired a generation of home cooks.

Leafing ahead to the article, I was captured by a full-page photograph of Edna Lewis—an elegant, white-haired woman in her eighties with skin the color of light brown sugar. Her muscular left hand rests on the edge of a wooden table that she appears to be leaning against for balance. With her right hand, Ms. Lewis cuts rounds from dough that she's kneaded and rolled out on the well-floured surface of the table. Pictured opposite is a down-home pot of simmered greens topped with cornmeal dumplings so flakey and golden they looked like they might fall off the page.

In a never-before published essay "What is Southern?" Edna Lewis writes nostalgically of local ingredients from her rural childhood in Freetown, Virginia:

> *Southern is a meal of early spring wild greens—poke sallet before it is fully uncurled, wild mustard, dandelion, lamb's-quarter, pursulane, and wild watercress.*

As if her prose was not nourishment enough for the soul, her plain and simple recipes for clay pot guinea hen, Brunswick stew, smothered steak, potato casserole, buttermilk cookies and fried apple pies are included in the *Gourmet* issue.

But more than the homey ingredients in Ms. Lewis's regional recipes, I love reading Ms. Lewis's tribute to the writers, musicians, and artists she felt had contributed to our understanding of the character of the South. "Southern," she wrote, "is Truman Capote." When dining at Café Nicholson, "he would request that I make him some biscuits."

Ms. Lewis gained acclaim cooking at Café Nicholson's on East 58th Street in Manhattan (1948-1954). Author and editor, Ruth Reichl, notes, "her broiled oysters, roast chicken with watercress, and chocolate soufflé attracted a glittering crowd of writers, artists, aristocrats, and movie stars." It is reported that during a Broadway run of *A Streetcar Named Desire*, playwright Tennessee Williams and actor Marlon Brando dined late at Café Nicholson, and then walked Ms. Lewis home.

Edna Lewis died in 2006 at the age of eighty-nine. After reading about her, I emailed Bonnie Slotnick at her vintage cookbook shop in Manhattan and purchased one of Ms. Lewis's early cookbooks. In subsequent emails, Bonnie and I have discovered we both love cooking with pears. She will soon receive my favorite recipe for upside-down pear cake and two dark chocolate bars enhanced with pear filling.

On my journey to find Edna Lewis—a unique woman who mastered the art of southern country cooking with fresh, seasonal, regional ingredients decades before "slow food" and "localvore" entered America's culinary vocabulary—I ventured into the cookbook shop in Manhattan that I had read about in *Country Living*. "You never know what you'll find," the article proclaimed. And that is precisely what every journey of discovery should be about.

(January 2008)

The Joy of Cooking and Small Kitchens

*I*N THIS ERA OF MEGA MODERN KITCHENS and six-burner, industrial Wolf stoves, I would like to speak of the simple pleasures and delicious hours that I've spent cooking in small kitchens over the past four decades. Whether I'm cooking for two or twenty, the journey is always a joy.

My first kitchen was in Thailand where I was a Peace Corps Volunteer (1967-1970). It had no stove, refrigeration, or running water. I cooked rice on an electric hot plate and kept non-perishable food in a pie safe. Water for cooking and washing dishes was collected from an outdoor water jar and boiled before drinking. Milk was the thick, sticky, condensed variety poured from a tin can. Meals were simple, and usually included sauces, fresh fish and fruit purchased daily at a local market. Ice was a luxury available in elegant hotels and restaurants that I could not afford to frequent on my Peace Corps salary of $75 a month.

When I met Kit a decade later in Los Angeles, our weekly movie dates were followed by a discussion of the film over dinner at a local restaurant in Westwood. This tradition of movies, meals and conversation continues to this day. As our romance developed, I was invited to join Kit and his children, Hayden (ten) and Heidi (eight), on Wednesday nights at his apartment. After repeated samplings of Kit's standard menu of meatloaf and mashed potatoes (skins included), I soon took over the cooking. A year later, I moved into an eight-hundred-square foot, 1920s canyon cottage in west Los Angeles with Kit, Hayden and Heidi, and my cats Tiggy and Muffin.

The Cottage, our cozy home for the next decade, had a tiny kitchen with an ancient gas stove at one end, a single basin enamel sink, almost no counter space and only a single open cupboard. The refrigerator was one step down in the laundry room that also served as a pantry. After adding a sturdy, two-tiered oak table that gave me an open workspace, I dove into the business of mastering the art of cooking for a family of four.

The quietude of that small kitchen was a balm for the body and senses after days spent teaching in a large urban junior high school in South Central Los Angeles. Once home and isolated from the noise of the city, I decompressed by gathering lemons and roses in our backyard garden and working my way through two of Martha Stewart's "quick cook menus" cookbooks. But on weekends, it was Julia's classic Boeuf Bourguignon and Reina de Saba (Chocolate & Almond Cake) recipes that I loved preparing for company.

These days, simple but equally delicious recipes reflect the national growth of local farmers markets and the cornucopia of exotic produce and ingredients readily available in grocery stores year round. Cooks have instant access to celebrity chefs through their cookbooks, TV shows, and websites. On command, I can print a recipe for hummus with edamame (soybeans). Tahini (sesame paste) and extra virgin olive oil, two of the ingredients in hummus, are staples in our kitchen pantry, and I keep frozen bags of edamame—available at most local grocery stores and Columbia's World Harvest International Gourmet Foods Market—on hand in abundance.

Last week, Nora Ephron's much anticipated film, *Julie & Julia*, opened nationally. It is the story of Julia Child and Julie Powell—two women who each developed a passion for cooking that changed their lives. Julia, who lived in 1950s Paris with her husband Paul Child, explored local markets and studied at Paris's famed Cordon Bleu. Teaming up with Louisette Bertholle and Simone Beck, she co-authored *Mastering the Art of French Cooking Vol. 1* (1961)—the first cookbook that explained how to create authentic French dishes in American kitchens with American ingredients.

Powell, an unhappy secretary, lived with her husband in a small apartment in Queens. There, she chronicled her own effort to prepare all five hundred twenty four recipes in Child's *Mastering the Art of French Cooking* in their tiny kitchen in three hundred sixty-five days. Ephron's film overlays Powell's 2005 book from her blog, "Julie & Julia," with Child's memoir, *My Life in France*—published by her nephew Alex Prud'homme two years after Julia's death in 2004.

These days, the venerable oak worktable from our tiny cottage kitchen in Los Angeles has center stage in our modest country kitchen at Boomerang Creek. Sixty years after Julia towered over her first stove in Paris, her buoyant spirit and classic recipes continue to bring joy no matter how small the kitchen or how large the gathering. As Julia would say, "*Bon Appetit!*"

(August 2009)

Edible Adventures with Clotilde

*C*LOTILDE DUSOULIER, A PARISIAN, has been sharing her passion for food through a fascinating food blog, she began in 2003 when she was twenty-four years old. For those who love Paris and dream of French travel, you can choose to read her food blogs in either French or English, depending on just how adventuresome you are feeling at the moment. In addition to publishing culinary tips in her monthly newsletter, Dusoulier is the author of *Chocolate & Zucchini: Daily Adventures in a Parisian Kitchen* and *Clotilde's Edible Adventures in Paris*.

On the first day of every month, Clotilde greets me with a newsy "C&Z" email from Paris. *"Bonjour Août!"* she wrote last week, welcoming August onto the scene. How timely, I thought, staring at the sizeable accumulation of dark green zucchini taking over our kitchen counter like squash vines snaking their way throughout a summer garden. That very morning, I'd already turned three of them into two loaves of spicy zucchini walnut bread—one shared with friends over morning coffee and the other frozen for a later occasion.

What now would I do with the surplus? For our longtime friends Pat and Gary who grow organic zucchini in their rooftop garden in Los Angeles, *ratatouille* is the perfect way to serve up their bounty of homegrown zucchini and tomatoes. In Clotilde's "C&Z" glossary of French cooking terms, ratatouille, a specialty from Provence, is defined as "a vegetable stew made with tomatoes, zucchini, eggplant, peppers, onions, herbs and olive oil."

However, you can only eat so much ratatouille, and as our friend Wally Pfeffer would be the first to point out, zucchini are ubiquitous.

This is the hot and steamy month of August, the garden is awash with squash and pumpkin blossoms of all varieties, and unless those blossoms are harvested, dipped in batter, and fried (a delicious thought), they will develop into an abundance of assorted squashes (acorn, zucchini, butternut, and yellow) and pumpkins (orange, white, green, and terra cotta).

Picked early, zucchini are tender and delicious when sliced thinly and tossed with angel hair pasta, lemony olive oil and fresh grated Parmesan. Left too long under leaves the size of elephant ears, they morph into thick-skinned, mega-zuke footballs and become legend at annual county fairs. Those that grow into tubular long boats are best prepared like a dugout canoe—seeds scooped out and interior filled with a mixture of chopped zucchini, onion, carrot, tomato, and cubed day-old French bread, generously topped before baking in a casserole dish with bread crumbs and Parmesan cheese drizzled with olive oil.

What else, I wondered, can one do with zucchini? What sweet and savory zucchini dish is Clotilde cooking up in her Paris kitchen these hot August days? Her August "C&Z" newsletter had the perfect answer. Clotilde claims not to have named her blog after a cake that includes the two named ingredients but has had fun testing recipes shared by bakers and readers of her blog over the years, blending the best of their suggestions with a family recipe for chocolate cake.

Why add grated zucchini? Clotilde's answer is simple—it provides moisture, reduces the amount of butter needed, and (she assures those put off by the strange wedding of ingredients in her "C&Z" cake), you won't taste the zucchini because it melts into the batter and disappears.

Clotilde's Chocolate & Zucchini Cake combines all-purpose flour, unsweetened cocoa powder, baking soda, baking powder, sea salt, light brown sugar, unsalted butter or olive oil, vanilla, instant coffee granules or strong cooled coffee, eggs, unpeeled grated zucchini, chocolate chips, and Confectioner's sugar (optional). For baking directions and a thousand other edible adventures, Clotilde's creative and informative foodie website can be found at chocolateandzucchini.com.

I share Clotilde's website with New Zealand friends, John and Sarah, who are spending the cold August winter months in the southern hemisphere much like Midwesterners do—planning a spring garden. "What's your favorite zucchini recipe?" I ask. "Thought you'd never ask," John responds.

Five months later, winter had shifted to the northern hemisphere and all traces of our August abundance of zucchini were gone. That is when a new conversation began with Clotilde via her monthly food blog that always feels like a friendly conversation:

"Bonjour Janvier! Happy New Year!" Clotilde's "C&Z" newsletter begins.

I settle in and read recipes, interviews on food, watch a documentary on French pastry, and take a virtual tour of Patrick Roger's chocolate factory in Sceaux, France—all in the comfort of our warming room at Boomerang Creek.

Clotilde describes her newsletters as "virtual table conversations." In that spirit, I tell her about *As Always, Julia,* a marvelous book chronicling the trans-Atlantic correspondence from 1952-1961 between Julia Child and Avis DeVoto—the period when Julia was working on her classic cookbook, *Mastering the Art of French Cooking.*

Then the subject moves to chocolate and I take Clotilde along on two edible adventures of my own. The first occurred in 1975 while I was on a month-long journey across Asia that included Hong Kong, Thailand, Laos, Burma, India, and Nepal. While in Nepal, I trekked for two weeks in the Annapurna region of the Himalayas with my sister Molly and a friend, Paul Langer.

Our trekking party's Sherpa cook, Pasang, prepared meals over an open wood fire using a cast iron Dutch oven much like those that cowboy cooks and my father used to make cowpoke beans and cooks in Provence use to make classic French cassoulet. What emerged from Pasang's oven depended on what seasonings he had packed along and what he purchased from local farmers each day—pumpkins, chickens, potatoes, onions, carrots, peas, lentils and cauliflower—as our party passed ever higher from one mountain village to the next.

On the inside cover of the pocket-sized journal that I kept during the trek is a recipe for Pasang's Tibetan bread. What made it magic was the subtlest of seasonings and most unexpected—two tablespoons of chocolate powder which he added to six or seven big eggs, two cups of wheat flour, one half cup of sugar, one teaspoon baking powder, one cup of water, and six to seven big spoons of butter. After rising, the bread dough was baked in Pasang's cast-iron Dutch oven over a wood fire.

Then, I tell Clotilde I recently came across a recipe for Cincinnati Chili published in *Saveur*, magazine. Described as "redolent of warm spices and an American classic," the recipe's ground beef, garlic and onions were seasoned with chili powder, ground cinnamon, allspice, cloves, cumin, oregano, nutmeg, celery seed, bay leaf, and an additional secret ingredient—unsweetened cocoa powder.

Surely Nicholas Lambrinides who founded the first of Cincinnati's chain of Skyline Chili restaurants in 1949 had his favorite family recipes with him when he immigrated from Kastoria, Greece to Cincinnati in 1912. I shouldn't have been surprised because the tradition of using chocolate as a seasoning had crossed the Atlantic centuries earlier. Elisabeth Rozin's book, *Blue Corn and Chocolate* (1992) reminds us that five hundred years earlier, foods like tomatoes, potatoes, peppers, chocolate and vanilla had been brought from the New World to the Old World.

Each food, Rozin writes, "has a story: how it was discovered, how it was greeted in its adopted countries and then integrated into the Old World cuisine, how it returned here in dishes that immigrants brought with them, and how it has become a part of mainstream American cooking."

In Rozin's chapter on chocolate and vanilla, the first recipe is Chocolate Chili served over rice. Nicholas Lambrinides served his

Cincinnati Chili over spaghetti with toppings of grated cheddar cheese, chopped onions and kidney beans. In Clotilde's spirit of edible adventure, the reader is encouraged to be epicurious.

So it is that I add a few tablespoons of cocoa powder to the January pot of chili now simmering in our kitchen at Boomerang Creek.

"Merci Clotilde!"

Your January admonition is perfectly timed. And after all, using chocolate as a seasoning truly is an American culinary tradition.

(January 2011)

Exploring the Tastes of Spain

*O*n a recent trip to Madrid and the Basque regions of Spain and France, the magic of traditional Spanish flavors and tastes was evident wherever Kit and I wandered. And wander we did under October skies as sunny and brilliant as the mustard-yellow, soaring arches of the architecturally spectacular Barajas-Madrid *Aeropuerto*.

Our daily explorations took the slow food route, allowing us ample opportunity to sample the rich variety of Spanish tastes that blend the robust Mediterranean flavors of garlic, olive oil, peppers and tomatoes with *tapas* (small plates) contributed by the Basques in the north as well as Eastern accents introduced by the Moors who ruled Spain for more than seven hundred years.

After a morning *cafe con leche*, fresh orange juice, toast and honey at our son Hayden's home in a suburb of Madrid, we caught a #146 bus into Madrid along Calle Alcalá to Gran Via. From there, our daily walking explorations commenced. Wandering grand avenues and winding backstreets now etched into my mental map of the city, we would emerge in a sunny plaza by two o'clock, just in time for lunch.

At the Plaza Mayor we ordered *Ensalada Mixta*—tomatoes, lettuce, sweet Spanish onions—made "illustrious" with the addition of tuna in olive oil, white asparagus spears, green olives and hard-boiled eggs. Relaxed and totally in the moment, we each nursed a cold *cerveza* (beer) enhanced with Schweppes orange soda while taking in the scenes playing out in the popular plaza.

Back home around six o'clock, we witnessed what energy it takes for Hayden, an urban architect, to help raise three active, tri-lingual children—Nicolas, Ines and Catalina. Our daughter-in-law Ana

Martín Salter, the marketing and advertising director for Madrid's recently refurbished Mercado San Miguel and Mercado San Anton, took us on tours of those two urban markets. She was also the source of fascinating conversations on preparing healthy family meals, and shopping daily at local neighborhood markets. Ana carries on the Spanish tradition of women—both stay-at-home and working moms—who prepare lunch and dinner for the family from recipes learned firsthand in their own mother's kitchen.

Ingredients are fresh, never frozen and "leftovers" are not part of the Spanish vocabulary. At lunch and dinner, dishes are shared, offering an endless variety of small plates (*tapas*) made with down-to-earth ingredients prepared in unusual ways. Dinner happens around nine o'clock and might be fresh hake (*merluza*) baked with olive oil and sweet white onions, served with a *tortilla española* (grated potato and onion omelet), followed by a simple salad of grape tomatoes from Hayden's backyard garden tossed with chopped sweet white onion, olive oil, salt, and pepper. And always there is fresh-baked crusty bread from the bakery of Ana's father, Marcos.

On a road trip from Madrid to the Pays Basque and Bay of Biscay, the seven of us stopped midway for lunch in Burgos in the Rio Duero wine region. For the next two hours we dined al fresco in an outdoor patio. Brunch was a delicacy that is a favorite of our son Hayden— fried eggs with grilled blood sausage patties mixed with rice. The dish, as he had promised, was as delicious and crisp as the sausage was dark.

By the time we had crossed the border into southwest France and located our charming French Basque farmhouse B&B in the seaside town of Bidart, it was dark, and we were sorely car weary. However, we quickly rallied and drove to the nearby seacoast town of St-Jean-de-Luz for dinner. After a stroll on the boardwalk, Ana chose a tiny restaurant down a small backstreet where the waiter proudly displayed and praised their line-caught fish. After ordering red snapper caught that morning, we grazed on appetizers of *gazpacho*, olive tapenade, *foie gras* (goose liver paté) and *gambas al ajillo* (garlic shrimp), while toasting Hayden's forty-fifth birthday with a Cabernet from the Rio Duero wine region we had passed through that very afternoon.

At journey's end, we had explored the tastes of Spain from Madrid north to the Rio Duero wine region and arid central tablelands (Spain's breadbasket) where wheat was being harvested, to the craggy green Basque country of the north that looks much like Switzerland, and finally to seacoast towns along the Bay of Biscay and the Océan Atlantique. Along the way, we tasted time-honored flavors of Spain that have survived the centuries, flavors I am now hoping to capture in our kitchen at Boomerang Creek.

(October 2011)

WHEN THE WOLF IS AT THE DOOR

*J*ANUARY CAN BE A COLD MONTH, long in weeks and spare in spirit. And so, I enter a soup phase this time of the year, working my way through the delicious pages of *The Soup Bible* cookbook and others on the shelves of our culinary kitchen library.

Sweet red peppers are sautéed in olive oil and simmered to tenderness with shallots, carrots, pears, chicken broth, paprika, and a few pepper flakes. Once puréed and returned to the pot, they are a soup, both easy and mysterious. Piquant with the sweet hint of pear, red pepper soup is a warm-the-spirit and feed-the-soul meal—heavenly when served with a loaf of crusty Tuscan country bread, butter and the simplest of green salads.

An onion sautéed with tomatoes, garlic, paprika, chicken broth, parsley and cannellini beans becomes a satisfying soup in no time. Whether preparing the most basic garlic and potato peasant soup or a mulligatawny soup flavored with exotic Indian spices made popular during the time of the British Empire, the possibilities are as endless and as simple as boiling water.

It is fitting then that while perusing a used bookstore recently, I discovered M.F.K. Fisher's early gastronomical classic, *How to Cook a Wolf*. While Mrs. Fisher spent a good part of her fascinating life as a housewife, mother and amateur chef, she also wrote novels, poetry, memoirs, a screenplay, and owned a vineyard in Switzerland, before finally settling in Sonoma Valley, California.

Mrs. Fisher's unique, prose-and-recipe rich cookbook was published in 1942 during a time of war and sacrifice—a time, Fisher noted, when for the majority, the wolf was at the door and the pantry bare. What was needed, she wrote, was "a practical guide to the art of living happily and well—even though close to starvation." Simply stated, *How to Cook a Wolf* is a how-to book on keeping the wolf at bay.

Written at a time of wartime rationing when "countless humans are herded together, as in military camps or schools or prisons," Mrs. Fisher's practical suggestions offered a happy medium between a diet that is balanced nutritionally and living on a steady diet of plain boiled water. In her chapter, "How to Boil Water," she writes that "a few herbs and perhaps a carrot or two and maybe a bit of meager bone added to boiling water combine to make something quite good." That something was soup.

Distaining the dictum of the great French chef, Maître Escoffier, who claimed that the origin of soups went back no further than the early years of the nineteenth century, Fisher believed soup to be "probably the oldest cooked food on the earth after roasted meat." She then described basic recipes for Chinese consommé, Parisian onion soup, Chowder, Cream of potato soup, and Gazpacho.

In Fisher's mind, *"Probably the most satisfying soup in the world for people who are hungry… tired or worried, or cross, or in debt, or in a moderate amount of pain or in love or in robust health or in any kind of business huggermuggery, is minestrone."* A thick, unsophisticated soup, she found it *"heart-warming and soul-staying"* as well as economical. She quotes an Italian friend as saying, "Topped with grated Romano, served with crisp garlicked sour-dough bread, a salad and a glass of wine, and *I have dined."*

After reading *How to Cook a Wolf*, I find this treasure of sage food writing and dietary advice to be surprisingly relevant today as it was during World War II. As we enter 2012, America continues to be deeply engaged in military conflicts abroad. Nationally, obesity is epidemic. Global economic uncertainty and political gridlock in Washington have many middle class Americans and families struggling to keep the wolf from their door.

It seems then the perfect time to be revisiting M.F.K. Fisher's timeless classic on living happily and well, even in the toughest of times. Her practical approach to healthy, economical, heart-warming and soul-staying meals continues to have an audience, just as it did seventy years ago.

(January 2012)

HOMETOWN APPETITES

*T*HIS THANKSGIVING, I pulled out the November 2002 issue of *Saveur* magazine and turned to an article about Clementine Paddleford—a forgotten food writer who spent decades traveling the country and chronicling how America ate. A post-it sized note on the cover hinted at the delicious contents of the issue—"Good, Old-Fashioned Roast Turkey." Most intriguing was the title of the feature article—"Clementine Paddleford: First Champion of American Regional Cooking."

Clementine who? I recall wondering. Apparently, I was not the only one. Kelly Alexander, the article's author, had also never heard of Clementine Paddleford before Alexander's husband discovered a dusty copy of *How America Eats* (Scribner 1960) in a used bookstore two years earlier. Intrigued with Paddleford's vivid descriptions of food, Alexander decided to learn all she could about the book's once internationally famous food writer.

After convincing her *Saveur* editor, Coleman Andrews, that Paddleford was worthy of a story, Alexander headed for Manhattan, Kansas, where she teamed up with Cynthia Harris, Kansas State University's manuscripts/collections archivist. Working together, the two Paddleford enthusiasts began organizing the voluminous body of the journalist's donated papers.

Virtually forgotten over the years since her death in New York City on November 13, 1967, Paddleford was for a time perhaps the world's most influential food writer. Born in 1900 on a two hundred sixty acre farm near Stockdale, Kansas, Clementine Haskin Paddleford graduated from KSU in 1921 before moving to the other Manhattan to study journalism at New York University.

For three decades in the years before the food empires of Martha Stewart and Rachel Ray and 24/7 cable TV cooking channels, Paddleford defined how America ate. Her food column appeared weekly in the *New York Herald Tribune* from 1936 until the newspaper folded in 1966. Concurrently, she wrote for *This Week,* edited *Farm and Fireside* magazine, and wrote for *Gourmet* magazine from 1941-1953. With an estimated twelve million weekly readers, she was called the "best known food editor" in America in 1953.

While Paddleford enjoyed covering international food stories behind events that included Queen Elizabeth's coronation and Winston Churchill's Iron Curtain speech in Fulton, MO, she also relished eating with crews on fishing boats and enjoyed sampling slum gullion at a Hobo Convention. She adored cats, especially her own cat, Pussywillow, that accompanied Paddleford to work at the *Tribune* and napped in the in-box on her desk.

Paddleford attributed her love of cooking to her mother, Jennie who "stirred-in joy" and "seasoned every meal with love." The food editor's extensive travels—over fifty thousand miles a year—taught her "we all have hometown appetites." "Every person is a bundle of longing for the simplicities of good taste once enjoyed on the farm or in the hometown they left behind."

Such stories and wisdom were shared in crisp, smart prose that stimulated the senses of her readers. "Chowder," she wrote, " breathes reassurance. It steams consolation." To her, the perfect soufflé responded, "with a rapturous, half hushed sigh as it settles softly to melt and vanish in a moment like smoke or a dream."

"How does America eat?" wrote Paddleford half a century ago. "She eats on the fat of the land. She eats in every language. For the most part, even with the increasingly popular trend toward foreign food, the dishes come to the table with an American accent."

Paddleford's 1960 work, *How America Eats,* was based on

personal interviews with more than two thousand of the country's best cooks who shared regional American recipes that are "word-of-mouth hand-downs from mother to daughter." In addition to recipes, it documents the way immigrants influenced American cuisine—concocting dishes that had been "mixed and Americanized."

In the forward to Paddleford's *The Best in American Cooking* (1970), a friend remembers the author: "These regional recipes are a harvest of Clementine's interviews, the windfall of her food reporting for over thirty years. Recipes carried in heads and in worn suitcases from lands around the world; recipes that fell into our national melting pot and emerged with a special flavor—American regional cooking."

Kelly Alexander's collaborative Paddleford research with Kansas State University archivist Cynthia Harris continued after the initial *Saveur* article, and recently the two published a biography of Paddleford entitled *Hometown Appetites*. In the book's forward, Coleman Andrews, *Saveur's* co-founder in 1994, writes about "Why Clem Matters":

> "As I started reading this obviously feisty, indefatigable Kansan's reports (the recipes) from half a century earlier... I was seduced by their unpretentious tone and evocative detail, but I was also quite astonished. Though her writing was new to me, Clementine Paddleford had apparently invented *Saveur* when I was still in my highchair—not really inventing it, of course, but concerned herself with exactly the same culinary issues and approached her subject matter from exactly the same point of view we did."

Alexander's *Saveur* article is filled with Paddleford's favorite Thanksgiving recipes—roast turkey with wild rice stuffing and old-fashioned pan gravy; her mother Jennie's recipe for milky, creamy Oyster stew that smells of the sea; Mrs. Orville Burtis's butterhorn rolls and sweet potato tipsy; minted cranberry sauce; and Paddleford's own 1937 black walnut pumpkin pie.

This Thanksgiving, some of her recipes—mixed and fused with my own mother-to-daughter, handed-down family favorites—will be recreated for friends who gather around the harvest table at Boomerang Creek. After all, sharing good cooking was what Clementine Paddleford's life was all about.

(November 2013)

MEMORIES OF MANGOS AND CURRY LEAVES

$\mathcal{R}$AIN. A RESPITE FROM ROUNDS OF WATERING that have kept the gardens hydrated this past dry July. Slow mornings on the screened porch listening with Kit to a sound we'd almost forgotten. Books piled on the long table before me. A rattan settee where I am anchored between our cats, Pooh and Fanny—each with an outstretched front paw firmly resting on my knees. A cup of steaming hot Kenyan black tea with a pinch of garam masala and dollop of milk.

Rain. The permission I have wished for, allowing me to come in from the noise of the world and the demands of an ambitious summer garden. With this the setting, a food journey begins. Before sipping my tea, I raise the cup to my nose and breathe in. Eyes closed, a list of spices—pods, seeds, powders, and pastes—spills forth. I mouth each as it appears. *"Fenugreek, turmeric, cardamom, ginger, cumin, black mustard, coriander, red chilies, green mango, curry leaves, cilantro, and tamarind."*

Most immediate is the fragrance of garam masala in my tea, connecting me to Madhur Jaffrey's 1975 cookbook, *An Invitation to Indian Cooking*, and her garam masala recipe reprinted in this month's India issue of *Saveur*. In a spice grinder, combine and grind together one quarter cup cardamom seeds and one and one-half teaspoons each of black cumin seeds, whole black peppercorns, whole cloves, four sticks cinnamon, and one whole nutmeg cracked into pieces.

This I've now done, relegating a former coffee bean grinder to a new purpose. A week before the issue arrived, I'd just finished reading two books—local author Nina Mukerjee Furstenau's memoir, *Biting Through the Skin: An Indian Kitchen in America's Heartland*, and

---

Richard C. Morais's *The Hundred-Foot Journey*. Reading back and forth from each, they became bookends between which I add food memories of my own. Like jars filled with spices, they are stored but not forgotten. Reopened, they connect me to journeys taken and remembered, just as they connect these two gifted writers to family and home.

Cilantro and kaffir limes. Pots of spicy sauces and curries bought in backstreet Thai food markets, carried home in plastic bags dangling by rubber bands from the fingers on one hand while the other grips an overhead bar on a crowded bus speeding across Bangkok. Reheated and enhanced with fish, squid, or chicken, they were eaten with jasmine rice cooked on an electric hot plate in the kitchen I shared with two students, Chomsri and Siripon, half a century ago.

My Thai food memories commenced five years after Nina was born in Bangkok when her Hindu Bengali parents worked there. Later, traveling in India and Nepal, I added to those memories—dal with cauliflower and potatoes and chocolate cake prepared in a cast-iron Dutch oven by a Sherpa cook on a trek in the Himalayas—my first indelible immersion into the flavors of the Indian subcontinent.

Reading *The Hundred-Foot Journey*, I am transported to Mumbai where Hassan Haji first tastes sea urchin, then breathes in and identifies for his mother the intoxicating mix of spices in her fiery fish curry. With his family, we journey to Lumière, France, where destiny introduces the young chef to classical French cuisine in the kitchen of Madame Mallory—preparation for the culinary journey that awaits him in Paris.

In our kitchen at Boomerang Creek, I open Nina's memoir to the final chapter and step-by-step prepare her family's Rainy-Day Khicuri (Rice and Lentils with potato and cauliflower) and Indian Vindaloo. First, six spices must be ground into a powder. Then oil is heated in a large copper stockpot until a bay leaf, cinnamon stick, whole cloves and cardamom pods come to a sizzle and pop.

I recall the first time I peeled a mango and cooked with curry leaves. It is then that I release a prayer of thanks for the August rains from whence sprang these deeply rooted food memories—rich, spicy, and indelibly delicious.

(September 2014)

Chapter Thirteen
FAMILY SNAPSHOTS

This year, April stormed the barricades set up by aging March to stem the flow of time. But alas, neither time nor spring rains can be kept from their destiny.

C.S. April 2014

TWENTY-NINE PUMPKINS AGO

HEIDI IS MY DAUGHTER. Well, in fact not exactly, but indeed, yes she is. What matters is that I think of her as so. There is a story, of course, as there always is with families, and this is ours. It began twenty-nine pumpkins ago, which is to say just before Halloween in 1977 when Heidi was almost nine, and I had just turned thirty-two.

That was the summer when I first met Kit while taking a summer class he was teaching at UCLA. At the time, Heidi and her brother Hayden were living with their mother up Beverly Glen Boulevard, that snakes up a narrow urban canyon off Sunset Boulevard in West Los Angeles. Kit was by then living on his own in a rented apartment not far from campus. Over the prior year he had built a bunk bed for those nights when the kids slept over.

By fall, patterns that evolve when families reconfigure were beginning to fall into place. The kids stayed overnight on Wednesdays and most weekends. Kit was chief cook and bedtime storyteller extraordinaire. At bunk time, Hayden and Heidi played a word game with Kit called "the cook and the king." The kids came up with dishes like macaroni and cheese or sauces like ketchup, and Kit would then make up a story about how the king's cook had come up with each recipe. If the king didn't like the results, it was off with the cook's head.

Games aside, Kit's personal repertoire of dinner menus was exactly one—"nurkle" (his creative variation on the subject of meatloaf), mashed potatoes (boiled with the skins left on) and frozen green peas. Pretty quickly, I saw my role in this close-knit circle of three. Most evenings, I cooked while Kit threw hardball with Hayden who was in Little League, and Heidi entertained herself making amazing little creatures out of Play-Doh.

Kit's apartment was next to a small urban park in West Los Angeles that was landscaped with large boulders for children to climb, sidewalks ideal for skateboarding, outdoor grills and picnic tables perfect for weekend cookouts. That October, while Hayden and Kit were playing catch, Heidi and I carried pumpkins, newspaper, magic markers and small carving knives outside to one of the tables. Thinking back on our history, I count this event as our first, just the two of us, Heidi and Cathy project.

I remember three things about that afternoon—Heidi's hair, her hat, and her bravery. Her hair was long and wild, untamably curly, and a rich dark brown. Brushing it would have been fussy, which Heidi was not. Instead, she opted to keep it under control by wearing a Cuffy cap turned backwards. Her bravery related to our pumpkin carving exercise that turned scary when Heidi's knife slipped and cut her finger.

"That's it," I said to myself as I sprinted to Kit's apartment in search of a hot washcloth, Bacitracin and Band-Aids. "I am now officially toast in the mother-daughter bonding department. One pumpkin and done! " But there was nary a tear nor sob from this brave eight-year old. Heidi, I learned, loved Band-Aids as much as she loved that old cap. I had survived my first test.

The following summer, the four of us decided to really test our new unit by driving across country in Kit's school-bus-yellow Volkswagen, pop-top Westphalia camper van. It was a six-thousand-mile journey, one of two cross-county trips the four of us took during our ten years living together in California. The trip was filled with memories but two in particular stand out in my mind as pure Heidi. The van had no hood ornament, so Heidi created one while we were camped at Bear Lake, Idaho over Kit's fortieth birthday. Her creation was a giraffe named "Noble Neck" that rode on the dashboard the remainder of the trip, guiding us on our way and keeping us safe from wild beasts and those weird creatures that go bump in the night.

The other moment came on our last day of the road trip. We had swum in rivers and waded through streams from the Pacific Coast to the Atlantic and back across the country's Heartland and Southwest. Our final swim was in the Colorado River where it forms the border between Arizona and California. It was a beastly hot August afternoon, and the river looked cold and inviting. Without a second thought, we pulled off the road and suited up for a quick dip. Hayden and Heidi, both good swimmers, plunged in first, but within seconds they were caught by a current that was moving faster than they could manage. In a flash, I swam toward Heidi who hung onto my neck as I swam toward the shore. Kit headed for Hayden and rescued him in the same fashion.

I think that that moment and the post-rescue picture we took of ourselves—dripping wet and happy to be alive—says it all. We were a team. Over time, we would work out the semantics of what to call our evolving family relationship. The important thing is that we became a family and remain one to this day.

Heidi turns forty-seven this November. She is a creative artist, a community college English professor in northern California, and the published author and illustrator of a children's book, *Taddy McFinley and the Great Grey Grimly*. A few summers ago, Heidi bought a Volkswagen van and completed a six-thousand-mile road trip to Canada and Alaska with her partner, Sugie, and their three dogs— Atticus, Jake, and Joaquin. Many life decisions, shared memories, roads and pumpkin harvests later in our journey together as Salters,

I am enormously proud to celebrate Heidi as the extraordinary daughter in my life.

(May 2015)

ON THE SUBJECT OF LANGUAGE

*I*N A BIOGRAPHY OF JOHN ADAMS, I came across a quote by Thomas Jefferson—"The earth belongs in usufruct to the living." A reader with any modicum of curiosity could not sail through such a sentence without backing up to chew awhile on the odd, antiquated, mouthful of a word that holds the key to Jefferson's meaning. *Us-u-fruct.* And so I did.

I went to my library shelf and pulled out David McCullough's 2001 biography of the Founding Father and second U.S. president, *John Adams,* and turned to page 450 to remind myself of the context of the word's usage. McCullough had been talking about a correspondence between John Adams and Thomas Jefferson in the spring of 1794— their first communication in two years.

The two had had serious differences with each other but it was spring. Jefferson had returned to Monticello and returned to farming *"with an ardor,"* he wrote to Adams, *"which I scarcely knew in my youth."* Adams, who spent summers at his farm in Quincy, Massachusetts whenever possible, agreed and wrote back of a summer "spent so deliciously in farming that I return to the old story of politics with great reluctance."

But, McCullough notes, Adams disagreed with his friend when Jefferson observed that the *"paper transactions of one generation should scarcely be considered by succeeding generations,"* that *"the earth belongs in **usufruct** to the living: that the dead have neither the power or rights over it."* Jefferson, McCullough explains, was writing of a principal that Jefferson believed to be self-evident.

At this point I turned to my dictionary for more on the subject of *usufruct*. Its Latin root is *usufructus*. In legal jargon, it refers to "the right to utilize and enjoy the profits and advantages of something belonging to another so long as the property is not damaged or altered in any way. Use and enjoyment."

It was a time of building revolutionary fervor in France. Jefferson felt "a little rebellion now and then to clear the atmosphere," was a good thing. Adams, McCullough observed, "refused to accept the idea that each generation could simply put aside the past...to suit its own desires."

Unspoken in these letters were Adam's suspicions of what Jefferson's "retirement" to Monticello would do to him. Jefferson much later acknowledged in a letter to his daughter Polly that during the period from 1793 to 1797 when he withdrew from the world of politics to his mountaintop at Monticello, he (Jefferson) had suffered a breakdown that left him "unfit for society, and uneasy when engaged in it."

I think of these two founding fathers, one a frugal New Englander, the other who designed a French villa atop a mountain in Virginia, and marvel at the enduring documents that reflect the combined legacy of their ideas and words. I am also fascinated with the nature of their friendship built around letters. Adams, according to McCullough, understood Jefferson. And though politics severely strained their friendship for periods of time, the two men corresponded regularly in the final years of their lives, sharing their thoughts once again as old friends.

Language has the power to connect us over distance and time. On a recent trip to Madrid, Kit and I visited our son Hayden, his Spanish wife Ana, and their three children—Nicolas (then nine), Ines (then four), and Catalina (then two). Hayden who has lived in Europe off and on for the past fifteen years is fluent in Spanish. When called upon in professional situations, he also relies on the French and Italian he picked up while living briefly in those two countries before settling in Spain.

Our grandson Nicolas speaks in animated English with us about soccer and quotes favorite lines from the quirky independent film *Napoleon Dynamite*. Conversations between Hayden and Nico move seamlessly from Spanish to English to French. They have also picked up some Portuguese from Vera—the Brazilian woman who has lived with the family since Nicolas was five.

When Kit and I visited Madrid two years ago, Ines was only two—an age when more time is spent crying than communicating. Now a charming and affectionate four-year old, she was eager to know her American *abuela* and *abuelo*—grandmother and grandfather. Fixing her enormous brown eyes on my face, she touched my mouth and hair, and then waited for me to speak.

Ines doesn't speak English. I don't speak Spanish. Desperate to communicate, I realized that our common language was French—the language Ines and Nico speak at school— the *Lycée Français de Madrid*. I last studied French in high school forty years ago.

"*Rouge*," I said, touching the rosy color on her beautiful face. "Red." Then reaching into my purse, I pulled out a compact and brushed her cheeks and nose with a touch of plum-colored powder.

From that moment on, French—however basic and rusty—connected us heart to heart in that magic way that only language can. For Ines, I became Abuela Cathy who lives on a farm with Abuelo Kit and three cats in a place called Missouri—one she hopes to visit someday soon.

(May 2006)

Nico's Excellent Adventure

$\mathcal{O}$ n his recent visit to Boomerang Creek, our grandson, Nicolas watched the Tom Hanks movie *Big*. A boy about Nico's age visits a traveling carnival and puts a coin in a fortune telling machine. The turbaned seer's eyes light up, smoke issues forth from his mouth, and a voice demands to know the boy's wish. "I wish I was big," the boy says, and the next morning when he wakes up, he is Tom Hanks with a twelve-year old's mind.

Seeing Missouri these past two weeks with Nicolas was a bit like *Big* in reverse for me. Watching and listening to Nico's expansive and fluently expressed thoughts on international politics, soccer, spiders, Mustangs, technology and all that he finds beautiful about Missouri has me feeling like a kid again. He tells his American grandparents, Abuelo Kit and Abuela Cathy, his ambitions when he is big and we understand them completely. "When I grow up," he says with certainty, " I want to live in Los Angeles, Paris, and then Missouri."

I told Nico whose home is in Madrid, Spain that Missourians can easily drive to Paris, Versailles, Japon, Mexico, Milan, and to a town called New Madrid—site of the strongest earthquake ever recorded in North America at a magnitude of XII on the Mercalli intensity scale of I (not felt) to XII (extreme)—without ever leaving the state. For a comparison, I add that 1906 San Francisco earthquake was only a VII.) Impressed, Nico tells us we are "super lucky" to live here, and when he is old enough to buy a Mustang, he'll drive around Missouri to them all.

Nico is a lean, Mediterranean-American, multi-lingual package of boundless energy who loves American hamburgers, Fruit Loops,

Coco Puffs, whole milk, chocolate ice cream, orange juice, and movie popcorn with butter. A visit to a Sonic drive-in led to a new food favorite—the American corn dog on a stick—proof positive of Nico's direct culinary linkage to his American grandfather, Abuelo Kit.

This grandfather and grandson are true pals. Driving to a matinee of this summer's *Star Trek* movie, Kit filled Nico in on the backstory, explaining that he had first watched *Star Trek* reruns with Nico's father, Hayden, and his Aunt Heidi when our son and daughter were little kids in Los Angeles. By the time Kit reached the movie theater, Nico could align his fingers deftly into a Vulcan "V" and recite Spock-speak like a true Trekkie— *"Live long and prosper."*

On Independence Day, I made Nico buttermilk pancakes with blueberries we'd picked the morning before at Greg and Carol Busacker's blueberry farm near Wilton. That same day, we attended the wonderful "Patriotic Pops" tribute at Columbia's historic Missouri Theater. Afterwards, we strolled with the Pfeffer family to Cold Stone Creamery for chocolate ice cream with sprinkles, and bumped into Paige Sommerer (Miss Columbia 2009)—the very same lovely and talented vocalist who had just dazzled the audience at the Pops Concert.

Even better than the sprinkles on chocolate ice cream was when we bumped into our friend, Sgt. Chris Kelley, riding on a police department Segway near the 10th Street Parking Structure. Next to Mustangs, Segways are currently the most super cool mode of transport on the planet in Nico's mind. "They don't exist in Madrid," he explained, "except on futuristic TV shows." I said we'd recently seen tourists on rented Segways in Washington, D.C., and Kit wondered if they were hard to ride. Sargent Kelley assured him he could learn to ride one in just two hours, explaining that a gyroscope keeps you upright and balanced on two wheels.

During summer visits, grandchildren and grandparents keep their balance by building breaks into action-packed days. What works for our trio are lazy breakfasts on the porch, occasional movie matinees to get out of the heat, afternoon naps under ceiling fans while Nico writes in his travel journal, and Kit's nightly reading aloud from Louis L'Amour's *Last of the Breed* until Nico finally nods off.

For his thirteenth birthday, we gave Nico a cell-phone sized, point-and-shoot camera. He immediately began capturing images to illustrate the daily entries he has been making in his journal of this summer's Missouri visit. Nico's first entry set the stage—"9:00 a.m. Madrid. I woke up, put the last things in my bag, had breakfast, told bye-bye to everybody and went to the airport with my granddad."

In a later entry from Boomerang Creek, Cocoa Puffs and Kellogg's Fruit Loops cereal box tabs were Scotch taped to a page in the journal. And there is a favorite picture of Nico standing next to a mustard yellow Mustang at Andy's Frozen Custard in Columbia and another of Nico in a super tall Stetson straw hat leaning against a giant round hay bale that had just been harvested along Liberty Lane in Ashland. Others will be added once he has penned in the details of each adventure.

As Nico flies back to Madrid, he will recall stories of spiders and tree frogs, his thirteenth birthday party, KOMU's morning *Pepper & Friends* TV show, American hamburgers, fireflies, outings to Arrow Rock and Kansas City, shared conversations and road songs, and adventures with our three adorable cats. Each is a part of the magic he has been capturing in his journal—memories from our "not quite 'big' yet" grandson Nico's "super wonderful" visit to Missouri. *Besos*, Nico. We miss you.

(July 2009)

Now That I'm Sixty-Five

$\mathscr{T}$HIS IS IT. IT IS OCTOBER OF THE YEAR 2010. The month I turn sixty-five and officially reach senior status. For months I've been the recipient of an avalanche of information from healthcare companies, AARP, Medicare and the Social Security Administration explaining new healthcare options, deadlines for making changes, and helpful hotlines should I have any questions. Already, I've used my Medicare card for my annual flu shot and made a plane reservation online with a senior discount. Having done so, I'm now officially in the system for the rest of the journey.

However, being a senior has its challenges. Kit and I recently changed our satellite service and can testify that the technological leap from our five-year old receivers and remote control devices to the newest technology takes a village to understand. The experience reminded me of our move to Breakfast Creek in 1988. It was our first home in the country where installing a massive satellite dish in the yard was the only way you could pull in channels beyond ABC, NBC and CBS. For us, PBS is a must.

We called Tom's Satellite on old Route K and a deal was put together. Tom and his assistant spent all afternoon digging a hole, pouring concrete, installing a steel pole, and attaching a space age dish we then dubbed our "yard art installation." It was dark by the time Tom came inside and began a rapid-fire tutorial in total techno-speak with remote controls blazing in both hands. Cross-eyed-tired, I took copious notes and hoped Kit was absorbing more of Tom's satellite patois than I was.

Whenever our nephews Adam and Christopher visited Breakfast Creek as boys, they could channel surf with a remote in each hand, not once looking at the buttons or seeming in the least lost in their search. I'm convinced it is a generational thing. When you get right down to it, I'd much rather be reading, outside watching an autumn sunset with Kit, or mentally traveling the world via my own imagination.

When I was preparing to teach a travel writing class in the fall of 2010, my first sojourn was an exploration into the world of books that exist on the subject of travel. Words took me places without a single reservation. In an instant, I was gone, transported by the mere mention of a place or city by name. Rome, Istanbul, Bangkok, Shanghai, Cairo, Buenos Aires, Kabul. The words alone were my transporter. My plane. My magic carpet ride. In class, our discussion of travel began with books and articles written by both past and contemporary travelers.

Soon our explorations led beyond a sense of place to a broad range of practical questions relating to contemporary travel. In search of answers, I explored websites that not only took me places virtually, but offered answers for travelers setting off for new worlds. Reading the daily *New York Times* online, I took a three-minute video tour entitled "36 Hours in Rome" and immediately shared it with my students.

Minutes later, an email arrived from Beijing. In words and pictures, my sister Kelly and her husband, Jack shared their first visit to China's Great Wall, the Forbidden City, the Summer Palace, a traditional hutong neighborhood with ancient housing soon to be replaced by high-rise apartments in this city of 19.2 million people, and a fog of pollution and automobile congestion. A day later, another email described an overnight train ride from Beijing to Xian, and a walk around Xian with blue skies overhead.

Having arrived at sixty-five, I still enjoy international travel and the vicarious adventures of others. But, even more, I love a country life that allows me the quietude to read, paint, garden, cook, reflect and write about the world—up close and with a little help from technology, from afar. As I take in the blaze of fall colors at Boomerang Creek, I cannot imagine a sweeter place to spend the next chapter of my life.

(October 2010)

LETTING GO

*O*N THE FINAL TURN OF MY MORNING WALK around the meadow at Boomerang Creek, I am suddenly aware of a stinging sensation on my arm. I've circled the quarter mile walking path six times, striding with walking poles that instruct me on where solid ground is before my feet are squarely planted, one ahead of the other, allowing me to move without fear of stumbling while lost in thought, invisible to all save the birds in the bluebird box on the fencepost that fly out to distract me from the nest that lies within.

I locate the source of the pain, a small biting fly on my arm that resists my efforts to pull it off. Swat! Gone now, all but the sting. My reverie interrupted, I turn my attention to watering the strawberry bed that has produced an abundance of ripe June berries following weeks of May rains.

The exercise of watering carries my thoughts to the desert world I left six years ago when I realized I could not put down roots in such a dry and distant place, even though my sister Molly and brother-in-law Jim had retired there the prior year. I made a choice, initially painful like a bite, returning to begin life anew in Missouri in hopes that the sting of our familial separation would in time lessen and eventually heal.

A year ago, Molly was diagnosed with stage three ovarian cancer. Since then I've returned to Albuquerque frequently to share what time I had left with her, each time preparing our mother Alice's incomparable meatloaf and mashed potatoes with whole milk and real butter in hopes that this magic combination might do what months of aggressive chemotherapy ultimately failed to do.

Each journey back, I found Molly physically weaker from the toxic chemicals that attacked her body while unsuccessfully targeting the inoperable tumors that remained following her surgery a year ago when she first learned of the silent killer just weeks after returning from a magical trip to Italy with Jim. For a year, they hung on to hope that she would win her valiant battle and in time be able to return to Tuscany the whole and vibrant woman she'd felt herself to be just months earlier.

On one visit, I brought a classy little black dress for Molly to wear to the annual dinner her doctor hosts for former patients who reach the five-year remission mark as cancer survivors. Molly held up the dress and decided it would be perfect with the pearl necklace our father brought her years ago following a trip to Japan.

I also brought a prayer quilt made by women in the Caring Ministry at Peace Church in Hartsburg. During a service, the quilt was passed from hand to hand around the congregation so that each member of the church might silently pray for Molly's recovery and tie a knot with the pieces of yarn left visible for that purpose on the quilt's cover.

In late May, I cut a cluster of fragrant peonies and carefully toted it in my hand luggage for what I knew would be my final visit with Molly, the sister who had been a part of my life for more than sixty-five years. Always beautiful and poised, smart and self-assured, she was a singular woman who was in fact many women to the circle of family members and friends who gathered in Albuquerque for her memorial service the first week of June.

Molly spent twenty-five years working to improve health care for poor women in developing countries—Pakistan, Indonesia, Kenya and Nepal—while she and Jim were on assignments with the U.S. Agency for International Development. She leaves behind a legacy of having truly made a difference in the lives of thousands of poor women who benefited from programs that Molly began. But first and always, she was my big sister, and I miss her powerfully at this painful time of letting go… and always will.

(June 2011)

Cathy Salter

JULIA AND ALICE: TWO EXTRAORDINARY WOMEN

*A*UGUST 15, 2012 WAS THE CENTENNIAL of the birth of Julia Child, the celebrated chef and cookbook writer who died in 1992 just days before her ninety-second birthday. My mother Alice will be celebrating her ninety-third birthday on August 21 in San Antonio, Texas where she was born at Ft. Sam Houston in 1919. What the two of them have in common gets to the meat and potatoes of my love for both of these extraordinary women.

Julia McWilliams grew up in a conservative, well-to-do family in Pasadena, California where meals were basic rather than continental. A towering six-foot-two-inch athletic figure full of the theatric, Julia ate merely to feed her energetic self, not caring a jot about the food she was ingesting or the act of cooking.

My mother Alice was the daughter of William Henry Kasten, a cavalry officer in the U.S. Army, and my Ohio born grandmother Florence who was seventeen when she married Granddad and moved with him to San Antonio at the end of World War I. Officer's quarters on U.S. Army posts in the 1920s came with a cook. Meals were similar to those in Julia's Pasadena home—meat, potatoes, gravy, garden-variety vegetables, rolls and desserts. Granny didn't do much of the cooking herself until later in life, but somewhere along the way she learned to make the best turkey gravy I've ever tasted. During World War II, my mother married my father—the seventh of seven children born on a small Pennsylvania dairy farm where home-cooked meals were served three times a day. Mother had never even fried bacon.

Similarly, Julia's introduction to food began when she met her future husband, Paul Child after volunteering with the Office of

Strategic Services during World War II. Paul had grown up in Paris and developed a taste for sophisticated continental cuisine, none of which was available in the military mess halls in Ceylon or Kunming, China where the two were later reassigned. Craving local cuisine, Paul drove Julia to local villages to sample regional Chinese dishes—a totally new culinary experience for this tall, gangly young woman from Southern California.

By the early 1950s, my mother was busily preparing meals for two adults and three little girls with the help of the *Good Housekeeping Cookbook* that lives in a handy drawer in her kitchen to this day. It was the original source of her matchless meatloaf and a spaghetti sauce spiced with cloves—two classics she passed down on three-by-five-inch recipe cards to all four of her daughters.

Over the course of my childhood, my mother cooked her way through that *Good Housekeeping Cookbook* in the kitchens of each Air Force base where my father was assigned, preparing breakfasts and dinners, and packing lunch boxes for four little girls. At the same time, Julia began her culinary training at the Cordon Bleu, explored the food markets of Paris, Marseilles, Bonn and Oslo, and invested a decade of collaborative testing and experimentation with Simone Beck and Louisette Bertholle that culminated in their best-selling classic, *Mastering the Art of French Cooking*, published in 1961 when I was in high school.

The awakening of Julia's palette occurred when the Childs docked at the port of Le Havre en route to Paris in 1948. The couple stopped for lunch at Paul's favorite restaurant, La Couronne, in Rouen. Sole *meunière* browned by golden Normandy butter, oysters *portugaise* on the half shell, salad greens, crème fraîche, a bottle of chilled Pouilly-Fuissé and *café filter* were served on a white table cloth—providing a memorable culinary experience Julia later described as her epiphany. It was, she recalled, the first food she had ever tasted.

During the first decade of my life in Los Angeles with Kit and his two young children, Hayden and Heidi, I cooked in a kitchen so small that it now seems impossible that I dared to prepare recipes from Julia Child's two-volume *Mastering* oeuvre (1961/1970).

Coq au Vin! Quiche Lorraine! But of course!

If I were to make a dinner tonight for these two extraordinary women who provided the diverse foundation for my own culinary explorations, it would be Alice's *Good Housekeeping* meatloaf with mashed potatoes and Julia's dessert recipe, *Reine De Saba* on page 677 of *Mastering the Art of French Cooking, Vol. 1.* Like Julia and Alice, both are classics that I love. Happy one-hundreth birthday, Julia. Happy ninety-third, Alice. As Julia would say, "*Bon Appétit!*"

(August 2012)

Behold the Waters

*T*HIS YEAR, APRIL STORMED THE BARRICADES set up by aging March to stem the flow of time. But alas, neither time nor spring rains can be kept from their destiny. Announcing her arrival with thunderous lightening and ominous clouds, April erasing morning light completely on the first day of the newly arrived month. Two days later, tornadic activity danced all around. Winds tossed hail grown big as ping pong balls up and down as if in a duel with the heavens. With Kit in Boston, I weathered the storms inside, a book in hand, and our cats Fanny and Pooh by my side.

"Behold the waters," I told the cats as rainwater rushed across the meadow toward a channel separating the shade garden and nearby woods. When lightening flashed, setting their ears on point, I assured them that Henry David Thoreau had found such days sharpened his powers of inward reflection—

> *I love very well this cloudy afternoon,*
> *So sober and favorable to reflection*
> *After so many bright ones.*
> *What if the clouds shut out the heavens,*
> *Provided they concentrate my thoughts*
> *And make a more celestial heaven below!*

When the cats fell into a deep slumber and there was a break in the rains, I slipped outdoors and headed down our long gravel driveway to collect the mail. Just short of the road, the force of the day's torrential rains lay evident.

For hours, rainwater had rushed across our sloping meadow

toward a four-hundred foot channel along the driveway, pushing forward any fallen leaves in its narrow path. Compacted into a rapidly multiplying mass, they had completely clogged both the end of the channel and a small culvert buried under our gravel driveway that directs rainwater into our boomerang-shaped creek through two massive culverts buried under our gravel county road. With the runoff's progress thwarted, the water's force dug a new channel across our driveway, displacing rock and strewing dense mounds of leaves as if a giant mole had been up to serious mischief.

As I beheld the water's aftermath, I saw the dense layering of leaves as chapters chronicling the storm's journey, creating volumes bound tightly by a layering of muddy glue. It could only get worse. Storms were forecast to resume soon and increase overnight. *"You know what to do,"* I heard my father and his brother Ralph whisper from on high.

I had been thinking about Uncle Ralph constantly since his passing two days earlier at the venerable age of one hundred one. He'd loved the dairy farms in West Finley and Bedford, Pennsylvania where he and my father grew up. After moving to Texas in 1945, the year I was born, and working at a steel mill for thirty years, Uncle Ralph and Aunt Lou—his wife of eighty years—built a house on forty-eight acres they called the Riggs Ranch. There they raised six children, a menagerie of animals and later welcomed a passel of grandkids who played in the barn, fished, and rode in the bucket of their Grandpa Ralph's Kubota tractor.

Buoyed by the spirited presence and memory of the strong hands of my father and Uncle Ralph, I put on my tall muck boots acquired during the Hartsburg flood of 1993, and stepped down into the channel with pitchfork in hand and wheelbarrow nearby. By the time rain began to fall again two hours later, water moved freely into the culvert.

Above me, thunder rolled, as if a rollicking barn dance was underway on the farm where Uncle Ralph was born on November

12, 1912. It was, I do believe, a celebration underway on high. And you can bet my father was at the barn door, eager to welcome his brother Ralph back to their boyhood home.

> Let me go where'er I will
> I hear a sky-born music still:
> It sounds from all things old,
> It sounds from all things young,
> From all that's fair, from all that's foul,
> Peels out a cheerful song….
> …in the darkest, meanest things
> There always, always something sings.
>
> Ralph Waldo Emerson

(April 2014)

Chapter Fourteen

ENCOUNTERS WITH THE NATURAL WORLD

I walked out to the meadow where fireflies danced as they magically do in mid-July when temperatures in the nineties cause the garden foliage to explode following abundant rain. Standing there under the stars, surrounded by the magical incandescence of firefly illuminations, I was once again anchored. Surrounded by the natural world I so love at Boomerang Creek.

C.S. August 2011

A NATURIST ON BOOMERANG CREEK

*O*N A RECENT TRIP, I CAME ACROSS a copy of David Kline's 1997 book, *Scratching the Woodchuck: Nature on an Amish Farm.* Kline tells of coming across a sleeping woodchuck while walking one summer day on land near his farm. Keenly attuned to the natural world, he extended his walking stick and scratched the sleeping creature that then arched its back with pleasure and appeared to genuinely welcome the attention.

Kline's eloquent gem of a book is this farmer's account of the rhythms of nature and the plants and animals he has witnessed over a fifty-year period in and around his Amish farm in northwestern Ohio where he grew up. Kline once wrote, "Sometimes I wonder whether I farm to make a living or whether it is all a front, just an excuse to be out in the fields looking at clouds."

I often feel the same way as I move about the five acres of garden and meadow, glade and woods at Boomerang Creek. As a writer, I feel a kinship with Kline who divides his observations into collections of discursive essays that move easily from farmstead to fields, woods and creek, and his local community.

Upon arriving back in the heartland from a weeklong trip to New Mexico, I was struck with the intensity of the lush green vegetation that had been fed by rain while I was gone. The sand tones of adobe walls and xeriscape gardens common to the dry, desert world were absent. Soybeans had grown more than a foot tall, and fields of tasseled corn lined stretches of the drive home from the St. Louis airport.

I walked out to the meadow where fireflies danced as they magically do in mid July when temperatures in the nineties cause the garden foliage to explode following abundant rain. Standing there under the stars, surrounded by the magical incandescence of firefly illuminations, I was once again anchored. Surrounded by the natural world I so love at Boomerang Creek.

The following morning, I asked Kit if he'd noticed any activity in the wren nest built in a planter on a wall of the house in late June. "Indeed," he replied, pointing out the barricade he had created on the porch railing to keep our cats from reaching the nest. "Fanny," Kit reported, "has been spending an inordinate amount of time focused directly on the three flower pots that provide cover for the cleverly constructed nest."

No sooner had I asked but a juvenile wren with spiky feathers atop its head popped out of the nest and stood wide-eyed and straight-backed as a barred owl on the rim of the planter, ready to receive food from the parent birds that were singing in a nearby tree. We made eye contact, and there the little creature remained that hot, humid day as its parents fed it in preparation for flying the coop. The next morning the young wren was gone and the nest empty.

I set out later that morning to cut flowers in the rose beds and gather in the last of this year's glorious array of daylilies and a few long wands of purple hosta flowers. Unlike the meadow garden, the shade gardens give without growing wild—remaining calm, offering calm, the perfect haven for our Thai spirit house where another pair of wrens made a nest early in the spring.

Squirrels dash to and fro, stealing pears from our orchard, while our three cats—tired from a morning of chasing about—collapse on whatever cool surface they can find and wait for the cycle of the rotating porch fan to stir a breeze their way. There they remain, slowed into sluggishness by the afternoon's languorous midsummer air. Perhaps like the sleeping woodchuck discovered by Amish farmer David Kline, they too might enjoy having their furry bellies scratched.

(July 2010)

Sweet Cat Grass and Dreams of Summer

*I*N FEBRUARY, WINTER DRESSES THE WORLD in layers. This week, temperatures reached into the single digits in the night, freezing hard the fresh layer of powdery snow covering ice that has gripped the ground for weeks now. Moving in and out this season calls for dressing in layers. Relaxed jeans and a light cashmere sweater are my winter uniform of choice. The older the better. Whether I am indoors or out, fleece-lined Ugg boots keep my feet toasty warm.

While it is still dark outside, I slip on a sweater, and an old blanket robe that speaks of the Painted Desert of the American Southwest. Around these layers, I add one final layer of warmth—a deliciously warm shawl that my friend Diane Peckham made from wool harvested from her own herd of alpaca.

Before stepping out into the freezing cold pre-dawn elements, the dripping of coffee into a glass carafe pulls me into the kitchen. Soon the sounds of steam frothing a pitcher of milk are added to the chorus. Eager to warm my hands, I pour the hot milk and coffee into my favorite mug, winding up with a dollop of creamy froth at the top. As the sun begins to wash across the world out our kitchen window, I warm my hands on the hot mug and let the aroma of just-brewed coffee tease my senses. There is just enough time to dash outside, burrow under the wool blanket on my Adirondack chair, and to watch the show of early morning's cold winter light on snow begin.

For the dicey, late morning walk to the mailbox on patches of ice-encrusted gravel, I stretch a pair of steel cleats onto the soles of my boots to keep from falling. I ordered them recently when an editor friend declared that he is convinced that this ice isn't going to melt

Cathy Salter

until April. A five-minute Google search on the Internet introduced me to Yak Trax and two days later David, our intrepid UPS driver, delivered them to our door.

These days, we all deal with the elements as best we can. Birds puff up, cows beef up, and horses grow shaggy winter coats. Our three cats venture out to chase squirrels, but don't stay long. In February, I grow small pots of sweet cat grass, because cats long for green just as I do. Green is our mutual connection to summer and warmth. Chewing sweet grass fuels the dreams of these felines as they sleep the winter away dreaming of grand exploits in the gardens and woods around Boomerang Creek.

While the cats sleep, tiny deer mice are busy in the woods relining old birds' nests for their winter homes, and white-tailed bucks have begun to shed their antlers. The snow cover provides insulation for burrowing animals that spend the winter underground. From January on, fox, raccoons, and beavers prepare for new birth that will come with the arrival of spring and summer.

Feathers and fur insulate, feet and bills are tucked in for warmth, and birds shiver to increase heat production. But animals and birds also need a good supply of nourishment to keep them warm on cold winter nights. As Kit and I watch the steady activity at our birdfeeders hanging in air that has traveled down from somewhere in the Arctic latitudes, I recall a conversation between Peter Rabbit and Tommy Tit, a chickadee in Thornton W. Burgess's, *Mrs.Peter Rabbit*, 1919—

> *"I thought it was your coat of feathers that kept you warm," said Peter.*
>
> *"Oh, the feathers help," replied Tommy Tit. "Food makes heat and a warm coat keeps heat in the body, Peter.... You are never really warm in winter unless you have plenty to eat."*

In their winter feasting, seeds are dispersed by all manner of birds. Woodpeckers are regulars at the suet feeder. Nuthatches hop tail over head on tree trunks, nabbing insects overlooked by the woodpeckers.

Cardinals harvest sunflower seeds on the ground where we broadcast a scoop of wild birdseed each morning, and chatty Juncos hop about with abandon near soft, doe-colored doves.

Like the birds and creatures at Boomerang Creek, we dress in layers. As winter marches on, we fill evenings with conversation and read our way through stacks of books with the same relish that our cats consume sweet grass. And at the end of the day, we burrow under a pile of quilts and lose our selves in dreams of wild roses and the warmth of a summer sun.

February
One month is past, another begun,
Since merry bells rang out the dying year;
And buds of rarest green began to peer,
As if impatient for a warmer sun;
And though the distant hills are bleak and dun,
The virgin snowdrop, like a lambent fire,
Pierces the cold earth with its green-streaked spire
And in dark woods, the wandering little one
May find a primrose.

Feb. 1, 1842: Hartley Coleridge

(February 2007)

DISAPPEARING BEES AND FIREFLIES

*M*Y MIND IS A BEEHIVE of activity this morning. It is a deliciously cool morning in a week that promises to be dry, sunny, and consistently in the eighties for days in a row. My morning begins with a walk to the edge of the meadow where at seven fifteen, the sun is fully focused on the raised strawberry bed filled with fast-ripening red orbs that birds, box turtles, and squirrels apparently think we have planted solely for their pleasure.

In my search under layers of green leaves for ripe berries, my attention is focused at the micro level inhabited by a stray blade of invader grass, an audacious dandelion, a furiously scampering fiery-orange millipede, and the occasional worm unearthed when I pluck a berry loose from its stem. Overhead in a nearby sweet gum tupelo, a red-winged blackbird cracks at me like a rifle shot, annoyed that I'm harvesting what seconds before might have been the noisy bird's plan for breakfast.

On my walk back to the house, I am already anticipating fresh strawberries on my morning cantaloupe, added to a lunch salad, or atop a bowl of French vanilla and Dutch chocolate ice cream after dinner. With that final delicious image, my thoughts segue to a Haagen-Dazs admonition to us all to "Bee a Friend" to honey bees that pollinate the ingredients that go into nearly fifty percent of their ice cream flavors.

Bees are attracted by scent and color—in particular to blue, purple, yellow, and orange flowering plants rich in nectar and pollen. But as bee colonies collapse and honey bee pollinators disappear at an alarming rate, ice cream lovers are encouraged to plant bee-friendly gardens, filling them with native plants that bloom from early spring to fall. Bee favorites in our garden include lavender, rosemary, coreopsis, violets, thyme, sunflowers, cosmos, and coneflowers.

In our bee-friendly backyard garden, there is plenty of room for wild violets, dandelions, and clover—weeds to some, nectar and pollen to honeybees. A birdbath in the shade garden and an earthen Chinese basin provide bees drifting between masses of bleeding hearts and columbine with the cool, continuous source of water needed to keep beehives healthy and active. A conical straw bee skep rests on a tree stump in the heart of the garden as a visual reminder of this petite pollinator's essential presence and alarming peril.

Locally, there has been a rise in the number of backyard beekeepers. A few facts remind us of the importance of saving honeybees. According to the Boone Regional Beekeepers Association, one-third of the human diet relies on pollination, much of it carried out by bees. Fifteen billon dollars worth of vegetables, fruits and nuts depend on bees for pollination. Our neighbor, Dan Kuebler—chairman of the non-profit Sustainable Farms & Communities and former president of the Columbia Farmers Market—used to see fifteen to twenty bees working the flowers around him on an early morning walk around his organic garden. Now he sees one bee every hundred feet.

I am alarmed to learn that fireflies are disappearing as well. It was in late May that fireflies first visited the gardens at Breakfast Creek— our first Missouri home—carrying me back half a century in time to summer nights spent in my grandparents' backyard in San Antonio. I remember my childlike wonder at seeing the magic glow of fireflies in the darkness that today can only be found in rural settings around the world where stars are still visible in a night sky.

The June 2009 issue of *National Geographic* reported dramatic declines in fireflies in Asia, Europe and North America, most likely due to habitat loss and light pollution. Thailand is one place that seems to be losing "the bioluminescent beetles, " according to the article. For centuries, *National Geographic* noted, fireflies blinked with such synchronicity along Thai rivers that "locals fished solely by their flashes."

These flickering images transport me back to still another backyard in the late 1960s when I was a Peace Corps teacher living on the distant outskirts of Bangkok. There, on the back porch of my little wooden house, I watched the light of each intense sunset compete with the saffron color of the robes worn by Buddhist monks living at a monastery beyond the canal just up the road. For two magical years, fireflies were the nocturnal fairy lanterns that lit up the darkness in a world that was still distant from the development that has now dimmed their light and changed the night.

In our own backyard at Boomerang Creek, I am keeping a tally of fireflies and will continue to add native plants that have a local historical relationship attracting bees to our gardens. Our reward will be counted in the harvest of Bartlett and Kieffer pears, Fuji apples, Montmorency cherries, Red Haven peaches, sweet peas, strawberries, raspberries, tomatoes, fava beans, squash, pumpkins, assorted herbs, roses, and flowers harvested in the months ahead.

To become bee friendly, plant native species, and let dandelions and violets grow in your grass. When night falls, you too can begin a tally of fireflies in your own backyard.

(June 2009)

The Tale of the Fox and the Egg

*A*ESOP'S FABLES—TIMELESS TALES told in a simple way—are attributed to a Greek slave born in approximately 620 BCE. Each of these short tales passed down from generation to generation and across the cultural landscape illustrates a moral and teaches a lesson to children of all ages. The characters in fables are usually familiar animals, loved by children. The animals act and talk as though they were people while retaining their animal traits.

One cold December night, I shared three tales from my personal storybook of fables with Fanny, Scribbles, and Pooh—our three adorable cats—as they curled around me in front of our hearth. The stories related to my encounters with three foxes—one in Idaho, and two in our local Missouri woods.

This summer, Libby Gill and I visited George and Helen Washburn in McCall, Idaho. Each evening, the four of us sat on their deck, talking over the day. At dusk, George would fetch an egg from the kitchen in anticipation of the arrival of their tortoise-colored, neighborhood fox.

"The fox," I explained to the cats, "would soon trot by at a safe distance before circling back to the edge of the porch where George had placed the fresh egg. Like a trained dog waiting for a promised treat, the fox sat obediently, then moved cautiously up to the porch steps, picked up the egg, inspected it, and headed off, egg in mouth, back to his den in the woods."

"Foxes eat eggs?" queried Fanny with surprise.

"In northern climates," I explained, "foxes squirrel away bird's eggs, hoarding them in nests or burying them in 'cold storage' for lean times."

When a magnificent red fox crossed our meadow shortly after dawn recently, the question of what constitutes a fox's diet reminded me of another morning some years ago at Breakfast Creek—our first country home in Missouri—when my ducks and geese were grazing near the pond.

While gazing over the pastoral scene from the porch of our house, I witnessed a brazen duck-snatching by a red fox that had been hiding under a cedar tree. Duck in mouth, the black-pawed, rusty-red rascal with a white ring around its bushy tale took off across the road, disappearing into the netherworld of Louise Dusenbery's woods.

I had known that Sheba, our black Lab, was an incorrigible egg-sucker with a reputation for sniffing out duck nests. Now I had to worry about Mr. Fox's taste for eggs and ducks as well. Foxes, I've read, are extraordinarily opportunistic, omnivorous feeders that spend about five hours a day searching for food—predominantly small animals (rats, mice, voles, the occasional squirrel, rabbits), birds, insects, earthworms, carrion, fruit, berries (especially autumn blackberries), and eggs whenever they can find them.

"But, do they eat cats?" asked Pooh, the smallest and most vulnerable of our cats. Also the oldest, she had followed the deadly drift of my fox and duck tale and was clearly worried.

"Kittens, perhaps," I answered, noting that a fox would probably give most adult cats a wide berth, especially Fanny—our rabbit-fast, Phantom-masked Manx. Kit reminded me that anyone who has ever tried to give a cat an anti-worm pill or a bath can testify to their explosive nature and the sharpness of their claws and teeth. "So beware," I told Scribbles, the gentlest of our felines, " should Mr. Fox reappear on the scene."

I then recited Aesop's fable, "The Fox and the Crow." A fox spots a crow up a tree with a piece of meat in her beak. When Master Fox flatters Mistress Crow about her beauty and lovely voice, she utters a loud "Caw," dropping the meat to the ground where it is snatched up by the cagey fox.

The next morning, I asked the cats what they should do if Mr. Fox compliments them on their beautiful fur and invites them to his den to see the eggs he's stolen from our neighbor's hens.

In unison, the three cats replied, "We should puff up like a porcupine, hiss like a snake, and tell Mr. Fox to save his devious flattery for the witless crow."

(December 2009)

Cathy Salter

Encounters with Tree Frogs

TALES BEGIN WITH THE SMALLEST OF THREADS. A word triggers a thought and that thought another. Lines form and a story begins to take shape. Like strands of wool spun into yarn, threads become the fabric of a writer's tale. This story of two memorable encounters with tree frogs is such a tale.

When Kit and I lived at Breakfast Creek some years ago, I assumed that the music heard on warm spring evenings was a chorus of crickets accompanied by an orchestra of bellowing bullfrogs. Invisible fiddlers and croakers exchanging notes like Pete and Repeat while fireflies danced with their reflections on the surface of our pond. That was before I found a tree frog trapped in a ball of fuzz in a dark corner of the front living room.

Busy with projects that had piled up on my desk, dust—a regular part of every well-lived-in country home—had collected in the less-traveled reaches of every room. That is where my encounter with the first tree frog comes in.

In truth, I don't know how the frog arrived in the house. In a cat's mouth most likely, although there wasn't a mark on the little fellow's motionless body and its limbs and E.T.-like digits were all still attached. I spotted it quite by chance, and thought it nothing more than unsightly dust.

At first, this grey mass appeared to be a dead mouse, but its surprising softness suggested that the hapless creature might still be alive. Upon closer inspection, it turned out to be a tree frog, only about an inch in length, just barely distinguishable in its dusty encasement.

To find out if it was still alive, I carried the motionless creature to the kitchen and dipped its back feet into a bowl of lukewarm water. Immediately the fuzz sagged and legs appeared. It definitely was a frog. What proved to be a more delicate challenge was removing the mess of soggy fuzz now plastered to its skin.

This wet, web-like layer clung tenaciously to the adhesive pads on the frog's elongated digits like glue, letting go only after I'd pulled each limb to an extension much greater than the tree frog's body length. Like a puppeteer, I maneuvered its thin arms and legs up and down, willing it back to life.

Finally, as if emerging from months of hibernation, the frog's color changed from gray to vibrant green, accented by streaks for yellowish orange on its soft underbelly. As its normal color returned, so did its spirit. "Take me out to the trees," the frog seemed to say, "and I will sing for you once again." And so, I did.

This week at Boomerang Creek, I heard another tree frog singing loudly somewhere on our porch. I mimicked its song and I am convinced that the tiny frog answered. We continued to exchange choruses until I was able to pinpoint the creature's location in a damp, ceramic urn on the deck. His throat was as bulbous as a booming prairie chicken until we locked eyes, at which point the tree frog shape-shifted into a flat grey mass that blended in with the interior of the urn.

For a few minutes, we continued staring at each other. It remained there for the next hour without moving a jot, allowing me to capture it from several angles with my camera. Not wanting the frog to leave, I sat down and relayed the story of my first encounter with a tree frog, long ago and a few hollers away at Breakfast Creek.

When I finished my tale, frogs high in the trees exploded in song. I answered, and the frog in the urn did too. Hours later, it was gone and, once again, the trees were silent. What's left now is this tale, woven into the fabric of the country life I love and hope to keep sharing for years to come.

(March 2010)

THE WRITING SPIDER

I SIMPLY CAN NO LONGER AVOID WRITING about the industry and habits of *Argiope aurantia*—the Golden Orb Weaver known as "the Writing Spider." Come September, Boomerang Creek is awash with spider webs cast out on land and in the air. Across the mown meadow, delicate gossamers of spidery silk woven in the night sparkle with dewdrops in the early morning light. Wherever there is a tree branch or porch post or roof gutter, there are spiders eager to begin their spinning work.

For that is the nature of spiders. According to Henry C. McCook—a popular nineteenth century naturalist and author on the subject—spiders derive their name from *spinder,* "the spinning one," root of both *spindle* and *spinster*—"by which the virgin mistress of the distaff was commonly known in the days of our grandsires."

In the case of recluse spiders that lurk in dark places, I have a healthy fear and hope never to cross paths with one. I prefer those that spin their webs in sunny places and care only about eating aphids, flies, grasshoppers, mosquitoes and wasps. Unlike my habit with cats, I have not until recently ever named or developed an affection for a spider.

But, like E. B. White, acclaimed essayist for *The New Yorker* and author of the children's book classic, *Charlotte's Web* (1952), I have of late developed more than a casual interest in spiders. In part, this comes from the fact that Kit and I have now lived a country life for close to a third of my life. In that time, I've learned to deal with all manner of insects and in some cases, how to treat the affects of their angry bites and stings when they are disturbed.

This brings me to Ziggy, the Golden Orb Weaver that took up residence on our porch in mid-August. Initially, the spider anchored its web by a single dry line to the porch gutter and from there to a spiky frond of a red grass palm on the deck below. From that fragile foundation, it spiraled out, creating a circular domicile two feet wide and promptly took up residence squarely at the web's center.

E. B. White studied spiders for a year while living on a farm in Maine before writing *Charlotte's Web*—the story of a small pig and his friendship with a large grey spider. In his notes on the engineering behind a spider's fly-trapping web, he wrote:

> *The first thing a spider does is stretch a thread from some high point. Then from the center of this, it stretches threads like spokes of a wheel. Uses 2 kinds of thread: dry and tough (for the guy ropes) sticky (for spiral).*

The body of a female Orb Weaver grows almost an inch and a half long, the male only about three quarters of an inch long. The head is small with silver hairs on it while the large back abdomen section is egg-shaped with distinctive black and yellow coloring. What makes this spider appear so massive is the length of its eight legs—each black with red or yellow bands and three claws on the end.

The female builds the large web, and a male builds a smaller web—a thick zigzag of white silk—on the outer part of her web. That bold, zipper-like pattern was the source of our Orb Weaver's name.

Ziggy, as we call her, has settled in just off the porch under a southern eave where she is protected from rain and wind. I greet her each morning and sense that she's grown easy with my presence. *"Has she been eavesdropping?"* I wonder, secretly hoping so.

In the closing description of Charlotte in his book, E. B. White wrote:

> *It is not often that someone comes along who is a true friend and a good writer. Charlotte was both.*

To date, Ziggy has not written a word. But then, our conversation has only just begun.

(September 2011)

Save the Last Dance

*W*HAT EXACTLY IS A PRAIRIE, and where does one find a relic prairie in Missouri? The word "prairie" preceded the 1804 arrival of Lewis and Clark. According to historical geographer Walter A. Schroeder, the French had earlier named Missouri's grasslands *prairie*, their word for meadow. Prairies represented open fields of wild flowers and occasional thickets of shrubs and brush. Forests provided borders on the horizon. Fires were common, natural or set by Indians, thus maintaining the openness of the grasslands.

Large game animals once populated Missouri's pre-settlement prairies, along with turkey, prairie chickens, golden plover, white pelicans, sand hill cranes, and grouse—killed regularly for sport and food. As prairies were converted for agriculture and other uses, the once plentiful prairie chickens declined. In 1944, biologist Charles Schwartz estimated their population to be only thirteen thousand, down from the tens of thousands in the 1860s when their population in Missouri was at its peak.

In April 2004, as few as five hundred to eight hundred of these colorful birds remained in Missouri. That was the spring when I witnessed my first dance of the prairie chicken. I'd been invited to join NPR reporter Catherine Welch and a wildlife biologist from the Missouri Department of Conservation (MDC) to witness an age-old spring ritual—the mating dance of the greater prairie chicken. Hours before dawn, our party left Jefferson City, headed for an ancient "booming ground" in a tall grass prairie to view the dawn event.

We arrived at Cole Camp, population one thousand twenty-nine in Missouri's Benton County shortly after six in the morning and drove directly to Hi Lonesome Conservation Site—six hundred twenty-seven acres of prairie acquired in 1987 by the Missouri Department of Conservation. The town sits at the edge of the Ozarks to the south and prairie to the north—tall grasslands that once extended, nearly unbroken, all the way to the Great Plains.

Just past the cemetery at the edge of town, we arrived at a pasture where a dazzling dawn ballet was already underway. This was the ancient booming ground or "lek" where male greater prairie chickens strut, spar, and call each spring hoping to attract a mate.

On an open rise in the center of the field, a dozen male prairie chickens approached each other in the fashion of an old barn dance. Strutting forward and back, the sashaying increased. When agitated, the birds displayed bright orange air sacs puffed out below a set of erect neck feathers at attention like a ring of rabbit ears. With tail feathers cocked and wings fanned out to their sides, they stomped about in the fashion of an Indian war dance, and then shot straight up into the air.

The male exhibiting the greatest strength and flair will mate with the hens attracted to the booming ground. Describing the ritual in 1944, Schwartz noted, *"Prairie chickens don't look for land, they look for sky"*—land unbroken by trees where predators might hide. Sadly, prairie chickens no longer dance or boom in Missouri's Hi Lonesome Prairie.

Efforts, however, are underway to restore prairies to fields where cedars have taken over. The Grasslands Coalition—founded by the Missouri Prairie Foundation and the Missouri Department of Conservation (MDC)—works with the Audubon Society, the Nature Conservancy, and other state and federal agencies and non-profits to acquire and manage prairie lands.

In addition, award-winning MDC nature/wildlife photographer Noppadol Paothong has been photographing the rapidly disappearing North American grassland grouse so that future generations, too, can marvel at their grace and beauty. More than a decade and seventy thousand miles since beginning his personal mission, Noppadol has published *Save the Last Dance*. This two hundred four page, 2012 publication is filled with stunning photographs by Noppadol and text by noted outdoor writer Joel E. Vance. It is their heroic effort to show the world what it stands to lose if these endangered species are allowed to disappear forever.

(July 2012)

When a Hidden Thrush Leaves His Solitudes

$\mathcal{O}$N THE FINAL MORNING OF A RAINY MAY, a solitary cinnamon-brown bird emerges from the leafy shadows at the edge of the woods. Its breast is boldly speckled, and its rusty tail long. Hopping about like a robin, it scrabbles for leaf-liter insects, never venturing far from the woods from whence it came. It is a wood thrush, cousin of the hermit thrush.

Some years ago, I rescued a tiny thrush that had flown into a window. The crash of bird and glass must surely have ended badly for the poor winged creature, I thought at the time. Imagining the worst, I stepped outside and into the drama unfolding in the leaves beneath my window.

There in the mix of fallen brown leaves was a small bird, still as a stone but not dead. The beak parted in quick panting breaths. Eyes open, the lids slowly drooped toward unconsciousness. Left on the still cold ground, it would have quickly slipped from shock into death. Without wasting a precious second, I lifted the stunned bird without resistance, wrapping its feathery lightness in the palms of my hands.

For the next twenty minutes, I gently rubbed its round head, visible between my thumbs. In that window of suspended time, I was witness to its incredible beauty, impossible to detail in rapid flight. An eye-ring circled the bird's large eyes. The color was a warm gray-brown with buff throat and spotted breast. The tail was a rusty red. Its rounded head and strong legs suggest it is part of the thrush family that includes robins and bluebirds. Later, my Peterson's *Field Guide to Eastern Birds* confirmed my speculation.

While in shock, the bird's melancholy song could be heard without singing. *Give me warmth. I will not fly away.* Finally, as if awakened from a deep sleep, the elusive thrush was once again alert. For a few seconds, it stood perched in my open hand out in the warm air. Then its wings slowly unfurled, signaling its slow, swooping flight from my hand to a nearby bush.

Now, back in the moment, I called my sister-in-law Jean, and told her I was being visited by a wood thrush "Oh, my dear," she says. "The thrush is one of the rarest and most melodious of birds. Mother once wrote a poem entitled 'Ode To A Hermit Thrush' in praise of their ethereal, flutelike song. I do hope your wood thrush will share its song with you."

When the wary thrush retreated to the solitude of the woods, I opened a red, leather-bound volume, *The Collected Poems of Katharine Hayden Salter.* There I found my mother-in-law's ode to this rare bird and heard its flute-like song through her words, written in a New Hampshire woods in the summer of 1934. I imagined her sitting alone in her studio at the MacDowell Colony, writing of the thrush's heavenly song—

> *...For never will he leave His solitudes,*
> *Nor bring his gift to any mortal throng.*
> *No one shall hear him save in deepest woods,*
> *And one must come along, to hear his song....*
>
> *...Blessed our hearts, if they have ever heard*
> *The sudden singing of the hidden thrush!*
> *Deep in among the trees the airy bird*
> *Strikes that long note, that melts into a rush*
> *Of falling trills—cluster of berries clinging,*
> *Amber and crimson, on some fairy bough!*
> *So clarion rich and pure those single notes,*
> *Held like enchantment on the world—and how,*
> *Breaking like silvery carillons set swinging,*

They end with that exultant, sudden singing
That over all the listening forests floats....

Visited this day by a wood thrush that momentarily left its solitudes, I am left with these gifts—a measure of its pure and perfect song, and a timeless poem written by Kit's mother that leads me now to the place deep in our own woods where I must go to hear its song.

(May 2015)

Chapter Fifteen
My Life With Cats

After Chutney, we never looked back, or to be more exact, we never looked for cats. It wasn't a question of finding a cat, cats simply appeared, 'out of the woodwork,' as the saying goes, and it was more a question of trying to decide which ones should be invited in. A preliminary test period was usually called for, which in some cases was protracted.

— Margaret and Michael Korda, *Cat People*
(2005)

Traveling Through Life with Cats

My MORNING RITUAL IS THIS. I awake shortly before five, walk bare-footed to the kitchen, and start the coffee machine Kit fills with fresh coffee grounds before bed each night. While black liquid percolates into a glass carafe and puffs of steam escape into the room, I open the door to the basement where our three cats—Scribbles, Fanny, and Pooh—spend their nights.

I move with stealth, yet when the door is open, they are all three sitting on the top step, looking straight up where they intuitively know I'll be.

"It's still dark outside," I tell them as I head back to bed with coffee in hand to read for an hour. "You know the drill." And with that, they pile onto our comforter and spend the next fifteen minutes purring, rubbing, kneading, and nuzzling, in an effort to steal my attention away from whatever I am reading.

I ignore the trio as long as possible. After traveling through much

---

Cathy Salter

of my life with cats, I've learned to think like one. Like children with their minds set on wearing their parents down, they patiently persist at being a presence impossible to ignore. Working as a coordinated team, each cat circles, cuddles, then shape-shifts into the narrow space between my book and body. Finally tiring of the contest, I give in knowing they won't. Then I slide open the door to the outside world, and the three are free to explore.

More often than not, I follow them outside and walk along the flagstone pathways through our hosta garden. I have gradually added roses, Tuscan rosemary and Spanish lavender, and sprinkles of color—vibrant verbena, lemon and tangerine-colored lantana, and various shades of pink peonies.

Focusing on the soil between plants, I look for signs of new growth emerging—ferns, columbine, and woodland violets. Pooh follows gamely in my footsteps, stopping to stretch at a thin persimmon tree that has become her outdoor scratching post. Scribbles trots to the edge of the yard, sits down, then cautiously weighs his options.

Fanny, our alpha calico Manx disappears through a small opening that leads to the netherworld under the porch deck—a space inhabited by an occasional field mouse and world of spiders.

Later in the morning, Fanny dashes inside, excitedly announcing herself as she heads into the kitchen with a mess of spider webbing trailing from the top of her head to her black nose. Sphinx-like, she spreads out on the cool kitchen linoleum floor, her head held high and one long black-stockinged foot thrust out ahead of the other as if striking a pose. Oh, the tales Fanny might tell were she any more human a cat.

Whenever company arrives, most cats instantly become invisible until they've sized up the guests. If a cat enters a room where guests are seated, it moves with studied grace, like a woman confident she is the most beautiful creature in the room. It's no wonder we love them. Unlike a dog that plops his entire head into the nearest lap, cats are selective—choosing without fail a non-cat person's lap where they curl uninvited and leave without saying thank you or good-bye.

Over our sixteen years at Breakfast Creek, I moved in the company of cats. I didn't choose them. They chose me. It happened, just as it did to cat artist, B. Kliban who wrote:

> I used to be a dog person. Then, somebody handed me a cat, just a small cat, and I tried it. It wasn't bad, sort of pleasant, in fact. So I had another, then another, and then another....

The barn at Breakfast Creek produced kittens with the same regularity as chickens lay eggs. When mom cats tired of a litter, I led their kittens along the edge of our pond to teach them about fish, frogs, snappers and our intermittently resident great blue heron. And over time, I introduced them to ice and the changing seasons.

At water's edge, I had them look at their reflection. *"If you look long enough,"* I said, *"you can learn a great deal about yourself and the world."* Soon, all of the sounds around us retreated. In that quiet instant, the kittens and I saw clearly through our reflections, all the way to the bottom of the pond.

At Boomerang Creek, we have no pond. When our trio of cats comes in for the evening, I am always relieved. They survived a move from their bucolic rural beginnings to an arid urban garden in Albuquerque, New Mexico. Now a year later, they are eagerly exploring the edges of their new country home.

"To see what is in front of one's nose needs a constant struggle," I remind them, quoting George Orwell.

Cuidado. Keep your eyes open. It's a jungle out there.

(April 2006)

On Becoming a Cat Person

*W*HEN YOU LIVE IN THE COUNTRY, you encounter all manner of critters large and small. According to my Webster's, a critter is defined as "a creature: specifically, a domestic animal, especially a cow, a steer, a bear, or a wolf." I love knowing there are critters like hedgehogs, and love witnessing deer in silent motion pass through our meadow.

Living in the country, we benefit vicariously from our proximity to herds of cows that graze in fenced pastures along local country roads. Three of our neighbor's horses occasionally trot over to have their noses rubbed if I am walking near the fence line. I love their presence and majestic beauty; Kit loves that someone else is responsible for their daily maintenance.

The tree canopy that shades our central yard belongs to the birds, squirrels, and tree frogs. Box turtles and creek frogs occasionally make the trek up the steep bank from our meandering creek bed, dry as a bone in summer, in search of water in the yard and gardens. Moles mimic the meandering movement of water beneath hardened topsoil, leaving a mounded map of their dark subterranean route as they munch their way from one tender root to the next. Catching these critters is the favorite occupation of our three Boomerang Creek cats—Pooh, Scribbles, and Fanny.

At a recent dinner party in Columbia, two regular readers of my weekly newspaper columns greeted me with "*Please write about your cats.*" Over the sixteen years that Kit and I lived at Breakfast Creek, cats entered our world and wove their way into my writing as regularly as the seasonal rotation of crops in the Hartsburg bottoms. We had a barn, farm friends with an abundance of cats, and we lived along a quiet country road. The combination was a perfectly wonderful storm that rained cats and kittens down upon our lives.

In exchange for feeding them and providing water in all seasons of the year, I was allowed to enter the barn, sit quietly for hours on a bale of straw, observing the mother cats as they took turns tending and teaching their caboodle of youngsters. I was Jane Goodall and they were my anthropological study for those sixteen years. Each member of the barn cat family had a name. Births were recorded, family trees drawn, and breeds as best could be determined were recorded.

Their names found their way into my columns and always brought a smile to our neighbor Louise's face—Oatmeal, Lilly, Bear, Willie Wag Tail, Jackson, Spot (Pooh), Pearlie Mae, Murphy, Scooter Boots, Fat Uncle Mellow, Coffee, Redford, Butterfly, Opie, Stubby, Granger, Dinky, Scribbles, Toby, Aggie Gray, Sherman, and finally, Phantom (Fanny).

As every cat person knows, cats find you—never the reverse. Step one: Enter the cat. Step two: The cat observes the person from a distance. Step three: Gradually that distance diminishes to an arm's length. Step four: The person drops to his/her hands and knees in an effort to allow the cat to approach. Step five: The extended index finger of the person's hand touches the cautious cat's cold, wet nose. Result: When that God-making-contact-with-Adam connection finally happens, you are from that moment on a cat person.

Three of the cats from Breakfast Creek moved with us to Albuquerque, New Mexico and back in 2005. Pooh, an odd-eyed (one blue, one gold) white cat, born with possible congenital patella hyperplasia, walks with wobbly gait but gambols with abandon like a lamb. Our tailless, rumpie calico Manx, Phantom (Fanny for short), has the powerful back legs of a rabbit and is unquestionably the most intelligent Alpha cat on the planet. Scribbles, a gentle grayish-tan and white seal point barn cat with slightly crossed blue eyes, was the absolute love of Fanny's life. Each is worthy of a chapter in a book. Michael and Margaret Korda, co-authors of *Cat People*—a delightful book about the special cats who have shared their 20 years of country life in upstate New York—would certainly agree.

I miss having ducks and geese, especially when a V of Canadas honk overhead in preparation for landing on Roy Richardson's nearby lake. But for now, I am content with the companionship of our three cats that stalk pesky grasshoppers and patiently stand guard at the mouth of emergent mole holes in our yard. Cats never beg to be walked, never tire of entertaining themselves, sleep for hours as though they haven't a care in the world, and only occasionally leave a trophy of the dead-critter sort in my bathtub when eager to impress me with their prowess.

Recently, we had a letter from our friend Dan Arreola, a true cat person. "Life is so much better with cats around," Dan wrote. He then mentioned William Jordan's memoir, *A Cat Named Darwin*, about how a stray cat changed his life. In the book's epilogue, Jordan explained, "I was born a Homo Sapiens. Then I became a biologist. Then I became a cat. In the end, because I became a cat, I became a human being." And so it is.

> *Again I must remind you that*
> *A Dog's a Dog—A CAT'S A CAT.*

T.S. Eliot, *Old Possum's Book of Practical Cats*
(September 2007)

January Dreams

*O*N THIS BITTERLY COLD JANUARY MORNING, an arctic high has extended its icy jet stream into the Deep South, making Atlanta colder than Maine. At the Miami Zoo, orangutans have been given wool blankets and tropical pink flamingos have eagerly flocked indoors. Sea turtles, cold-stunned and lethargic, were immersed in warm water to restore their circulation.

Locally, last night's low of minus three degrees had only risen nine degrees by mid morning. A powdery snow that fell from early afternoon yesterday and into the night led to school closings in much of the area. When I awoke, the world was utterly silent.

After throwing another log into the Buck stove, I brought my coffee and a slice of toasted pumpkin-raisin bread in by the fire. Instantly, all three cats headed for the couch, each one hoping to get to my lap before the other two. I explained how cold it was outside, and that strong winds predicted for afternoon that would make the air feel like minus twenty-five degrees to minus thirty degrees.

"How cold is that?" asked Fanny, our inquisitive Manx cat.

To answer her, I recounted a drama that unfolded on the coldest January morning I can remember at Breakfast Creek, the place where all three of our cats were born.

"Early one morning," I began, "I came upon a great blue heron lost in dreams of soft water. We had both come to a spot along the western edge of the pond that was the last place to freeze in the night. The heron had seen two geese and a small paddling of ducks circled around what looked like an opening in the ice. But sometime during that frigid night, the mischievous old moon had reached out its icy fingers and pulled the pond's zipper tight.

"It isn't easy to surprise a heron," I assured the cats. "Silent and stately in their movements, they hunt for food alone. So glacial are their movements as they wade around the edge of a pond, herons often appear to be asleep. In reality, they see all. Pencil-thin and periscope sharp, they ever so slowly investigate the possibilities that move beneath the pond's surface. Fish, frogs and other small pond creatures quickly fall prey to the lightning-fast spear motion of their long pointed bills.

"But that night, winter showed its mean streak and made the search for food hard. Made everything hard, but most of all, the pond itself. To stay warm, the heron reduced itself by half. Facing rearward, the solitary fisher bird had periscoped its great head and bill tucked around and under the warmth of its own wing. By morning, all that appeared to remain was a cold blue shadow balanced atop a single stick on the ice.

"The heron," I continued, "had rendered himself invisible and drifted into a deep sleep. Perhaps he was remembering the soft feeling of warm water against his long, spidery legs, and the silken feeling of pond muck between the digits of his thin, bird feet. In that dreamy warm-water port, the heron was a thousand miles away when I stepped out onto the ice."

"*Then what happened?*" all three cats asked.

"At that instant," I concluded, "the motionless, steel blue shadow on the ice lifted upward with the drama of Arthur's Excalibur emerging from the stone that had held it captive for mythical ages. For a moment, the surprised bird seemed to hang in the frigid air while his long spindly legs unfolded and arched his long neck downward into his shoulders. Finally, in the curious posture of heron flight, he lifted upward with the quiet power and grace of a Concorde jet, banked slightly westward, and flew off into the cold morning."

And with that, the cats curled up on the couch, resigned to another morning of hibernation near the fireplace. Within minutes, like the great blue heron now large in their minds, they were lost in warm January dreams of their own.

(January 2010)

Cathy Salter

SCRIBBLES

*T*HE SNOW BEGAN WITH MORNING LIGHT. Soft, soundless, and feather light, it soon transformed the decaying vegetation of late autumn into a sparkling white wonderland. Forest green cedar boughs capture snow like children with arms extended. Juniper berries not yet harvested by birds and woodland foragers are nature's ornamentation.

Out early to follow animal tracks in the snow, I gaze back at the studio and house through a veil of falling snow. The snow-covered windshield of the old Ford truck resting on blocks in the meadow completely hides the happy passengers inside—tropical plants too big for the house and too tender to winter over in the yard. Snug as bugs in a rug, they will ride out the winter until the last hard freeze of spring 2013—our first truck garden.

Back inside, I toss my wool sweater and neckscarf into the dryer long enough to melt the wet snowflakes they captured while I walked. Pooh, our wobbly, pure white cat, dashes out and in seconds is reduced to nothing but whiskers, toes and nose moving across a snowy canvas. Fanny, our imposing calico Manx, dives at a squirrel busily digging for buried nuts. There is not a jot of wind. Grosbeaks, flickers, and doves gather in like assemblages beneath the feeders, moving without birdsong as they harvest seeds, nuts and cracked corn.

Inside, Scribbles—the second oldest of our three cats—is sleeping the morning away. It is his habit these days to remain detached from the dramas of nature taking place outside. This precious male cat, frail from lungs damaged by asthma that almost killed him two winters ago, is lost in dreams that have him revisiting the chapters of his decade-long life. Born in one of the horse stalls in the barn at Breakfast Creek, he stood out immediately from the passel of rough-and-tumble gray and yellow tabbies, solid black, and pure white kittens born the summer of 2002. With champagne-colored fur marked with soft gray on his face and ears, he was as limp as a rag doll when I lifted him from the straw nest where his wild, untamable mother had tried to hide him from me.

From the beginning, Scribbles' passive and gentle nature made him a favorite of all who visited that magical world. He would be one of three cats to accompany Kit and me on our brief move to Albuquerque and back in 2005. Like Fanny, Pooh, Kit and me, he was disoriented by the Southwest and instantly took to the green woods, open meadow, and creeks at Boomerang Creek where we settled upon our return. We were a family that had come home, eager to explore a new chapter of life together.

Most of the year, we five are dispersed hither and yon around our five acres made up of woods, creek, house, studio, porches, gardens, meadow, and pathways that link them all. Still, I know instinctively where each of our cats wanders, sleeps, and hides. In winter, they each nap in favorite chairs or sunny window perches and vie to be first in line when the wool lap blankets are unfolded for an evening in front of the fire. With only two of us and three of them, guests who are cat lovers are encouraged to visit.

It is now mid afternoon and snow is falling steadily. As his health continues to decline, Scribbles is not focused on much beyond the occasional drink of water or tuna juice, and the pile of warm blankets that are his soft place to fall throughout the days and nights that remain. He is but a whisper of himself, light as he first was as a kitten, disappearing a trace more each day as this snowfall by nature surely will.

Shifting his long bony frame, a paw reaches out and drapes across my lap. *"Still there?"* Scribbles queries without making a sound. Reassured, his eyes close and mirroring the January landscape outside, his breathing is as silent as the falling snow.

(January 2013)

WHEN CATS SPROUT WINGS AND FLY

*E*ACH JANUARY, THE WORLD IS ONCE AGAIN GIVEN a new start. Last year's calendar is retired and replaced with a brand new one filled with hope and promise. Quickly the squares that represent its three hundred sixty-five days begin to be filled in with notations of upcoming activities, appointments, and events. Some part of me wants to spend the entire year curled up by the fire, reading the year away. But of course, life quickly gets in the way, stands me on my feet, and puts me squarely in motion.

January temperatures rise and fall like gas prices. When the same swings affect the spirit, we fight to keep our balance. Brilliant blue-sky days are a joy whether it is freezing cold or balmy outside. On mild days that feel like early spring, sunlight on my shoulders kneads out the tightness that sets in when January holds me hostage in a heavy fog of gray. Sunlight is nature's Bengay and Blue Emu oil therapy for the body and soul.

The world at Boomerang Creek fell out of balance recently when our gentle cat Scribbles began his final passage one January night, leaving us with an emptiness that only memory can fill. In hopes of capturing shards of his rapidly waning life, I penned this ode early the following morning —

> *Sometime in the night*
> *Scribbles quietly slipped away,*
> *weightless, still forever free;*
> *light as goose feathers now is he.*

The Creek's furry trio
is now only two—
our formidable Manx, Fanny
and wobbly, white Pooh.

Upon quiet reflection
at dawn's rosy light,
we found comfort in recalling
Scribble's decade-long life.

Born in a horse stall
in the Breakfast Creek barn,
this tan and gray Seal Point
was soft as mohair yarn.

Among our herd of many cats
from Breakfast Creek to Boomerang Creek,
Scribbles was the gentlest of all,
with the sweetest of cat speak.

A languorous lap draper extraordinaire
that flowed like melted Brie,
he loved watching Downton Abbey.
A cultured cat was he.

His hiding spot in the garden
was never easy to see,
still an imprint of his body remains
in the ivy beneath his favorite tree.

Transfixed by nuthatch, wren, and flicker,
Scribbles feigned he was a sleeper;
while whiskers he could not still
marked him as a Tomcat peeper.

Cathy Salter

But cross-eyed and utterly passive,
a bird stalker never was he.
Instead he preferred to lie quietly
watching birds flit about, tree to tree.

In his endless quest to mimic birds,
Scribbles climbed—but never high,
for he was just a feline,
and he knew he couldn't fly.

But when his life at last expired,
Scribbles threw off his earthly tethers.
Forevermore this sweet angel cat
will soar on catwings with feathers.

As this whimsical remembrance worked its way from mind to pen, the weight of losing Scribbles ebbed as ink flowed on paper. Finally standing to stretch, I felt a lightness that I hadn't earlier. Then suddenly, the honking of geese cut through the chill air outside—a sound instantly familiar from our years at Breakfast Creek where barn cats chased or were chased by our resident gaggle of domestic geese.

Outside, flocks of flapping Canadas appeared from all directions, noisily honking as they converged directly overhead and re-assembled in a single, broad V formation. Had this splendidly attired flock come to escort Scribbles back to his barnyard beginnings at the edge of their pond world, a few miles and hollers to the south and east? Looking up at their soft, goose-feather underbellies, I imagined Scribbles riding the thermals on catwings, looking down at his entire life from beginning to end.

Never again will I see a formation of geese without feeling the presence of this feather-light feline whose spirit now soars untethered.

Nor will I walk these grounds without feeling his presence. For in sunshine, shadow, snow and rain, his earthly footprints—now indelible as memory—remain.

(January 2013)

Cathy Salter

The Tale of a Most Unusual Cat

THE DAY SHERMAN WALKED INTO OUR LIVES began like most days. Kit and I were having breakfast on the back deck after I had finished feeding the house cats, barn cats, ducks, and geese. You don't live in a place called Breakfast Creek without being attentive to the food needs of all creatures great and small before pouring your first cup of morning coffee. It just wouldn't work. This way, they are happy, and we can enjoy a bowl of our friend David Allen's divine homemade granola topped with fresh blackberries, while listening to a chorus of contented quacks and purrs out in the yard and in the meadow.

But on the particular morning about which I am writing, one walkon addition to the chorus had not been invited to breakfast. "Do you hear that strange meow?" I asked Kit. "It's not coming from our clowder of cats."

After breakfast, I headed for the fenced-in vegetable garden to do some weeding. The air was cool as I worked my way from the lemon thyme at one end of the herb bed to the oregano at the other, extracting leggy sprigs of grass—one invader at a time—from the dense weave of herbs. With feet planted firmly in the straw pathway that defines the bed, it was an exercise in bending, stretching and losing myself in thought.

Near the rosemary, I noted a single yellow primrose in a section of the garden interspersed with Missouri wildflowers. Then I heard the strange meow again, closer this time and louder, coming from the base of a nearby bush. From where I stood, the area under the bush appeared to harbor nothing more than a play of shadow and light until something moved—something big and black and white.

"What an unusual looking breed," I remember thinking to myself when the creature that cautiously emerged into full sunlight could clearly been seen to be a cat. "Must be lost, or more likely, someone dropped him off."

I continued to weed for a while longer under the cat's watchful eye until he stood up, arched his back and stretched as if mirroring my motions inside the garden. When I straightened up to get a better look at him, he sat down and stared directly back at me. A solid mask of black ringed his eyes and square forehead. His hind legs were especially long and his chest stocky and wide. But his most distinguishing feature was the absence of anything more than a knob for a tail.

"I'm calling him Sherman," I told Kit a week after the cat had become a regular fixture on the back deck, "because he's built like an army tank. The only problem is he's a girl… and if I'm not mistaken quite pregnant. We'll have to keep him…that is her… at least until the kittens are born."

With that settled, Sherman took up residence on an old towel in a chair on the porch, eating every last kibble that came her way and growing rounder by the day. Knowing she would need a sheltered nest for her kittens, I hauled a fresh bale of straw into the old chicken house behind our barn that served as a brooder house for all of our ducks and geese. After vacuuming out the cobwebs, I set it up with a heat lamp for cool nights, a small rotating fan for hot afternoons, a litter box, and bowls for kibbles and water.

Finally, I carried Sherman into her cozy quarters and set her down on the bed of straw. Two days later, she delivered four beautiful offspring, rolled over, pushed her solid body into the soft straw, and purred adoringly at her precious kindle of kittens. The largest was a gray male with a white underbelly and no tail; the others were all calicos, only one of which had a tail.

"You are Manx cats," I explained to Sherman and her sleepy caboodle one afternoon, described as "intelligent, friendly, rumbustious creatures, very solid and British of breed with a rabbity gait because your hind legs are longer than the front. You are also especially easy to train and love playing with children."

"British lore" I continued, "has it that your tails were cut off to decorate the shields of Irish warriors. To prevent this, anxious mother cats bit off their kittens' tails at birth. Others say the tail of the last cat to race onto the Ark was cut off when Noah slammed the door. A Manx with no tail whatsoever is called a 'rumpy' and those with a wee bit of a tail like some of you are 'stumpies.' "

"Goodnight, little darlings," I said realizing the kittens were all sound asleep.

This ends my tale of Sherman—Breakfast Creek's most unusual, almost tailless Manx cat. A wonderful family from Macon, MO adopted Sherman and two of her kittens. We kept one—a true rumpy with a black facemask and intelligent, black eyes. We named her Phantom, soon shortened to Fanny because of her non-tail rump. At age eleven, Fanny has grown to be a hefty cat like her mother, and does her fair share of napping these days. Oh the stories Fanny and I could tell of her growing up years, first exploring Breakfast Creek, then in the high desert of New Mexico, and now back in Missouri where she was born.

Like Kit, Pooh, Scribbles and me, Fanny loves the world where we landed a decade ago and turned a new page of life together on five acres in the country surrounded by woods, meadow and creek—a magic place in southern Boone County, Missouri we call Boomerang Creek.

(Updated "Notes from Breakfast Creek"
Columbia Daily Tribune, August 2004)
August, 2015

Chapter Sixteen
THE NEW OLD WEST

"A writer, like a sheriff, is the embodiment of a group of people, and without their support both are in a tight spot."
— Craig Johnson, *Another Man's Moccasins*

THE AMERICAN COWBOY

*I*N THE DAYS BEFORE COMPUTERS, my father typed a note and tucked it inside a book by Charles Siringo—born in Matagorda County, Texas in 1855 to an Irish immigrant mother and Italian immigrant father. After retiring in San Antonio in 1975, my parents often browsed local estate sales and used bookstores. Siringo's classic, *A Texas Cowboy: Or Fifteen Years on the Hurricane Deck of a Spanish Pony* must have been one of his treasured finds.

Recently, I found Dad's yellowed and faded note but not the book. This led to a search for information about Charlie Siringo—the cowboy detective who was the fascinating subject of my father's page-long note. This is what I've learned.

Siringo was an American lawman, detective, and agent for the Pinkerton National Detective Agency during the late nineteenth and early twentieth centuries. At the age of 15, he began working on local Texas ranches as a cowboy and taking part in cattle drives. He settled down in 1884, got married, and opened a merchant business in Caldwell, Kansas where he wrote *A Texas Cowboy*—published a year later to wide acclaim. After moving to Chicago in 1886, he worked for the Pinkerton National Detective Agency—operating undercover, infiltrating gangs of robbers and rustlers, and eventually making more than 100 arrests.

As a detective, he crossed paths with Wyatt Earp, Pat Garrett, Tom Horn, Clarence Darrow, Kid Curry and Butch Cassidy and the Wild Bunch gang. After retiring in 1907, he wrote two books—*A Cowboy Detective* and *Further Adventures of a Cowboy Detective*—that alienated him from the Pinkerton firm. In 1916, Siringo became a New Mexico Ranger, and then moved to Los Angeles in 1918 where his relationships with western heroes like Wyatt Earp made him a celebrity. His final autobiography was published in 1927, a year before his death.

The following is my Dad's review of Siringo's book, *A Texas Cowboy*:

> The cowboy in history and the cowboy in myth has had a great romantic appeal to most American youngsters and oldsters alike. What was it really like in the beginning? My knowledge of the cowboy has come from songs ("Oh, Bury Me Not on the Lone Prairie"); art (Fredrick Remington, Charles Russell), dime novels and books (Owen Wister's *The Virginian* and the Zane Grey library I grew up with); movies and movie stars (Tom Mix, Randolph Scott, Gary Cooper, John Wayne). Motion pictures more than anything else helped fix the image of the cowboy in the American scene.

> The range cattle industry developed with astonishing rapidity after the Civil War. Between 1866 and 1886, it began, matured, and collapsed. During that short period, nearly nine million cattle were driven in trail herds from Texas to shipping points in Kansas and new grazing ranges in the northern plains. Technological developments and refrigeration made it possible for residents in eastern cities to consume those cattle in the form of fresh beef.

> At the very root of this industry was a new kind of American— the cowboy. In those twenty years he became the object of fascination for easterners and westerners alike. He emerged as a new popular hero, symbolizing an old American ideal: unrestrained personal freedom.

Suddenly the open range ranching system collapsed. The terrible blizzard on the northern plains in the winter of 1886 resulted in the death of approximately five million cattle. By 1890, the open range was gone—fenced into organized pastures and planted with feed crops.

The day of the trail drive had passed, but the cowboy remained. He has been a part of American life in one form or another, real and mythical, for the past century. What was he really like in his heyday? I recently came across this book by Chas. Siringo. For me, it vividly recounts those days as well or better than anything I have ever read.

WER (*William E. Riggs*)

Boy howdy, Dad! What a great story!

(July 2015)

FOREVER WEST

$\mathcal{W}$YOMING'S OFFICE OF TOURISM loves to share maps and travel information about their beautiful state. One advertisement features buffalo grazing in grassy fields with Yellowstone's Old Faithful in the background and this message: "Come. Behold. Roam Free. There is no telling how Wyoming will affect you. Just know that it will." Just back from an eight-day road trip from Boomerang Creek to Buffalo, Wyoming, I can say with absolute certainty, boy howdy, will it ever! This is the backstory behind that journey.

A few years ago, my longtime Wyoming pal Pat Fennell called from Los Angeles and said, "You've got to read western mystery writer Craig Johnson's Longmire books." My response was that western detective novels were just not my genre. But when A&E cable network began filming the *Longmire* series—set in the small western town of Durant, Absaroka Country, Wyoming (actually Buffalo, in Johnson County), Kit and I began watching the show. Filmed in sites around northern New Mexico and intelligently scripted, we were hooked before the end of the first episode.

While watching *Longmire* during seasons two and three, we read all of Craig Johnson's novels, starting with *The Cold Dish*—the first of his eleven Longmire mysteries—and found ourselves captured by compelling human dramas, storms blowing down the Big Horn Mountains and a cast of characters that have become as real as family. The storylines are dynamite, filled with Johnson's natural cowboy wisdom and writ large with his gift for intelligent, contemporary storytelling.

To be a good writer, Johnson tells his devoted international fans,

---

you must be a reader. He avidly supports libraries and bookstores big and small across Wyoming and in cities that he visits on his wildly popular U.S. and European book tours. Last week, Johnson shared with his fans the news that the Longmire books as a series are up for the 2015 Will Rogers Medallion Award for Western Fiction. He went on to say that the nomination "truly tickles me in that ol' Will has long been a great hero of mine, celebrating humor, intelligence and westerns in media.

Johnson's fans are not surprised by the nomination. When A&E made the incredibly wrong-headed decision to drop the *Longmire* TV series after three seasons, incredulous fans formed support posses in every state, Canada, Australia, and in Europe. Using social media, thousands of *Longmire* supporters went on Facebook and Tweeted their irritation with the cable network. After four months of weekly stampedes of support for the series, Netflix came to the rescue and began filming season four, set to debut September, 10, 2015.

After playing a role in the social media "#LongLiveLongmire" effort, Boomerang Creek's local Missouri posse of two began making plans for a July road trip west to celebrate with author Craig Johnson, the *Longmire* TV cast and fans from near and far during the fourth annual Longmire Days in Buffalo, Wyoming. Seconds after author Craig Johnson posted the event dates, I called the Buffalo Chamber of Commerce and began following the schedule of events taking shape. AAA maps were ordered and driving routes planned with overnights en route in Council Bluffs, Iowa and Rapid City, South Dakota. Immediately, four nights were secured at a Buffalo inn and a table reserved at the historic 1880 Occidental Hotel's restaurant named after writer Owen Wister's western classic, *The Virginian*—written while he was a guest at the hotel.

As our July 14 departure grew near, we packed our best western boots, hats, and jeans, as well as a boomerang for the TV actors and author to autograph and an audio recording of Johnson's latest Longmire novel *Dry Bones*. With the voice of Sheriff Walt Longmire and his friend Henry Standing Bear to keep us company, our 1,059-mile forever west roadtrip to Buffalo at last got underway.

A writer, like a sheriff, is the embodiment of a group of people and without their support both are in a tight spot.

—Craig Johnson, *Another Man's Moccasins*
(July 2015)

CROSSING SOUTH DAKOTA

*D*RIVING ACROSS INTERSTATE 90 with a South Dakota state map as our guide, Kit and I are welcomed by Governor Dennis Daugaard to the land of "Great Faces and Great Places"—friendly people, a rich variety of wildlife, and scenic landscapes filled with natural and man-made wonders. Crossing into the state's southeast corner on Interstate 29, we felt the spirits of explorers past as we approached the hill and monument where the Corps of Discovery buried Sergeant Charles Floyd, the only man to die during the Lewis and Clark Expedition (1804-1806).

South Dakota's informative state map takes modern-day travelers on an American journey—one made by early explorers bound for the headwaters of the Missouri—North America's longest river. From Montana to the Dakotas, through Nebraska to Iowa, and south to Kansas City, it flows eastward, passing just five miles from Boomerang Creek on its two thousand, three hundred forty-one mile journey from the Rocky Mountains of western Montana before entering the Mississippi River north of St. Louis.

Driving across South Dakota to the fourth annual Longmire Days in Buffalo, Wyoming, we stopped near the Fort Pierre National Grasslands—one of the filming sites in the 1990 movie *Dances With Wolves*. There, a sun-faded yellow South Dakota Central Railroad engine sits in an open field with adjoining passenger cars that seemed to be frozen in time. Standing next to it, the high plains wind turned my light cotton pants into billowing sails. Unlike the Missouri River that flows past Ft. Pierre with direction and authority, the train was going nowhere. We, on the other hand, proceeded west to Chamberlain for buffalo burgers at a local café named Al's Oasis.

Crossing South Dakota, we passed periodic Wall Drug highway signs reminiscent of the old Burma Shave ads. Today Wall Drug claims to be the number one roadside attraction in America. In 1931, Ted and Dorothy Hastead purchased a pharmacy in the town of Wall east of Rapid City. It was the middle of the Depression. Like the train going nowhere that we'd seen earlier that day, Wall Drug was not attracting much business because it was off the beaten path. Then, in 1936 Dorothy came up with the idea of advertising free ice water for motorists and put Wall Drug signs up along the highway. The ploy worked and literally put Wall Drug on the map. Located at the northern edge of Badlands National Park, it is a seventy-six thousand square foot tourist mecca with a museum and restaurant seating five hundred twenty customers.

Leisurely travelers can bypass I-90's straight shot across the state and exit I-29 at Vermillion, SD and mosey west along the three hundred eighty-eight mile Oyate Trail to the Wyoming border. "Oyate" in the Dakota/Lakota language means "a people" or "nation." Either route, the state offers a spectacular variety of geographic landscapes—loamy farmland in corn, soybeans, sunflowers, alfalfa, rye, oats, and durum wheat; rangeland with grazing cattle; and open prairies wild with big bluestem grass, buffalograss, flaxseed, segolily, soapweed, switchgrass, and tufted evening primrose.

The Badlands and Black Hills region has its own unique geography with buttes and ancient landscapes awash in the red earth tones of the American west. Here Americans come with their families to stand in awe at the monumental carved faces of Mount Rushmore National Memorial and Crazy Horse Memorial. Tourists are also drawn to the historic towns of Deadwood and Lead, once frequented by some of the Old West's most famous and infamous characters—Wild Bill Hickok, Calamity Jane, and Jack McCall.

After an overnight in Rapid City, we drove to Sturgis—home of South Dakota's annual Motorcycle Rally—ahead of the predicted million plus motorcycle enthusiasts expected this week for the event's Seventy-fifth anniversary rally. After a down-home-delicious pancake and sausage breakfast at Weiner's Diner and Doughnut shop, we continued west to the Wyoming border. With Buffalo in our sights, our one thousand fifty-nine mile journey west was almost over and Longmire Days 2015 was about to get underway. Boy howdy!

(August 2015)

At Long Last...Buffalo

$\mathcal{F}$OR THOSE READERS and fellow *Longmire* fans who have traveled with me in spirit on my recent journey to Buffalo, Wyoming, this is it. "We" have arrived. I say "we" because this adventure is a shared one in many ways. Kit and I—as loyal fans of author Craig Johnson's dynamite Longmire western mystery book series, as well as the TV series based on the books—had become part of an international support group dubbed the Longmire posse. This July's fourth annual Longmire Days brought fans together with the author and TV series actors in Buffalo, Wyoming for three days of fun events.

Friday, July 17, 2015 opened with a down home parade along Main Street with horse drawn floats and antique classic cars carrying the author and actors from the *Longmire* TV show, recently picked up by Netflix. Free *Longmire* episodes played at the Buffalo Theater, and summer fest vendors and food trucks filled Crazy Woman Square throughout the weekend.

That morning, we had tickets for an autograph session with the author and actors—Robert Taylor (Walt Longmire: the laconic and introspective long-time sheriff of Absaroka County); A. Martinez (Jacob Nighthorse: local businessman building a casino on the Cheyenne reservation); Zahn McClarnon (Mathias, chief of the Cheyenne reservation's tribal police); Adam Bartley (the Ferg: awkward, but hard-working young deputy), Louanne Stephens (Ruby: the dispatcher and manager of the sheriff's office).

For several hours, Kit and I visited with fans waiting in line to have books, hats, tee shirts, event programs and posters signed by the actors. I'd brought a splendid boomerang, now signed by them all. Robert Taylor (Sheriff Walt Longmire to the core) is Australian and actually knows how to throw a boomerang. When I handed it to him and explained the Australian name origins of Breakfast Creek, our first home in Missouri, and our current home Boomerang Creek, he rubbed it pensively, stood and walked around the table toward me. Standing at an imposing six-foot-two, ruggedly handsome, and looking as if he were born in the saddle in the Australian outback, I feared he was about to launch my boomerang then and there.

After lunch at the downtown Busy Bee Café (1927), we attended a two-hour conversation at the Buffalo Theater with Johnson and the actors. During the Q & A, Kit stood and explained I'd been so flummoxed over the possible outcome of a boomerang being launched inside the Bomber Mountain Civic Center where the autograph session had taken place, that he'd forgotten to ask Taylor to autograph our copy of Johnson's newest mystery, *Dry Bones*. "Bring it up here," Taylor said, which is how I got the inscription to die for—"To Cathy, my boomerang won't come back. Regards, R. J. Taylor."

Friday evening, the actors played in a Cowboys vs. Indians charity softball game in Prosinski Park. Hot dogs and Rainier beer (Sheriff Longmire's favorite) fit the bill. Saturday we explored Buffalo's downtown shops and businesses, admired the town's public art and historic buildings, and enjoyed barbequed pork from a food truck in Crazy Woman Square. When it began to sprinkle, we headed back to the Buffalo Theater, bought a Dr. Pepper and bag of fresh popcorn, and watched two *Longmire* episodes.

That evening, as six of us were enjoying a libation in the Occidental Hotel's saloon, actor A. Martinez (Jacob Nighthorse) stopped for twenty minutes of conversation about his complex role as the sheriff's nemesis in the Longmire series. After dining at the hotel's Virginian Restaurant we joined the dancing underway outside on Main Street. We danced amidst the locals, fans, and actors, and before the evening was over, I'd gotten a hug and kiss from the sheriff himself. Boy howdy!

Sunday's events included a skeet-shoot and horseback ride with the actors, Native American dance performances, a closing charity concert, and BBQ at the South Fork Lodge. *Longmire* Season four debuts on Netflix September tenth. Will we return to Buffalo next year? Stay tuned!

(August 2015)

EPISTOLARY JOURNEYS

*W*HEN DOES A LIFETIME OF LETTER WRITING BEGIN? For me, it first happened in the mid 1950s when I attended Camp Bonnie Brae in the Berkshire Mountains of Massachusetts—now the oldest continuously operating Girl Scout camp in the United States. The collective experiences of living away from home for the first time in my life, sharing a cabin with a tribe of five other ten-year-old scouts, tasting campfire cooking, swimming in a cold mountain lake, and studying the woodland plant and animal life filled letters that I wrote by lantern light each night and mailed to my parents at the camp store's post office.

Fast forward a decade to Bangkok, Thailand where I had just begun a three-year assignment as a Peace Corps Volunteer (1967-70). In that era before computers and cell phones, my epistolary communications with my family were filled with as much detail as was humanly possible to pen onto an onion-skin, fold-and-seal aerogram. Mother saved them all and returned them to me later as a chronicle of that extraordinary chapter of my life.

I love the process of writing letters—the stationary, fountain pens, pots of ink, and the army of black squiggles and swirls that line up to form the letters that become words. I treasure the conversations captured within each stamped and sealed envelope that I present to our local post mistress for her final stamp of approval before its journey to the addressee is officially underway.

Writing postcards at café tables in cities and small towns from Madrid to Buffalo, Wyoming. is a way to share our travels with family and friends in a way that is both visual and personally meaningful.

Cathy Salter

Emails quickly evaporate into the ether. Like personal journals, penned postcards and letters capture treasured moments that last a lifetime.

Returning recently from Buffalo, Wyoming, Kit and I wound our way south past Casper and Cheyenne before heading east on Interstate 80 across Nebraska. Before crossing the Missouri River at Nebraska City, we made a planned detour that took us map-in-hand to the home of an epistolary acquaintance—a Nebraska poet I'd not yet met—who lives tucked away down a winding country road in a hilly region just northwest of Lincoln.

Several years ago, I'd written to Ted Kooser, former United States Poet Laureate (2004-2006), after reading his quiet treasure of a book, *Local Wonders: Seasons in the Bohemian Alps* (2002). Since that time, the poet and I have exchanged letters, postcards with watercolor landscapes of his farm recording the changing seasons, favorite books, and tranquil observations on the gardens and critters (orb weaver spiders in particular) that inhabit our respective country homes.

When we arrived, Ted and his sweet old snow-white Labrador Retriever, Howard were waiting for us on the porch. "It's National Ice Cream Month," Kooser said after greeting us. "Would you like ice cream, or can I offer you iced tea and cookies?"

For the next two hours, we shared easy conversation about books, writing, poetry, life in the country, and we learned about the nature of Ted Kooser's life as a former United States Poet Laureate. It was as if we'd known each other for ages. I delivered a copy of *Gone West*— poetry by our friend Walter Bargen, Missouri's first Poet Laureate. In return, Ted presented me with two books from his personal library that he felt I'd enjoy—*Nature a Day at a Time: An Uncommon Look at Common Wildlife* by Cathie Katz, and *Little Things in a Big Country* by artist-writer-naturalist Hannah Hinchman.

Tucked in with them were two small publications enclosed in forest green, card-stock paper covers. One, a pocket-sized journal reminiscent of one Lewis and Clark might have carried, is Kooser's long poem *Pursuing Black Hawk (2012)*. The other is *Two Years in the Catbird Seat: My Experience as U. S. Poet Laureate*. The poet's literary gifts are now notations in a chapter in this ongoing epistolary journey—one shared by two kindred spirits across time and miles.

(August 2015)

Acknowledgements

$\mathcal{L}$IFE IS A MIXTURE of sunshine, rain, and occasional times of drought. Thank you to my family and the various tribes, clans, corps, societies, communities, neighbors, sisterhoods, salons, writers, and artists who have welcomed me into their worlds over the years. Our shared journeys have made all the difference. To you all, I give my heartfelt thanks—

To the Riggs family where my journey began seventy years ago and the bonds of kinship continue true and strong; to the extended Salter clan who welcomed me into their remarkable world forty years ago; and to the Gingerich folks from Goshen to Albuquerque, I extend my deep-felt love to you for providing the collective support that has enriched my life and allowed my writing to flourish.

To my Peace Corps Thailand pals who set out with me in 1967 to change the world and returned enlightened, inspired, and changed themselves by the experience. To Chomsri Lewinter, my student fifty years ago and sister ever since, with whom I continue to travel the world.

To my Wyoming/Nebraska sister Pat Fennell and my Riggs sister Kim Chandio, with whom I ventured west forty years ago in search of that magic place called California. To my little sister Kelly and her true love Jack, whose selfless deeds make the world a better place. To my sister Molly whom I loved and miss in my life. To my darling father who taught me to swim on my own and continues to fly with me in spirit, and to my amazing mother Alice who has always been a faithful champion of her four daughters and steadfast keeper of the family home.

To Gilbert M. Grosvenor and the National Geographic Society that entrusted Kit and me with the mission of expanding the horizons of geography teachers throughout the country, and to Oliver Payne, my editor at *National Geographic* magazine, who gave me the opportunity to write about the historic Missouri River of Lewis and Clark (April 2002).

To my editors and fellow Algonquinistas—Kit Salter, Hank Waters, Jim Robertson, Vicki Russell, Jane Flink, and Bruce Wallace. A special thanks to the *Columbia Daily Tribune* and the *Boone County Journal* for having allowed me to share my voice as a columnist in the pages of their newspapers every week for the past two decades. Those stories are the heart of this book.

To Yolanda Ciolli, my multi-talented publisher, editor-in-chief and tribe at Compass Flower Press/AKA-Publishing, and her stalwart editorial assistant, Von Pittman.

To the artists in my life. To Suzanne Dunaway, whose friendship, illustrated cookbooks, and spirited drawings that illustrate the pages of my books are joyous treasures. To Heidi, a daughter whose wit and artistic talents bring conversations and stories to life. To Hayden, a son whose international architectural creations and Spanish family—Ana, Nico, Ines and Catalina—are gems one and all. To Billyo O'Donnell, Missouri's premier plein air artist, who gave me the courage to paint the light of Italy. To Vicki White, who captured me with her watercolors in Siena's Piazza del Campo. And to my friend Wayne Meyer, whose quiet photographer's eye transforms corroding paint on an old truck into works of art.

To the writers in my life. To Katherine Shepard Hayden Salter, Jean Roetter Salter and Patricia Learned Salter—master weavers of words, stories and poems across time. To Ted Kooser, U.S. Poet Laureate from 2004 to 2006, for sharing his epistolary musings and world in Nebraska's Bohemian Alps. To Walter Bargen, Missouri's first Poet Laureate. To Michael and Margaret Korda, for writing about the pleasures and tribulations of country matters—and for being fellow cat people. To Matthew Goodman, for traveling to Missouri with a grip sack and sharing Nellie Bly and Elizabeth Bisland's remarkable historic race around the world. To Todd Kliman, for writing the story of the wild vine, Missouri's Norton grape, and for being epicurious in the extreme. And to Uri Shulevitz, whose Caldecott-winning, illustrated children's books have inspired me across forty years of friendship.

To award-winning author Craig Johnson for giving the world Sheriff Walt Longmire and the very best of modern western mystery writing. Special thanks to the Longmire posse, Robert Taylor and the cast of the *Longmire* TV series—a devoted tribe that has found a new home at Netflix. To Paul Theroux for *The Tao of Travel*. To Daniel James Brown for telling the magnificient story of the boys in the boat. And to David McCullough for celebrating the life of the Wright Brothers and so many other great Americans.

To Nina Mukerjee Furstenau, for bringing garam masala and tamarind/date chutney back into my life in her award-winning food memoir. And to the chefs and writers who have been champions of schoolyard gardens, farmers markets, slow food and edible adventures over time—M. F. K. Fisher, Julia Child, Suzanne Goin, Alice Waters, Clementine Paddleford, Edna Lewis, Clotilde Dusoulier, Jamie Oliver, Michael Pollan, Suzanne Dunaway, Jenny Grabner, Melinda Hemmelgarn, Michael Odette, Craig and Sarah Cyr, and America's First Lady, Michelle Obama.

To Alex George and my fellow Unbound Book Festival champions, my thanks for your tireless spirit of community and purpose in bringing a national book festival to Columbia April 23, 2016. To all who support Columbia's Osher Saturday Morning Book Talks—MU's Osher Life Long Learning program, Columbia Parks and Rec, local writers, poets, readers, book clubs, editors, publishers, and bookstores large and small. And to Diana Moxon and the Columbia Art League for "Interpretations"—a brilliant blending of art and writing.

To Keija Parssinen, Mary Kay Blakely, Laura McHugh, Marlene Lee, Gladys Swan, Carolyn Mulford and Eric Praschan for embracing and sharing the craft of writing. To Margaret Sayers Peden for her incredible life in translation. To Steve Weinberg, whose generous counsel, sharp critic's eye, and beautiful prose make his fellow writers feel blessed to know him. And to George Hodgman, a new old friend, for sharing Betty and Paris, Missouri with the world.

To Louise Dusenbery, my long-time neighbor, sidekick, and mentor in all that has to do with southern Boone County life. To Orion and Barbara Beckmeyer, and Terry and Mary Neuner—friends who taught me about the nature of farming and the wonders of a vineyard. To Dale Coble, our constant friend and keeper of the grounds, and to Greg and Carol Busacker for a friendship writ in Haiku and shared meals.

To Marjo Price for reintroducing tea time into my life. To Judith McCandless, who followed us to Spannocchia and amazed its seasoned cooks with her knowledge of Tuscan fungi. To Grady Clay, a prince of a journalist, storyteller and pal. To Alex Innecco who gave us music and the spirit of carpe diem. To Noppadol Paothong for your tireless efforts to save America's prairie chickens. And to Gary Fisher, for your genius in inventing a hydroponic device for growing cat grass.

To Jane Duncan Flink, my dear friend and mentor in writing. To the Magnificats, Salonistas, and Tiger Tales Book Club for their collective brilliance, curiosity, energy and positive take on life. To Lisa Loporto and Columbia's Barnes & Noble Bookstore for creative outreach efforts in our community. To the Daniel Boone Regional Library for sponsoring more than a decade of One Read community events. To David Wilson, Paul Sturtz, Ragtag Cinemacafé and the True/False Film Festival that has put Columbia on the map for all who create and love international documentary films. And to Paul Pepper, James Mouser, David Lile, and Darren Hellwege—the voices of community radio that keep us connected.

To the Hamoodi family, who introduced an international world of cheeses, olives, and foods to Columbia over a decade ago. The humanitarian actions, family struggle and personal sacrifice of Dr. Shakir Hamoodi, my friend and brother, continue to remind us of the need for tolerance, change, understanding, and international peace.

And above all to Kit, my partner in life and an editor extraordinaire. You have made my life a grand adventure every single day for the past forty years. Boy howdy!

ABOUT THE AUTHOR

Photo by Kit Salter

CATHY SALTER LIVES IN MANY WORLDS, as all authors must. When she is not traveling, she commutes one hundred sixty-five steps from her home to her studio, an inviting and warm writing library. Her studio space is the stage for the dramas of her writing. Alternately, she spends time in her compact but well-stocked kitchen. Through the intertwining of her writing and travel experience, and her culinary and cultural observations, she is able to create a *garam masala* that brings pleasure to readers and diners alike.